DATE DUE			

Land and social change in East Nepal

Lionel Caplan

Land and social change in East Nepal

A study of Hindu-tribal relations

UNIVERSITY OF CALIFORNIA PRESS

Berkeley and Los Angeles · 1970

UNIVERSITY OF CALIFORNIA PRESS
Berkeley and Los Angeles, California

Standard Book Number 520-01400-6
Library of Congress Catalog Number: 73-81801

To my Mother
and the memory of my Father

Contents

Tables

Illustrations

Maps

Preface

This book examines the changing relations between members of an indigenous tribal population in the Himalayas and the Hindus who have entered their region during the past two centuries, following its incorporation into the Kingdom of Nepal. The data on which this study is based were gathered during the course of a thirteen-month field trip in 1964–5. The research was made possible by a grant from the London-Cornell Project for East and South-east Asian Studies, which is supported jointly by the Carnegie Corporation of New York and by the Nuffield Foundation. The Service de l'aide aux Étudiants of the Quebec Government, Canada, provided an additional award to finance the preparatory stage prior to my departure for Nepal. I am deeply indebted to these bodies and their officers for this generous assistance.

While in Nepal my work was encouraged and facilitated by a number of persons to whom I here express my warmest appreciation. I am especially grateful to my friend, Dor Bahadur Bista, who was my host and guide in Kathmandu. Helpful in other ways were the officials in the Protocol Section of the Nepalese Ministry for Foreign Affairs, and the members of the district administration in Ilam, where my field-work was conducted. My thanks are also due to Sri Mahesh Chandra Regmi for allowing me to read his manuscript on the kipat land system before its publication, and to Sri Damodar Sharma and Sri Lakshmi Prasad Kaphle, who acted as my assistants at various stages of the work. I take particular pleasure in recording my gratitude to the people who live in and around the group of settlements in Ilam which I have called the Indreni Cluster. The experience of living amongst them has enriched me more than I can say.

Others have contributed in different ways to the preparation of this book. I owe much to Professor C. von Fürer-Haimendorf, who not

xiii

only stirred my initial interest in Nepal, but read the manuscript at several stages in its development, and generously made available his considerable knowledge of the Himalayan region. I am also grateful to Professor Adrian C. Mayer, who, in his roles as teacher, colleague and critic, has been a constant source of encouragement and stimulation. My thanks are due to Professors F. G. Bailey and E. Gellner, Dr. M. S. A. Rao and my wife, Dr. A. P. Caplan, all of whom offered helpful suggestions on an earlier version of the manuscript, and to Dr. A. Cohen, who read and commented on the final draft.

Finally, I express my appreciation to Mrs. Helen Kanitkar for preparing the index and seeing to a variety of publication details during my absence abroad.

Kathmandu,   LIONEL CAPLAN
January, 1969

Transliteration

Some Nepalese words are treated as though they are English, are given a plural form where necessary, and are not italicized. Certain proper names are also left in their English version. All other terms in the vernacular are rendered as close to their proper pronunciation as possible and italicized in the text; they are then transcribed in the Glossary according to the system devised by Professor T. W. Clark in his *Introduction to Nepali* (1963).

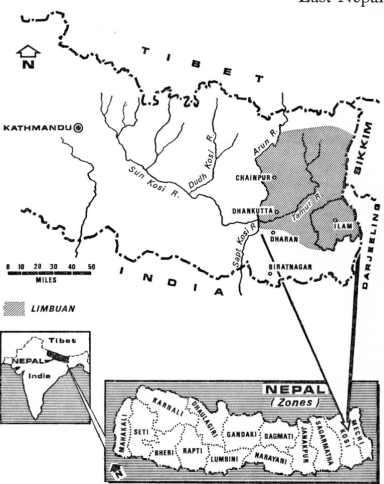

LIMBUAN

Chapter 1

Introductory

The spread of Hindu civilization throughout most of South Asia has taken place over many centuries. An important aspect of this process has been the manner in which the Hindus, advancing here by military conquest, there by migration, have interacted with the tribal communities lying on the route of their progression.

The interpenetration of Hindu and tribal[1] populations has attracted much attention. British administrators and their advisors in India were for many years concerned with the practical problems of protecting tribal peoples from what were regarded as the undesirable effects of association with Hindus. Objections to such association were phrased in terms of the breakdown of tribal character, evidenced in the loss of vitality and self-confidence, or in the assimilation of such 'Hindu habits' as child marriage or caste consciousness. On the other hand, arguments against this view suggested the positive effects on the tribal peoples of exposure to such 'Hindu influences' as improved agricultural techniques or more attractive bathing and dietary habits, and so on. These opposing contentions eventually crystallized into two main proposals for dealing with the tribal populations: one favouring their isolation from the Hindus; the other their total assimilation into the society of the latter (cf. Elwin, 1943: Ghurye, 1959).

More recently, anthropologists have turned from this debate to concern themselves with the more meaningful cultural component of the contact situation. Some have noted the ways in which tribes adjust their cultural symbols to conform with the Brahmanical model (Bose, 1953). Others have emphasized, rather, the two-way exchange of cultural traits: in other words, the manner in which the tribe is

[1] It will be evident that I am here using these two terms for convenience of description only, and not to imply that each represents a clear structural or cultural type.

increasingly 'Hinduized' while the Hindu group is correspondingly 'tribalized' (cf. Srivastava, 1966).

But to say that tribesmen have given up polluting dietary habits or taken to propitiating Hindu deities and that Hindus now worship local tribal gods is to tell only a part of the story. Hindu-tribal contact involves more than the mutual transmission of cultural elements.[1] It implies relationships between members of two groups within a single society. It can mean a significant change in tribal social institutions as a result of the impact of Hindu domination. These are the kinds of problems to which a social anthropologist might address himself in a study of Hindu-tribal interaction. This book seeks to present such a study. Its setting is east Nepal.

In the latter half of the eighteenth century that part of the Himalayas between Kumaon and Sikkim – containing a number of tribal peoples of Mongolian racial stock – was united, mainly by force, under a Hindu dynasty into what became the Kingdom of Nepal. There followed, in the wake of the conquest, a large migration of Hindus into the tribal areas. But despite the creation of a multi-ethnic society, relations between the tribal populations and the immigrants have frequently been characterized by seemingly opposed tendencies: cleavage, on the one hand, and interdependence on the other. To this day, this is certainly true of the ties between the Limbus, a tribal people residing in the easternmost portion of Nepal, and the Hindu settlers in their midst.

The cleavage between the Limbus and their Hindu neighbours arises not only or primarily out of racial and cultural differences between them. Rather, this aspect of their relationship can best be understood in the context of a confrontation over land. The story is simple and told repeatedly by the Limbus in a multitude of different ways: they were already settled in Limbuan – the country of the Limbus in east Nepal – when the Hindus came as immigrant settlers. Ever since, the latter have tried, by fair means and foul, and with conspicuous success, to 'eat' Limbu land.

A Hindu-tribal land struggle is not unique to Nepal. In India Hindu settlers entered tribal areas and often 'succeeded in acquiring large stretches of the aboriginals' land' (Fürer-Haimendorf, 1967,

---

1 A generation ago, in a different ethnographic context, Fortes warned anthropologists away from a too narrow concern with culture contact: 'Individuals and communities react under contact; and not customs' (1938, 62).

184). The observation by Bose (1964) that land-alienation was the chief problem facing the tribes of Andhra Pradesh could be echoed wherever Hindu groups penetrated tribal areas in substantial numbers (cf. Ghurye, 1959; Banerjee, 1963). Despite – indeed, to a certain extent, because of – the introduction by the British of laws attempting to arrest the trend, tribal lands continued to pass into the hands of Hindu outsiders (Roy, 1931).

The dynamics of the struggle for land have gone largely unrecorded by anthropologists. There is plenty of evidence to demonstrate that the social consequences of land-alienation were severe. A number of tribes in India rose against the Hindus who had taken their lands. As Fürer-Haimendorf notes, these risings were a 'reaction to the exploitation and oppression of the aboriginals by Hindu landlords and moneylenders who had established themselves in tribal areas . . .' (1967, 184). Unfortunately, the detailed processes of interaction which led to these manifestations of disaffection have not been systematically analysed. We know only what the final outcome has been: that tribal groups have generally been rendered landless and powerless, and have come to be dominated by the descendants of the original Hindu immigrants. Why and how did land change hands? To what extent did government legislation play a part in this process? Did the legal and social force of the surrounding Hindu society favour the interests of the Hindu immigrants and, alternatively, work against those of the tribal group? Finally, and most important of all, what effect did the land struggle and the alienation it led to have on tribal institutions and on the relationships between tribesmen and Hindus?

In most parts of Nepal, as in India, time appears to have buried the answers to these questions. The Nepalese authorities have, over time, brought all tribal lands, with the exception of those belonging to the Limbus, under a uniform system of tenure, akin to freehold and known as 'raikar'.[1] Traditionally – that is, before the establishment of the Kingdom and probably for some time afterwards – all tribal groups held land under a customary form of tenure which has come to be known as 'kipat'.[2] The conversion of these lands to raikar

1 Raikar has been described as a system of 'state landlordism' under which the rights of an individual to utilization and transfer of the land are recognized by the State so long as taxes are paid (Regmi, 1963).
2 Briefly, under this form of tenure an individual obtains rights to land by virtue of his membership in a series of 'nesting' kin groups. See Chapter 3 for a discussion of kipat tenure.

allowed for their alienation to Hindu groups. What took place echoed the Indian experience outlined by Hutton: 'Tribal customs which regulate the ownership, usufruct or transfer of land are normally superseded by a code in the application of which the tribe is deprived of its property, generally in the name of law . . . by alienation to foreigners . . .' (quoted in Elwin, 1943, 12).

In Nepal the outcome was similar, although certainly not so severe as described for India's tribal groups.

In the far-eastern part of the Kingdom, however, the situation was quite different. As I have stated, in Limbuan the kipat system was not abolished. Indeed, the government has always followed an equivocal policy towards this region. Legislation has reduced considerably the area held under kipat, but the Limbus have been allowed to retain at least a portion of their ancestral lands under this form of tenure.

In Limbuan, therefore, the struggle for tribal land is not a phenomenon of the past, but an ongoing process which continues to affect social relations in the region.

The government's adoption of a special policy towards the Limbus derives, at least in part, from the relations between the Hindu rulers and the semi-independent Limbu chiefdoms at the time of the invasion. The incorporation of Limbuan into the Nepal state was a result both of negotiation and of conquest. The expansion eastwards of the Hindu armies in the 1770s resulted in a series of alliances with potentially troublesome Limbu chiefs flanking them on all sides. In a royal declaration issued by the first king of Nepal, Prithvi Narayan Shah, the Limbus, in return for their support, were assured a measure of internal rule under their chiefs and guaranteed their rights to ancestral lands.[1] Limbuan's strategic location has played some part in holding subsequent rulers in Kathmandu to this initial pledge.

The Limbus are thus identified with the kipat system of tenure, and for some time now only Limbus have been able to own this kind of land. All other groups, Hindu and tribal, possess land under the raikar system, which is the dominant form of tenure in the country.[2] Both systems exist side by side in Limbuan.

1 Royal order to the Limbus of Far Kirat (Limbuan), 1774 (quoted in Regmi, 1965, 151–2).
2 A variety of land tenure forms have been noted for Nepal. Most were abolished after 1951. Cf. Regmi, 1963, 1964, 1965, for a description of these systems.

But however much the Limbus have been singled out for special treatment, the Hindu settlers have benefited even more from government legislation reducing the area under kipat tenure (and correspondingly increasing the amount under raikar tenure) and have succeeded in becoming the ascendant section of the population in east Nepal. The Limbus, moreover, have been hard-pressed to retain the cultivation rights to their remaining kipat lands. Land pressures and excessive social expenditure, among other things, have forced them to turn for assistance to the wealthier Hindus in their midst. They have grown dependent on the latter for credit. To obtain these loans the Limbus have had to pledge their lands. Under the system prevailing in this part of Nepal, the creditor, in lieu of interest, gets the right to cultivate the land for as long as the loan is outstanding. The Hindus, for their part, are anxious to have cultivation rights to these kipat lands, since their own raikar lands are in short supply. In consequence, the Limbus have been deprived of the usufruct of their lands. On the surface, therefore, their plight is not very different from that of the tribes who have lost lands outright to the Hindus. But the reality is not so simple. Kipat land is not permanently alienable. This means that however long a Hindu creditor retains the usufruct of the land belonging to the Limbu debtor, he cannot become the owner of the land. The Limbu has only to repay the loan to repossess the land. Until recently this possibility was remote. It is no longer so. Two main developments are responsible.

During the past fifty years Limbus have taken on a large scale to service as mercenaries in the 'Gurkha' regiments of foreign armies. This has provided a significant source of cash income and enabled a number of Limbus to repossess lands pledged generations ago to Hindu creditors.

A second main source of earnings stems from the considerable expansion in government services and economic activity since the overthrow in 1950–1 of the Rana régime and the emergence of the country from almost a century of isolation and stagnation. A variety of local commercial opportunities have been created and these have at least mitigated Limbu dependence on Hindu sources of employment and credit.

Thus such factors as State land policy, army service and the economic growth of rural areas have affected the struggle for land, and shaped the relations between the groups involved in this struggle.

In the district of Ilam, where this study was conducted, there is little new jungle to break or virgin land to bring under cultivation. Given the existing level of technology and pattern of cultivation, the land is unable adequately to support the population. Nevertheless, over 95% of the district's inhabitants still depend for a substantial part of their livelihood on subsistence agriculture. Hence the need to obtain land or to retain lands already in one's possession.

For more than a half-century the amount of cultivable land in east Nepal has remained more or less static. During the same period the population has increased substantially, due both to natural growth and to immigration. The figures for Ilam alone have risen from an estimated 89,000 in 1920 (when tentative figures first became available) to 124,000 at the time of the 1961 Census. These figures do not take account of population movements across the eastern borders of the country.

Pressure on land was recognized as the principal cause of emigration as early as the 1890s. At that time, one visitor to Sikkim remarked of the Nepalese: '. . . it is because every bit of the land in their country is taken up that there is such a steady emigration into Sikkim' (Donaldson, 1900, 208).

By 1891 over half the population of Darjeeling was of Nepalese origin, and one-third had been born in Nepal (O'Malley, 1907, 43). Nepalese have provided the greater part of the labour force for the tea estates of Darjeeling.

According to the 1941 Census of India, Nepal provided 45% of the foreign immigrants into India. One author suggests that there are 3 million people of Nepalese origin regularly resident in north Bengal and north Assam alone (Patterson, 1962, 193). Another estimates that 2 million Nepalese live in India, Sikkim and Bhutan (Rose, 1963, 117).

To take Sikkim alone, Nepalese immigration into that state began in the latter half of the nineteenth century, and reached such proportions that laws were promulgated by the Sikkim authorities to check the flow (Nakane, 1966, 260). Still, by 1951 77·2% of the people spoke one of the languages of Nepal as their mother tongue (Davis, 1951).

The decision to emigrate is not taken lightly. It means severing ties with kin – although many retain links with relatives in Nepal for many years – and can lead to even greater difficulties than those left behind, especially for the first generation of migrants. Nakane describes some of the hardships faced by Nepalese who go to Sikkim. Many become coolies in bazaar towns and hope in this way to earn enough to purchase land and settle down in a hamlet. In her words, 'It normally takes many many years from the time one leaves home until the final place for settling down as a peasant is found. . . . Some fail to become peasants and remain as coolies all their life' (1966, 255).

Those who have left their homes in east Nepal do not fall within the scope of this study.[1] But no examination of social life in this part of the country can ignore the ever-present possibility of having to emigrate. It is this threat which provides the edge to the struggle for land.

The problems to be considered in this book will be discussed in relation to a cluster of four contiguous settlements situated in the Ilam-Darda sub-division of Ilam district in east Nepal. They are referred to as the Indreni Cluster.

The Cluster is not a definitive residential unit, surrounded as it is on three sides by other settlements, into which it merges (see map, p. 18). Nor is it a unit in any administrative sense. It has sociological significance, however, in that it is recognized by people in the surrounding area as the place where the Limbus live, and is referred to by everyone as 'Limbu *gaon*'.[2]

There are many such Limbu clusters in Ilam district. The location of their settlements in the midst of non-Limbu populations reflects both the manner in which the district came to be settled and the effects of State land policy.

During the years prior to the creation of the Kingdom Limbu settlements had been established throughout the district. These settlements were generally situated on the tops of ridges, and the inhabitants laid claim to large tracts of forest and uncultivated bush surrounding the areas they inhabited.[3] Following the Hindu invasion, large-scale migrations of non-Limbus entered the district.

1 In the settlements where I conducted field work approximately 17% of all household heads could name at least one close male relative – son, brother, father's brother – who had emigrated to India and with whom all contact had been lost.
2 '*Gaon*', usually translated as 'village', is in fact used in a variety of contexts. See p. 23.
3 There is evidence to suggest that prior to and for some years after the arrival in east Nepal of the Hindus Ilam contained a sizeable population of Lepchas, whom the Limbus either drove out or intermarried with (cf.

The Limbus made generous grants of land to accommodate the immigrant settlers. Towards the end of the nineteenth century the government changed to raikar the system of tenure on those lands which had been granted, thus effectively removing them from Limbu control. By and large the Limbus were left the lands they had not granted the immigrants, which in effect meant those they were cultivating and living on themselves. This historical process is mirrored in the settlement pattern which finds Limbu inhabitants now living on lands held primarily under kipat tenure, surrounded by and occasionally interspersed with non-Limbus who enjoy rights to land under raikar tenure. About one-fifth of the inhabitants of the Indreni Cluster are members of non-Limbu groups.

The majority of those receiving Limbu grants were Brahmans. It is difficult to say precisely why this was. Several possibilities suggest themselves. They were among the earliest of the immigrants in Limbuan. They were certainly the most numerous: indeed, for some years now they have outnumbered the Limbus in Ilam. Undoubtedly they brought skills and labour resources which the Limbus needed. According to some informants, Brahmans frequently succeeded, by a variety of devious means, in obtaining for themselves lands initially granted to others by the Limbus. And, finally, Brahmans were by virtue of their ability to read and write and because of their high caste status, best placed to take advantage of any administrative regulations designed to reduce the area under kipat tenure.

I have chosen to concentrate on Limbu ties with the Brahmans because the latter are the most numerous and the wealthiest – in short, the dominant – segment among the Hindus, and because the struggle for land is essentially the struggle between these two groups. As I have noted, it has both divided and linked them. The cleavage created by the land-confrontation is expressed in and reinforced by attitudes of hostility, by the absence of reciprocal, co-operative relations and marriage ties, the lack of participation by members of one group in the social or religious ceremonies of the other, and by their overall cultural apartness.

But cleavage and division represent only one aspect of the con-

---

Rock, 1953; Nebesky–Wojkowitz, 1956). Whatever the case, the Lepchas no longer exist as a separate community in Ilam. When I refer to the Limbus as the indigenous population I mean only that they preceded the Hindus.

figuration of relationships. Interests in scarce land create ties of interdependence. Brahmans and Limbus are linked as creditors and debtors, landlords and tenants, farmers and agricultural labourers. These two groups are interdependent in a political context as well. The political hierarchy created two centuries ago by Brahman dependence on Limbu land grants gradually collapsed and was replaced by one in which the Brahmans have become the most powerful group.

The relationships between the Limbus and the Brahmans and the changes which are taking place in these relationships are presented essentially from the standpoint of the Limbus. It is the Limbu sector within the Indreni Cluster which provides the focus for the discussion, and an important theme in the book relates to changes in Limbu institutions resulting from confrontation with the Brahmans.

From the documents and writings I have seen and from personal observations made during visits to other parts of the region, I am satisfied that the type of social changes here described are not confined to any one section of east Nepal. Even so, I am not concerned to argue that the detailed processes of change recorded in this study of one cluster of settlements are typical of changes in the district of Ilam or Limbuan as a whole.[1] This is because factors such as the ratio of Limbus to Brahmans or any other dominant Hindu group, the availability of land, the impact of government legislation, or the existence of economic alternatives to agriculture vary from one locality to another. In other words, the magnitude of these 'variables' and the manner of their combination are not everywhere the same. This means that the degree and pace of change differ from one settlement cluster to another. But to the extent that many of the elements present in this single locality are to be found wherever Hindus have entered tribal areas it is to be hoped that the present study will contribute to an understanding of Hindu-tribal relations in other parts of South Asia.

In a different direction the problems discussed in this book have a universal relevance, in that they relate to the ways in which a community reacts to domination by a more powerful interloper. The Hindu-tribal confrontation provides an appropriate setting for a

1 For a discussion of the problem of 'typicality' in studies of this kind see Cohen, 1965, 176; Stirling, 1965, 25.

consideration of this question. It represents, *par excellence*, a relationship between groups of unequal endowment. The Hindus are now
economically, politically and educationally the tribesmen's superiors.
In the south Asian context the tribes are regarded as synonymous
with the backward, the exploited and the dispossessed; the Hindus
are those who exploit and dispossess them.[1]

These are the kinds of conditions which, in various parts of the
world, have given rise to religious movements (cf. Mair, 1959;
Worsley, 1957). In east Nepal the Limbus have been able to come to
grips with their dilemma, not by directing social disenchantment into
religious channels, but by organizing a political struggle to preserve
ancestral lands under the kipat form of tenure.

To defend this vital economic interest the Limbus must reiterate
their common identity and cultural apartness from the rest of eastern
Nepalese society. Moreover, because the system of tenure is fused
with and articulates the culture, the very survival of the Limbu way
of life is seen as bound up with the preservation of kipat land. This
book, then, apart from its concern with Hindu-tribal relations, ex-
plores the link between culture and politics in a tribal community
dominated by an alien group and threatened with what it regards as
economic disaster and cultural annihilation.

The next chapter provides the relevant background to the discussion
which follows. Chapter 3 describes the kipat system of land tenure as
it relates to the structure of Limbu kin groups. Chapter 4 then looks
at the cleavage between Limbus and Brahmans, and this is followed
by a consideration of their interdependent relationships: first in an
economic and then in a political context (Chapters 5 and 6). Before
concluding, Chapter 7 examines the Limbu movement to defend their
interests in land, and the role of culture in this struggle.

---

1 I ignore, in the interests of introducing the discussion, the more complex
reality. Tribesmen (who may claim to be Hindus) share a variety of problems in common with other depressed sections of the population (also
Hindus) who are exploited by dominant groups. I side-step the com-
plexities by using Hindu to mean the Brahmans and other high-caste
groups.

Chapter 2

The setting

Ilam district

The settlements of Angbung, Bharapa, Chitok and Dorumba –
which for shorthand purposes I call the Indreni settlement cluster –
are situated in the district of Ilam in east Nepal. The greater part of
the district falls in the middle ranges of the country, a strip of rugged
hills reaching to heights of 12,000 feet above sea-level and stretching
from east to west along the 500-mile length of the Kingdom. The
hills of Ilam rise sharply from the Terai to the south, a twenty-mile
wide belt of low-lying flatlands which is a continuation of the Gangetic
plain of India.

Ilam encompasses an area of 540 square miles. It is bounded on the
east by Sikkim and the Darjeeling district of West Bengal, while to
the west and north lie the districts of Dhankutta and Panchthar. The
area is mainly characterized by irregular terrain and poor soil,
necessitating the use of terraces for cultivation.

Paddy, maize and millet are the principal crops grown in the
district. Paddy – as many as twelve varieties are cultivated – is
planted in irrigated terraces (*khet*) along the mountain-slopes, mainly
in the lowlands close to river valleys. A comprehensive system of
irrigation channels directs the mountain streams into the paddy
terraces, which store the water. During the first two weeks of May,
prior to the commencement of the monsoon rains, seed-beds are
ploughed, inundated, and levelled, after which they are seeded and
fertilized with green leaves. Five to six weeks later, when the seedlings
are about 12 inches high, they are transplanted into the paddy
terraces, which have in the meanwhile been prepared as were the
seed-beds. During September, the fields are weeded and the paddy is
ready for harvesting in November. Most cultivators in the district
grow only one paddy crop a year. There is little attempt to plant

Ilam

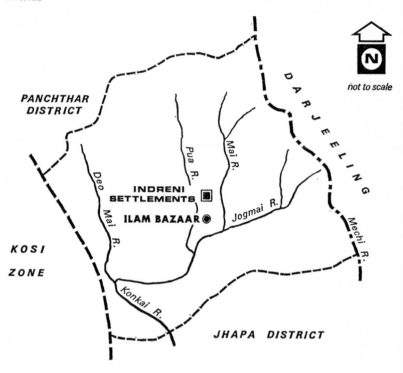

not to scale

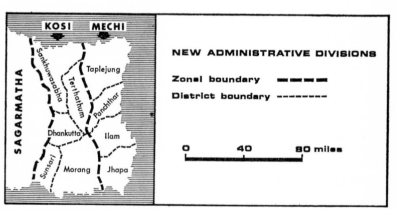

NEW ADMINISTRATIVE DIVISIONS

Zonal boundary ▬ ▬ ▬ ▬
District boundary -------

0   40   80 miles

winter crops for fear of their effects on the paddy yield. Only a few wealthy men grow small quantities of wheat in paddy lands at higher elevations. They are able to do so because of adequate livestock holdings which enable them to manure the fields.

Maize is the chief crop grown in dry fields (*bari*), generally situated on higher ground and mainly on plots surrounding homesteads. The fields are first fertilized with a mixture of straw, leaves and manure, which is then ploughed into the soil. In March, with the onset of the brief and intermittent spring rains, the seed is broadcast. About eight weeks after planting and again four or five weeks later the fields are weeded. The maize is ready for harvesting in late August or early September.

Millet, the third most important crop grown in Ilam, is sown in seed-beds on dry land in July, and transplanted about four weeks later. Some cultivators plant the seedlings in the shade of the maize stalks, while others prefer to clear a small plot beforehand. One weeding, in September, is sufficient, and the crop is reaped in November.

The district of Ilam experiences a moderate climate, temperatures seldom rising above 85 °F. during the warm season from April to September, or falling below 45 °F. during the cool months of January and February. From mid-June to mid-September the monsoon rains persist, and leave a precipitation of some 60 inches. Ilam contains a small basin, drained by four rivers – Mai, Pua Mai, Deo Mai and Jog Mai[1] – which dissect the district into four main sub-divisions (*thum*).

The Indreni settlements lie in a contiguous belt along the eastern slope of a 4,500-foot ridge in the Ilam-Darda sub-division of the district. Ilam-Darda, with an area of 55 square miles, comprises about 10% of the total area of the district. It is bounded on the east and west by the Mai and Pua rivers respectively, which meet south of Ilam Bazaar, the district capital, and join with the Jog Mai and Deo Mai rivers to flow southward into the plains as the Konkai.

Ilam-Darda sub-division contains a population of about 16,200, or roughly 13% of the district's total. This makes Ilam-Darda the most densely settled of Ilam's four sub-divisions, with a ratio of 294·5 persons per square mile, as against 235·2 for the district as a whole.

Ilam is one of six districts in east Nepal which constitute what is known as Limbuan – the country of the Limbus. Lying east of the Arun River, between the high Himalayas and the plains, Limbuan

1 Ilam is often referred to as *Char Khola* (Four Rivers).

comprises an area of approximately 4,500 square miles, or about 8% of the total area of present-day Nepal.

The Limbus are generally regarded as among the first inhabitants of east Nepal. Together with the Rais, they are thought to be the descendants of the ancient Kiratis.[1] In the *Mahabharata* the Kiratis were said to dwell in the eastern Himalayan regions. In many contemporary government documents the area of east Nepal is still referred to as Kirat. The country inhabited mainly by Rais lies in the mid-region of east Nepal between the Dudh Kosi and the Arun rivers and is termed 'Middle Kirat', whereas the Limbu country east of the Arun river, i.e. Limbuan, is called 'Far Kirat'.

The Limbus enter recorded history about the eighteenth century, by which time a number of small chiefdoms in Limbuan were subject to the kingdom of Bijayapur, ruled by a branch of the Sen Dynasty of Muckwanpur.[2] Hamilton (1819, 8) notes how the Kirati tribesmen 'formed the principal strength of these Rajput chiefs ... and the Rajputs, who were united with them, did not presume to act as masters, to invade their lands or violate their customs'. The tenuous control of the Sen rulers over their hill subjects led one missionary resident in the Valley of Kathmandu in the mid-eighteenth century to refer to the 'independent' nation of the 'Ciratas' lying to the east of Kathmandu (Giuseppe, 1790, 308).

By 1772 the armies of Prithvi Narayan Shah, having subdued the Valley of Kathmandu, began their advance into Kirati country.[3] In 1774 Ilam fell (D. R. Regmi, 1961, 96). The invaders erected there a series of forts to secure communications with the plains and from which to launch an eastern offensive. By 1810 they reached the banks

1 There is some disagreement over the proper designation of the term 'Kirati'. Although most writers include both Rais and Limbus, Vansittart (1915, 7) says that it belongs properly to the Rais, but because of intermarriage between Rais and Limbus he includes the latter within the 'Kirati group'. Chemjong (1952) suggests that all Mongolian peoples inhabiting the Himalayas and parts of south-east Asia as well are descendants of the Kiratis.

2 Chemjong (1952) argues that there were a number of Limbu chiefdoms which were not subservient to Hindu kings.

3 The growth of Shah power began in Gorkha, one of the petty kingdoms which had arisen in west Nepal following the large migration of high-caste Hindus from north India who fled in the path of the Moslem invasion. About 1768 the reigning Shah king took advantage of wars between the Newar rulers in the Valley of Kathmandu to further his own political ambitions.

of the Tista River in Sikkim. Only the intervention of the British stopped their advance, and in 1817 Nepal's eastern boundary was put back to the Mechi River, where it has remained since.

From the time of its incorporation into the Kingdom, Ilam, largely because of its natural boundaries and strategic location, has remained a distinct unit of administration. During the quarter-century following the conquest Ilam was administered separately by its own military authorities (Hodgson, 1880, 201). During most of the nineteenth century Ilam was nominally part of a larger unit of administration, with headquarters at Chainpur, but the district continued to be governed by the military, who collected customs and revenues and dispensed justice. Hodgson, writing about a century after the conquest, notes that the head of the Ilam garrison

is a captain and has a hundred soldiers under him, with eight artillerymen and one cannon of small calibre. This officer is also the civil authority of the arondissement, and raises the extraordinary revenue thereof to meet the local expenses, sending the balance, if any, to Kathmandu. The land revenue is wholly assigned to his troops in pay (1880, 204).

By the end of the nineteenth century the civil authority had largely replaced the military in Ilam. In 1890 the district was removed from the nominal control of Chainpur and the governor (*Bada Hakim*) was made directly responsible to the government in Kathmandu. In that year a magistrate's court was established in the district capital. Only revenue matters continued to be handled by the militia until about 1910, when a branch of the treasury department (*mal*) was set up in the district.

In 1952, following the overthrow of the Rana régime, which had ruled the country for over a century,[1] the government established a 'Panchayat' system of local committees and courts. In Ilam, the Panchayat lasted four years in the first instance, and in 1962, under a reconstituted system, was reintroduced and was still in effect at the time of field-work.

The various committees established under the Panchayat system were grafted on to but did not replace the traditional administrative structure. At the national level, the locus of power in the country remained the monarch and his appointees who head the various departments and ministries in the government.

Administration in the districts is still effected under the supervision

1 For a good account of the events of 1950-1 and following see Driver, 1963.

of a governor appointed by the monarch. The governor is primarily responsible for the maintenance of law and order in the district, and retains command of the militia and police. He also co-ordinates the activities of the various local departments and initiates such pro-grammes and activities as may fall outside the scope of these district branches. Traditionally, due to poor communications between Kathmandu and Ilam, the governor's authority was virtually absolute and extended to all matters of local administration. Recently the boundaries of jurisdiction between the office of the governor and the various departments have become more clearly defined. With the gradual improvement of communications between Kathmandu and the districts, central departments are tending to exercise firmer control over their local branches than in the past. As a result, the role of governor is more and more restricted to 'general supervision' of the various district departments (Malhotra, 1958).

To coincide with the establishment of a new Panchayat system in 1962 administrative boundaries in the country were redrawn. The country is now divided into fourteen 'development zones'. Each zone is divided into a number of 'development districts' – there are seventy-five throughout the country – which are further subdivided into administrative 'villages'. Together with the districts of Jhapa in the Terai and Panchthar and Taplejung to the north, Ilam became part of the Mechi zone, easternmost of the country's zonal divisions. The creation of new districts, however, did not affect Ilam's boundaries. Although the 1962 reorganization foresees emphasis on zonal rather than on district programming,[1] in 1964–5 the primary unit of development and government was still the district. Ilam as we know it today has remained a constant administrative entity since its in-corporation into the Kingdom some 200 years ago.

The Indreni Cluster

The Indreni cluster of settlements is contained in the village[2] of Syawa. The heterogeneous population of the village is probably not

1 Governors are gradually being replaced by area commissioners responsible for zonal affairs, each of whom may have one or more assistants to deal with district problems.
2 Wherever the term 'village' is used, I shall mean only the administratively-defined area under the jurisdiction of the recently created Panchayat Committee. See pp. 163 ff.

untypical of Ilam's. It contains thirteen different groups. Their numbers are given in Table 1.

TABLE 1
Syawa village population

	Population	*Percentage of population*	
Hindus	—	—	52·9
Brahmans	929	32·5	
Jaisis[1]	359	12·6	
Chetris	223	7·8	
Limbus	523	—	18·3
Other tribal groups	—	—	15·4
Rais	220	7·7	
Sunwars	90	3·2	
Gurungs	62	2·2	
Magars	42	1·5	
Tamangs	23	0·8	
Newars	158	—	5·5
Untouchables	—	—	7·9
Blacksmiths	95	3·3	
Tailors	68	2·4	
Cobblers	64	2·2	
	2,856	100·0	100·0

At the time of field-work the Indreni settlements contained a population of 511 men, women and children. The ethnic breakdown is shown in Table 2.

TABLE 2
Indreni Cluster : population breakdown

Settlement	*Brahmans*	*Jaisis*	*Limbus*	*Magars*	*Blacksmiths*	*Total*
Angbung	–	–	120	–	–	120
Bharapa	12	–	115	24	11	162
Chitok	22	–	112	–	3	137
Dorumba	23	7	62	–	–	92
	57	7	409	24	14	511

1 See p. 70.

3

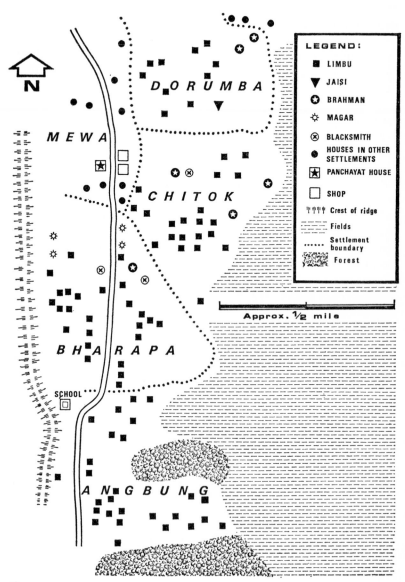

The Indreni settlements are located between three and four miles north of Ilam Bazaar, the district capital. They straddle a road which leads from the capital to a point about eight miles away, where the district's only lake is situated. Although vegetation in the area is lush, especially during and immediately following the monsoon rains, there is a conspicuous dearth of woodland. The dense bamboo forests which once covered the greater part of the ridge slopes have been denuded, leaving only sparse groves dotted sporadically around the hills.

There is no central square or meeting-spot which serves as a gathering-place for Indreni residents at the end of a working day. At one point on the main road to the west of Chitok there is a tiny hut which shelters the Panchayat Committee when it meets, and at most times of day a few men may be found there relaxing and trading news. Opposite the hut are two small shops with a combined inventory of about Rs 500. These provide a few items of stationery for local schoolchildren, religious articles, kerosene, tobacco and paper, sweets and a few staples, such as spices, sugar and salt. They are visited by Indreni residents only to replenish unexpected shortages, and then usually by persons living in the immediate vicinity of the shops. Most people prefer to combine their shopping with the excitement of market day in Ilam Bazaar.

The capital is only a one-hour walk south along the main road from Angbung, the southernmost settlement in the Cluster and just under a two-hour walk from the northernmost – Dorumba. On Thursdays, and to a lesser extent Sundays, hundreds of petty traders from the surrounding settlements set up 'shop' in the main square, squatting on blankets and bamboo mats to sell their wares. Shoppers can buy from these small traders as well as from the permanent shops and stalls situated along the main street of the town. There are about ninety such shops and stalls offering a wide variety of consumer items – imported mainly from India – and services.

TABLE 3
Shops in Ilam Bazaar

28 cloth shops; most carry other goods, such as kerosene, sugar, metals.
21 tea stalls; most sell cigarettes and sweets; some also sell liquor clandestinely.
29 general shops, carrying both Western and Ayurvedic medicines, stationery, toys, torches, lanterns, batteries and food staples.

1 hardware shop, selling various copper, iron and aluminium cooking
   vessels.
1 shoe shop.
1 watch- and torch-repair shop.
1 'pharmacy', carrying mainly Western patent medicines.
12 stalls for shoe-repairs, tailor, smith, barber, laundry, etc.

Between Angbung and Bharapa, on a small rise beside the main
road, is the only school for the children of the Indreni Cluster and
settlements to the north of it. Built of mud and stone, with a thatched
roof, the school has three teachers for its five grades. Beside the
school there is a large playground, the only flat spread of land to be
seen in the area, but only the schoolchildren use it for exercises or
games. None of the adults in the surrounding settlements are ever to
be seen playing on the field.

The Indreni settlements suffer from no shortage of water for drinking or bathing and every house is within easy reach of at least one
water-source (*dhara*). Water is usually tapped from a spring and run
through a split bamboo 'pipe' to an area which has been cleared and
laid over with stones. At such water-sources women are frequently
found washing clothes or filling copper or earthen jugs with water,
and passing the time by exchanging gossip.

Although several houses in the Cluster are situated alongside the
main road, most are set back a distance and can be reached only by a
series of narrow footpaths. The houses are constructed on unirrigated
plots along the crest of the main ridge at altitudes between 3,500–
4,500 feet. Households usually reserve a small section of their homestead sites to grow mustard seed, potatoes, squashes, cabbages,
cauliflowers, spinach, pumpkins, cucumbers, tomatoes, etc. Bananas
are the most commonly kept fruit.

An area in front of each house is cleared and levelled to provide a
courtyard, in which most domestic chores are carried out. Often a
raised platform on which the household's maize crop is stored is
placed in the centre of the yard. During the dry season men weave
wicker baskets, repair ploughs or pass the time away in the open
courtyard. Here women pound and polish rice, wash utensils or brew
millet beer. Grains are left to dry on long mats of split bamboo, and
rice for the daily meals is winnowed in the courtyard.

Unlike the practice followed in some parts of Nepal, cattle and
domestic animals are not kept inside the main house. Cattle-byres,
pig- and goat-pens are constructed on the edge of the courtyard,

while chickens are kept under baskets or in other containers out of the way of preying jackals.

Most people live in one-room houses built of stone with a thatched roof and a partly-enclosed verandah facing the courtyard. In none of these dwellings are chimneys or proper ventilation found. Windows are the exception and are usually covered by wooden shutters. As a consequence houses are generally dark and smoke-filled. The lower part of the outside walls are covered with red earth and the top may be whitewashed with lime. The floors of the inner house and verandah are covered with a mixture of red earth and cow-dung and re-plastered at the beginning of each Nepalese month and on other special occasions.

Even in the most well-to-do houses furniture is minimal. Beds are uncommon: people sleep on hay or bamboo mats laid out on the floor. While some of the wealthier households can afford a few chairs, most people sit on small round mats made of maize coverings or on locally woven blankets.

The characteristic residential pattern is one of wide distribution of dwellings, a pattern broken only occasionally by small clusters of houses. Instead of nucleated villages, we find dispersed settlements which merge into one another. The settlement is never accurately defined. Its name locates a man's place of residence, but except where distinctive geographical features divide a settlement from its neighbours, the boundaries between them are vague and, for the people themselves, quite unimportant. I have seen documents referring to the same man, living in the border area between settlements and written with his knowledge, citing his place of residence as Angbung on one occasion, Bharapa on another, and a third settlement outside the Cluster on yet another. A brief description of settlement boundaries in the Indreni Cluster will illustrate the residential pattern.

Angbung, the southernmost settlement in the Cluster, is the most compact of the four, so that every house is within easy reach, via a network of footpaths, of every other house in the settlement. Angbung has also the most definitive boundaries of any of the settlements in the Cluster. It is bordered on the west by the main road to Ilam Bazaar (only one house is situated on the western side of the road, atop a small rise). On the north and east Angbung is bounded by fields, and on the south by a wood. It is not completely isolated, however, for the houses of Bharapa continue along the ridge, on both sides of the main road, from where those of Angbung leave off.

There is a wider distribution of houses in Bharapa than in Angbung, save for one cluster of six dwellings to the west of the main road. Whereas the ridge-top to the west and fields down the eastern slope of the ridge bound the settlement on two sides, it 'fades' into Angbung on the south, into Chitok on the north-east, and into yet another settlement outside the Cluster – called Mewa – on the north-west.

The residential pattern in Chitok is similar to that of Bharapa: again, with the exception of one cluster of four houses and another of five, most houses tend to be widely dispersed. Residents of Chitok have clear ideas about the boundaries of their settlement to the east (fields extending down to the Mai River) and to the north (a glen between two hills). The boundaries with Bharapa to the south and with Mewa to the west, however, are ill-defined.

Houses in Dorumba are more widely spaced than in any of the other settlements in the Cluster. Although the boundaries are clearly demarcated to the south (the glen north of Chitok) and to the east and north-west (fields) there is no clear boundary between the houses of Mewa which extend westward up the ridge to the main road and those of Dorumba, nor between those of the latter and the dwellings of yet another settlement to the north-east.

Settlements are neither exogamous nor endogamous units. Nor are the inhabitants of any one settlement bound together by any common rituals. Because of the necessity of subdividing scarce plots, sibling groups tend to live on adjacent lands and thus to inhabit the same settlement. In several cases, however, siblings do live in different settlements. Moreover, links to kin units beyond the sibling group extend regularly into neighbouring settlements within the Cluster. Those persons who pay taxes to a headman are linked across the vague boundaries of settlement. Similarly, mourning obligations on the death of an agnate crystallize Limbu groups without reference to settlement.

In day-to-day contexts the persons with whom one interacts most frequently are neighbours. A household which runs short of salt or cooking oil borrows from a neighbour; those without a foot-pestle for pounding rice or millet use their neighbour's. During the agricultural season neighbours exchange labour. They are among the first to be invited to weddings or funeral rites. On warm evenings neighbours gather in one another's courtyards and tell stories or chat leisurely. But because of the settlement pattern a man's neighbourhood does not always coincide with his settlement. Those in the fringe areas between settlements count neighbours on both sides of the boundary. In a sense, then, neighbourhoods are egocentred and must be conceptualized as a series of overlapping circles which cut across settlement boundaries, unless these are prominent geographical barriers.

There is no Nepalese word which specifically denotes those units here called settlements. The word *gaon*, usually translated as village, is employed in a variety of contexts. It can refer to the general area, so that a man out for a stroll will say simply: 'I am going to the *gaon*.' It may denote the named unit of residence, i.e. what I have meant by settlement. The region subsumed by the new Panchayat Committee is called a *gaon*, although it includes a number of settlements. Within the confines of any settlement a small cluster of houses may be called a *gaon*. Finally, because the Indreni Cluster contains a substantial concentration of Limbus, it is generally referred to as 'Limbu *gaon*'.

Chapter 3

Land and kin groups

How does an individual obtain rights to kipat land? In this chapter I consider the question by describing the structure of Limbu kin groups – clan, lineage and household – and their relationships to land. It is then shown how, over time, these groups have been compelled to define their criteria of membership more rigidly in order to defend their interests in scarce land. This has led to the existence in the Indreni settlements of a category of Limbus who have no rights to kipat lands in the Cluster.

Clan and local clan segment

The Limbus are divided into a number of named units which may be referred to as sub-tribes, although they normally allude to these units as *thar*, which is the same word they use for the clan. Vansittart (1915, 117–23) lists over eighty such sub-tribes among the Limbus. Some, such as the Nembekes found in the Cluster, have no sub-divisions and so constitute both a sub-tribe and a clan. The sub-tribe Tamling is represented in the Indreni settlements by two clans, the Chongbung and the Kambo.[1] Members of these Tamling clans claim not to marry with several other Tamling clans, but they contradict one another about which ones. It can be assumed that the clan and not the sub-tribe is the basic unit of exogamy.

Over the years the clan has become dispersed, and its segments have cleared and laid claim to virgin lands in a number of areas of east Nepal. In much of Limbuan, certainly in Ilam, rights to occupy particular

---

1 All the sub-tribes and clans mentioned in the text, like the settlement cluster, have been given fictitious names.

areas of land under kipat tenure derive not from direct royal grants nor from 'estates of holding' conferred by superior authority, but by virtue of being 'first settler'.[1] These first settlers, migrating from areas of relatively high population density, or for political or security reasons, led small groups of kinsmen into what was mainly jungle and staked out claims to vacant lands. Following the Shah conquest the government allowed that Limbuan was a kipat area, hence Limbus who had cleared the land and brought it under cultivation 'by their own hoe' or would subsequently do so could claim the land as their own kipat. The legitimization by a royal decree of these claims to land by first settlers came much later, sometimes generations after the fact.

The Chongbungs of the Indreni settlements express clan dispersion in a kinship idiom which designates each settlement cluster known to harbour some members of the clan as the place where one Chongbung sibling founder settled after leaving the original (unspecified) clan territory north of Ilam. Thus, the second Chongbung brother is said to have gone to Jidhpur, a settlement cluster to the south-west of the Indreni settlements; the third brother ended up in Phungetapa, in the western part of the district, and so on. The Indreni Chongbungs reserve for their own apical ancestor – whose name, Sai Kemba, can be cited by only a handful of the more articulate Chongbungs – the position of senior sibling (*jetha*) of the original group which staked out lands in various parts of east Nepal.

The justification for the presence of Kambos in the Indreni settlements presents something of a problem for the inhabitants. Since no other Kambo groups are known to exist outside the Indreni settlements, the Kambos cannot claim that they are part of a wider clan. Several explanations are offered for their presence. One suggests that the Kambos are in fact the descendants of the fifth Chongbung sibling who came to the Indreni settlements with his eldest brother. Another relates that Chongbungs and Kambos were one clan until a severe famine occurred. Some members of the clan are a species of stinging nettle found in the hills, and these people came to be known as Chongbungs. Others ate soil, and they became Kambos.[2]

A third explanation, more commonly heard, ties together elements

---

1 This notion of 'first settler' also exists in parts of Zambia (cf. White, 1958, 127).
2 The letters *KAM*, which also appear in the true name of this clan, is the Limbu word for soil. The word for nettle (*sikya*) bears no similar relation to the true name of the group here called Chongbung.

of the first two with the early presence of Lepchas in Ilam.[1] I quote the version of one Chongbung informant:

This was the place of the Lepchas. There was a fish-trap at the confluence of the Pua and Mai rivers. Some Chongbungs from Panchthar arrived there and asked the Lepchas if they could borrow the fish-trap, since they were hungry. The following morning the Lepchas came to ask for the trap. 'We won't give it back,' the Chongbungs said. 'Why not?' the Lepchas asked. 'We'll teach you to make one and you can go somewhere else.' But the Chongbungs would not leave. So they fought there. Many Lepchas were killed, but they fought on. They came to Bharapa [in the Indreni Cluster] and still they fought on. Then the Lepchas said: 'We won't leave until you eat this soil.' What to do? So the Chongbungs sent for a kinsman and one came from Dharan.[2] He ate the soil, and his descendants became Kambos.

This last legend, like the first, emphasizes the seniority of the Chongbungs in the Indreni settlements. They are recognized as the first arrivals, the conquerors of the Lepchas, and the most prestigious of the descent groups in the Cluster. This status is bolstered by the fact that the majority of the Limbu population of the Cluster are Chongbungs. The third legend also points to the fact that the Chongbung who did eat the soil could not have been the apical forefather of the Indreni Chongbungs. On the contrary, it was an 'outsider' who was imported for the unsavoury task of soil-eating. And since he lived in the Terai, which is not a part of Limbuan, the implication is that he had lost contact with his ancestral kipat lands. This tends to support the private speculations of some informants that the Kambos were probably outsiders who came to the Indreni area after the Chongbungs, and were granted kipat land by the latter.

The Nembekes, with the second largest Limbu population in the Cluster, have links with a wider clan unit, but I have not heard any legends dealing with their arrival in Ilam. The two descent groups with the smallest populations in the Indreni settlements, the Phatras and Syelings, originally settled uxorilocally in the Cluster as affines of the Chongbungs. The latter conferred on them small kipat grants which are now inherited in the male line.

I refer to a group the members of which share the same clan name

---

1 See footnote on pp. 7–8.
2 Dharan is in the eastern Terai, just north of Biratnagar.

and trace descent patrilineally from a common 'first settler' in a cluster of settlements as a 'local clan segment'.[1]

The population of the five local clan segments with rights to kipat land in the Indreni Cluster are shown in Table 4.

TABLE 4
Population of local clan segments

Local clan segment	Population
Chongbung	256
Kambo	37
Nembeke	48
Syeling	5
Phatra	5
	351

By virtue of membership of such a local clan segment a Limbu obtains rights of ownership[2] to kipat land in the territory with which it is associated. Rights to a share in the kipat land of one local descent group, however, do not accrue to members of another even where both are part of the same clan. In other words, the bearing of a particular clan name does not of itself entitle a Limbu to attach himself to any local clan segment whose members happen to have the same name. The importance of locality is borne out by the following instance:

In 1953 a man came to the Indreni Cluster and asked to speak to a Chongbung headman. He stated that he was a Chongbung and wished to settle in the Cluster on kipat belonging to the Chongbungs. He was questioned closely about his kin ties, and it became evident that the man was not the descendant of an Indreni Chongbung. It transpired that his forebears had migrated to India many generations before and that he no longer knew where his kipat was located. He only knew that

---

1 A case could be made for using the term 'maximal lineage' to describe such units. But given the fact that beyond three or four generations Limbu genealogies become obscure, it seems preferable to distinguish between local clan and lineage in terms of *stipulated* and *demonstrated* descent (cf. Kuper, 1947).

2 The term 'ownership' refers to the 'possession of a certain quantum of rights in respect of land' (Lloyd, 1962, 66). What these rights are in the context of the kipat system will emerge during the course of the chapter.

he was a Chongbung Limbu, and when he heard that there were members of his clan in the Indreni settlements, he had come in the hope of being given land. The man was refused and went away.

This instance highlights the fact that clan membership is not a sufficient credential for pressing a claim to kipat land. It is membership of a localized clan which validates a Limbu's right to land. As long as agnatic links can be remembered and traced, a member of a local clan segment, even if living away from the territory of the group, can exercise his rights to a plot of land. Thus the local clan segment must be seen to include those who are not in fact permanently resident in the group's territory.[1]

Lineage

When segmentation occurs within the local clan segment the unilineal descent groups which emerge can be called lineages. No special term is used for the four- to six-generational unit which traces genealogical links to a common ancestor. Like the clan and clan segment, it is referred to as *thar*.

The lineage is the core of and to a large extent synonymous with the tax-paying unit. Kipat taxes[2] are levelled without reference to the amount of land owned or cultivated. A Limbu pays tax as a member of a kipat-owning group provided he builds a homestead and establishes a right to a plot of the group's land. Taxes are paid to government-approved tax-collectors or headmen (Subba).

The Shah rulers did not create Subbas among the Limbus. They only absorbed the traditional headmen into the administrative structure of the new state. As pointed out earlier, first settlers had staked out claims to land and later their patrilineal descendants sought confirmation of their rights to hold these lands as kipat. Authentication by government automatically absorbed the Subba into the tax-collecting machinery and made him responsible for taxes due from lineage members.

The first written evidence of Limbu rights to hold kipat in the

---

1 Fried speaks of corporate functions of unilinear kin groups which 'lie dormant . . . but continue to exist if strangers who can identify themselves as members of the kin may move in and enjoy the benefits of unilinear kin group membership' (1957, 25).
2 For the amount of taxes paid see pp. 78–9.

Indreni Cluster dates to the first half of the nineteenth century.[1] The Chongbung Subba was the first to receive a royal decree (*lalmohar*) in 1825; this was followed by similar decrees to the Nembeke Subba in 1832, and to the Kambo Subba in 1852. Each '*lalmoharia* Subba' – as they are termed – was able to choose a number of lesser functionaries[2] from among his lineage mates to assist him in his duties, including those of tax-collection, and the functionaries were granted a measure of tax-relief by the government. With the growth in lineage numbers some of these functionaries were able to secure government approval to submit the taxes they collected directly to the revenue office. In this way, new lineages emerged as separate entities, and the functionaries at their head would then be regarded as Subbas. Thus, for example, in 1872 the Chongbung Subba applied to have subordinate titles granted to three of his father's classificatory brother's sons. The eldest of the three later became recognized as the first in a line of new Subbas for what is now a separate Chongbung lineage.

The Subba, then, articulates the fissiparous tendencies of the descent group. By this dual process of segmentation and validation of new tax-collectors by government, five Chongbung lineages have emerged. Because of a dispute, however, the details of which I was unable to learn, the headman of one of these lineages was dispossessed and attempts to replace him apparently were not sanctioned by the government. Instead, his tax-collecting duties were assigned to the Subba of another Chongbung lineage – the one genealogically closest. The members of the first lineage now recognize the latter Subba as their own headman. As a result, the Chongbungs now have four recognized tax-collectors, each of whom is regarded as a Subba, although in fact only one holds the title by official grant of a decree. No special status accompanies either the officially-appointed Subba or his lineage.[3] The differences between the latter kind of Subba and the lesser functionaries is known, but rights and obligations attending all those called Subba are identical. There is also the fact that all enjoy government approval. The Limbus themselves make no point of emphasizing the distinction, although the fact may be remembered when it seems worthwhile to do so. In the remainder of the text

---

1 The dating tends to confirm the statement by a former Governor of Ilam that only after 1820 were such written decrees issued to Subbas in the district (Lama, 1959).

2 These functionaries are called *rai, karta, karbari* and *budyauli*.

3 To receive a decree a Subba had to make certain payments. See p. 57.

'Subba' will be used to refer to all Limbu headmen regardless of the circumstances surrounding their initial appointment.

The Nembekes have not experienced fission as have the Chong-bungs. Their apical ancestor is traced back only five generations, so that the lineage has remained coincident with the local clan segment. The Nembekes consequently recognize only one Subba.

The Kambo group is divided into two lineages, each with its own Subba.

Lineages vary in size and extent of kipat ownership. Chongbung lineages average 51·2 persons, Kambo lineages 18·5, and the Nembeke group totals 48 persons. The percentage figures for lineage land ownership and population are given in Table 5.

TABLE 5
Lineage land ownership and population

Lineage	Percentage of kipat land owned	Percentage of kipat-owning population
Chongbungs		
Lineage 1	12·1	11·1
Lineage 2	11·0	12·5
Lineage 3	14·2	26·5
Lineage 4	4·2	5·7
Lineage 5	21·2	18·5
	62·7	74·3
Kambos		
Lineage 1	11·5	8·2
Lineage 2	7·8	2·8
	19·3	11·0
Nembekes	15·1	11·1
Phatras and Syelings	2·6 99·7	3·1 99·5

Lineage lands, especially irrigated fields for paddy, are scattered over an area of several square miles. Lineage dry plots, situated on higher ground and on which inhabitants construct their houses, though not as widely spaced as paddy lands, tend to be distributed

Distribution of dry lands in the Indreni Cluster

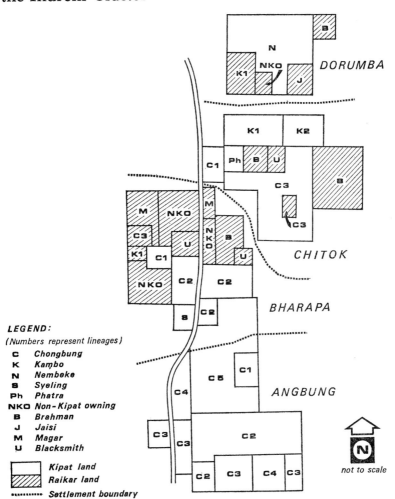

DORUMBA

CHITOK

BHARAPA

ANGBUNG

LEGEND:
(Numbers represent lineages)

C   Chongbung
K   Kaṃbo
N   Nembeke
S   Syeling
Ph   Phatra
NKO   Non-Kipat owning
B   Brahman
J   Jaisi
M   Magar
U   Blacksmith

     Kipat land
     Raikar land
.... Settlement boundary

not to scale

through more than one settlement in the Indreni Cluster. Chongbung lineage 1, for example, owns dry land in three settlements – Angbung, Bharapa and Chitok – while dry lands belonging to Chongbung lineages 2, 3 and 5 are found in two settlements (see map, p. 31).

The pattern of kipat dry-land distribution indicates that members of more than one kipat-owning lineage are usually neighbours within a single settlement. However, lineage land in a particular settlement is not distributed haphazardly among all lineage mates, but is likely to belong to a branch of the lineage. So that siblings and extended families incline to subdivide adjacent holdings and thus to occupy the same settlement. In some cases land associated with a particular lineage or lineage branch extends across the vague boundaries of settlements, so that members of one lineage branch might live in the same neighbourhood, but in different settlements.

Household

As we have seen, an individual obtains rights to kipat land by virtue of membership in a patrilineal descent group. These rights, however, devolve through the mediation of the household with which he is affiliated. By a household I mean a group of relatives sharing a common kitchen and budget. The same word – *ghar* – is used to refer both to this group and to the dwelling it occupies.

Composition

The great majority of Limbu households – 90.6% – can be classified as of 'simple' type. By this is meant that the core is an elementary or simple family. Such households may consist only of a core and include no other persons. Over half of all Limbu households are of this kind (see Table 6). Others may include widowed mothers or unmarried brothers of household heads. Because of the stress on virilocality and patrilineal inheritance, households tend to be composed of agnatic kinsmen along with in-married women. Just over a tenth of Limbu households, however, include other kinds of relatives as well. Generally, the attachment of affinal or matrilateral kinsmen is regarded as a temporary arrangement. By and large, economic difficulties rule out the permanent incorporation of kin who are not born or married into the household.

Table 6 lists six kinds of simple-type household found in the Indreni settlements. 'Joint'-type households are those which include a married couple or widower and at least one of their/his married sons and spouse. As the table shows, 9·4% of Limbu households containing 13·7% of the population fall into this latter category.

TABLE 6
Household composition

	Number	Population
Simple type:		
(a) Husband and wife and their child(ren)	43	208
(b) Husband and wife and their child(ren), and husband's widowed mother	4	22
(c) Brothers, one married with child(ren), other(s) unmarried or without wife (wives) with him/them	3	13
(d) Brothers, one married with child(ren), other(s) unmarried or without wife (wives) with him/them, and brothers' widowed mother	4	23
(e) Widow or widower and unmarried children	9	28
(f) Man or woman living alone	4	4
(g) other kinds of simple-type household	10	55
	77	353
Joint type:		
(h) Husband and wife or widower and their/his married son(s) and spouse(s)	8	56
	85	409

There is some reason to suppose that the incidence of joint-type households was higher in former times. Informants insist that in only rare instances would a son have separated from the main household before his father's death. The partition of households probably did occur at a later stage of the developmental cycle, since young men who were married around the age of puberty could not hope to establish new households until they and their wives were sufficiently mature. Perhaps, too, the greater economic viability of households before the turn of the century and the absence of alternative sources of income for the young men would have given the family elders greater sanctions to keep the household group intact. But whatever the truth of these contentions about the past the case today is that Limbu households seldom remain at the joint stage for more than a few years. And those that do are generally the wealthiest. Fraternal extended families, in particular, are exceedingly rare. At the time I conducted a census there was not a single Limbu household in the Indreni settlements containing two married brothers and their wives.[1]

Separation and inheritance

Separation from the main household (*mul ghar*) is generally in sequence, with the eldest son leaving first, followed by his younger brothers as they marry and bring their wives to join them.[2] It is not unusual, however, for youngest sons, after marriage, to remain with their parents or widowed mother once their elder brothers have separated.

The tendency towards early separation is usually rationalized in terms of the strained relations among the wives of brothers within a single household. One informant, two of whose sons had recently established their own households, described the process of separation in these words:

When our eldest daughter-in-law first came to the house seven years ago she was quiet and obedient. She did her work as her mother-in-law told her to do. Then two years later the second son was married and the two daughters-in-law were brought together. They worked without troubling each other for a time. Then the younger one had a child, and she had to stay home and take care of it. So she did less work, but she needed the best food. At first the eldest daughter-in-law understood, but soon she complained to her husband that she worked too much, and that her sister-in-law did nothing. When another child was born to the younger one, the daughters-in-law quarrelled often, and then even their husbands began to have bad feelings. The eldest son repeated the words of his wife that the younger brother's family was getting more to eat, even though they con-

1 By contrast, of the six Brahman households in the Indreni Cluster, four are of joint type. Two contain married brothers and their widowed mother; one a husband and wife and their two married sons, spouses and children; and another a husband and wife and one married son and his wife and children.

2 A married man serving in the army usually remains part of his father's household until he leaves the service. But during this time he enjoys a special status within the group. See pp. 117–18.

tributed less to the household. So last year they both said they wanted to build separate kitchens (*chulo*) and we did this. It is better now. They do not fight any more.

This description traces the growth of nuclear units within the larger group, and the strains between these units which lead to the break-up of the household.

Although household partitions are most frequently attributed to disputing daughters-in-law, another, not uncommon, explanation is the tension arising out of the co-residence of wives and married sisters. When women leave their husbands and return to reside, sometimes permanently, in their natal homes – a not infrequent practice – conditions are created which can lead to strains between sisters and their brothers' wives and, ultimately, to the break-up of the household. Daughters are indulged to a much greater extent by their parents than are the latters' daughters-in-law. It is commonly admitted that a woman, however kindly she may be disposed to her son's wife, will invariably favour her own daughter in any intra-household squabble. Arguments often arise when married daughters living in their natal households are allowed the customary privilege of earning a private income over which no other members of the household can exercise claims. Although in-married wives also have certain rights to possess property outside the household estate, it is not until they are mistresses of their own households that they can fully exploit their rights. As long as their activities continue to be controlled by their mothers-in-law, little time is available for personal business. As a result, daughters-in-law see themselves as contributing their time and energies for the benefit of all household members, while their husbands' sisters are free to spend much of their time accumulating a private equity, and thereby neglecting obligations to the household unit. In such circumstances, the pressures for partition are strong. It was generally acknowledged, for example, that when the only son of a Bharapa man established a separate household[1] in the spring of 1964, the determining factor was the constant quarrelling between the young man's wife and his two married sisters who were living in their natal household.

Finally, in addition to the disputes among brothers' wives and between the latter and their husbands' sisters, the strains inherent in

---

1 Frequently only sons establish households away from their parents. The heads of four households in the Indreni settlements are only surviving sons whose parents are still alive.

mother-in-law–daughter-in-law relations also contribute to household splits. Indeed, the belief in the inevitability of hostility among the women of a single household occasionally leads the parents of a recently married girl to refuse to allow her to join her husband until arrangements have been completed for the establishment of a separate household by the young couple.

The creation of a new household usually, but not invariably, implies its independence as a land-owning unit. The rules of inheritance practised by the Limbus resemble somewhat those prescribed by the Mitakshara system found in north India. Under this system, a household estate is conceived as being shared equally by a man and his descendants – in the case of the Limbus his male descendants – and each male offspring secures his rights at the time of birth.[1] In effect, this means that a man's sons can claim their share of the property – which is divided equally[2] – at any time, although in practice such claims are pressed only after marriage. The Mitakshara rules proscribing the rights of a man to dispose of lands belonging to co-sharers are reinforced among the Limbus by legal rules prohibiting the sale of kipat land. However, a man can, with impunity, pledge and thereby give away, at least temporarily, the usufruct of lands which are the shares of his sons: unless, of course, they are mature, in which case the decision would be a joint one. Alternatively, where a Limbu creditor assumes the usufruct of another Limbu's kipat lands, the former may transmit the usufruct of these lands to his heirs. When the debt is repaid the principal is regarded as part of their inheritance.

When the partition of a household is accompanied by a final property settlement, the son who sets up a separate household renounces any claim to property accumulated at a later stage by his father's household. His rightful inheritance may be augmented after the death of his parents by that portion of the property (called *jiuni*) which a father puts aside for himself and his wife to sustain them in old age. A father can determine who is to inherit this property after his death and that of his wife.[3] Generally, it is decided to share it out equally amongst the sons, but if the youngest son lives with and helps to support his parents in their old age, he may get the entire *jiuni* after their death.

1 Vijnaneshwar, who expounded the Mitakshara system, spoke of the 'principle of ownership by birth' (cf. Karve, 1965, 344).
2 Both *per capita* and *per stirpes* rules coexist side by side. See pp. 41–2.
3 Claims to *jiuni* constitute a frequent cause of quarrels among brothers. See, for example, pp. 140–1.

The exercise of inheritance rights by Indreni Limbus occasionally proceeds by stages, so that the separation of a son from the main household will not coincide with a final division of property. A temporary settlement might be arranged pending the marriage of his younger brothers. In such cases he takes only that amount of property necessary to provide an adequate living. Much of the property will be left undivided and under the supervision of the head of the main household. This arrangement satisfies the desire of a young couple for a separate household and yet the unit remains only partially independent in terms of property. In this, as in all stages of division, the kitchen and budget of the new household are quite separate from the main household. All income remains the property of the household and its expenses and debts are its own responsibility. Nevertheless, where this kind of property division occurs the amount of co-operation between the main and the new household can be extensive. The two units maintain a continuous interdependence and an interest in each other's affairs not usually found between households where the division of property is more complete. Indeed, in many respects they continue to act as a single unit. In the Indreni Cluster this kind of relationship tends to exist between the agnatically related households of the few wealthiest Limbus. In other words, the wealthier households can be seen to delay the division of property longer than the less affluent Limbu households. In the case of the latter, the household head can apply no sanctions to forestall the early division of the group's estate, so that household separations usually coincide with the division of the household property. But the sons of wealthy men are reluctant to force a division of what may be an expanding estate. In questions of inheritance no rigid distinction is made between ancestral and self-acquired property, since a household head is not expected to maintain a private estate separate from that of the household. By holding out the prospect of a larger inheritance in the future, a man can hope to delay the final division of his property, despite the partition of the household. Thus the wealthiest Limbu households in the Cluster are either of joint type or co-operate as if they were.[1]

Although, as pointed out, a division of the estate can be arranged on a variety of bases within the household, a final property settlement, to

1 In this regard it is worthwhile noting a remark by Freedman concerning Chinese households: '. . . co-operation between closely related households of a kind to make them seem to resemble one household was more likely to occur among the better-off' (1958, 30).

be valid in the eyes of the community (and the law) must be effected in the presence of several respected elders. Such settlements generally occur after all the sons of a man have married and established separate households, and occasionally it is delayed until after their father's death. At this time, a written document is usually prepared, setting out the terms of the agreement, and it is then signed and witnessed by the elders. Fifty-eight of the eighty-five Limbu households in the Cluster have made what can be regarded as a final property settlement, and thirty-seven of these have prepared documents attesting to the agreement, while the rest have relied on verbal settlements, backed up by customary knowledge of boundaries. Many in the latter category suggest that a written agreement will some day be made.

But even a final settlement may leave some lands undivided so that more than one household head would have a stake in the same fields. The inclusion of tracts of undivided property in a settlement is a function of the large-scale pledging of kipat lands to obtain credit. Lands to which the Limbu owners have long lost usufructuary rights are passed on from fathers to sons, sometimes with only cursory attempts to define the boundaries of each parcel. Thus, it is not entirely uncommon to find sons of one father sharing some undivided lands, and descendants of a common grandfather sharing others. These questions are usually clarified at the time of a revenue settlement when households and their irrigated fields are registered, and the boundaries of the latter defined.

The pattern of household fission is also influenced by the system of tax-collection on kipat land. This requires that kipat owners pay taxes according to the number of households and not in relation to the amount of land owned or cultivated. But households are counted and registered only at the time of a revenue settlement, and no amount of increase or decrease in the number of households between settlements need be reported. The last revenue settlement in Ilam in 1936 registered thirty-nine kipat-owning households in the Indreni Cluster. Today there are seventy-five. The taxes assessed on a registered household are shared amongst those households which separated off and divided the lands of the former after the revenue settlement. Thus, in the case of Chongbung lineage 5, twelve households share the tax assessment on six registered households in the manner indicated in Fig. 1.

The taxes payable by Chongbung lineage 5 households are distributed as follows: households 1–6 share the tax on *A*; households 7–9 share

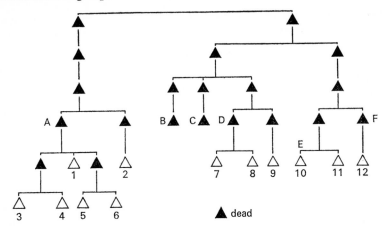

Registered households are lettered. Existing households are numbered.

Figure 1

the tax on B, C and D; households 10–11 share the tax on E; household 12 pays the tax on F. The tax burden is transmitted in a manner akin to property. Thus, the tax on A would be distributed as follows: household 2, $\frac{1}{2}$; household 1, $\frac{1}{6}$; households 3 and 4, $\frac{1}{12}$ each; households 5 and 6, $\frac{1}{12}$ each. And so on.

It can happen that the number of registered households is greater than the number of existing units. In the case of one Kambo lineage, for instance, the household population has decreased due to a number of household heads dying without heirs. As a result, two existing households must pay the taxes assessed on five households registered at the time of the last revenue settlement.

It would seem that the method of taxing kipat-owning households might have put a brake on the partition of households in the past. Because all households registered at the time of a revenue settlement were taxed without regard for the size of the estate, a conflict arose between the desire to establish an independent household and the realization that such a step would mean a heavy tax burden for the household. Since the turn of the century, however, with the drop in the value of the rupee,[1] taxes no longer represent a significant expenditure, so this is no longer a serious consideration in the calculations of

1 Since 1914 the price of paddy has risen approximately fourteen-fold in Ilam.

potential householders. Even so, I have been told that at the time of a revenue settlement some households 'merge' in order to avoid being registered separately.[1]

The system of kipat taxation also serves to stress the links among closely related households within the same lineage or lineage branch. Despite the tendency towards early partition and the fragmentation of estates, the very persons who are the protagonists in such divisions are potential heirs of one another's property. The eclipse of a household, whether through emigration or the absence of male heirs, results in the transmission of its tax assessment to the nearest agnatically related household, which also assumes ownership rights in the former's estate. In Fig. 1 the heads of households *B* and *C* died without sons to inherit their property and obligations, which then passed to the nearest collateral line, represented in the Cluster by the patrilineal descendants of their fathers' youngest brother.

Women's rights in land

The foregoing discussion of property division has suggested not only a stress among Limbus on the patrilineal transmission of land but on the exclusive inheritance rights of males. Even the word *aputali*, which indicates one who is childless, is used to refer to a man who has daughters but no sons, and implies that he is without heirs. What rights, we might ask, do women have in kipat land?

On marriage, a woman forfeits all rights to the lands of her natal household. Unmarried daughters, however, on reaching the age of thirty-five have a claim to a share in the estate equal to one-half the inheritance of each male sibling. In the event of the woman being an only child, she assumes rights in the entire estate following the death of her parents. These rights, however, are hedged by three main stipulations. In the first place, a daughter can only press her claims if she establishes a separate household. As long as she resides with her father or brother her status is similar to that of an unmarried brother, and her share remains in the custody of the household head. Spinster daughters, in fact, seldom urge their prerogatives, since the difficulties

1 During a Panchayat-instigated household count in 1963, the census-taker, a Brahman from another part of the district, was astonished when he was told by people in the Cluster that the only Limbu households were those registered by the revenue settlement of 1936.

of managing a household and an estate alone are considered formidable. Besides, property divisions among sons take no account of the
possibility that a female sibling might remain unmarried. By the time
a woman reaches the age of thirty-five the estate has usually been
allocated to her brothers, and she could only with the greatest difficulty
obtain her rightful share. I have heard of no cases of such a redistribu-
tion to accommodate an unmarried sister actually taking place. In the
Indreni settlements there were three spinsters in this age-bracket and
one, an only child, inherited rights to the lands of her father, from
which she maintained a separate household. The other two were
residing with their brothers.

A second condition concerns rights of transmission. The land
cannot be gifted or in any way transmitted permanently to anyone
other than the male agnatic heirs. When the spinster mentioned above
died in the early part of 1965 her mourning rites were performed by
three agnates of the nearest collateral line who were to divide her
lands. A young married woman, who was the dead person's sister's
daughter, and who had been living in the same household, was regarded as having no claims whatsoever to the spinster's lands.

Even to pledge lands to a third party an unmarried woman must have
the permission of the potential male heirs. Her rights, by and large,
are restricted to the use of the land during the course of her lifetime,
provided – and here a third condition applies – she remains unmarried. On marriage her rights would be forfeited.

In some respects, the rights of a wife to land are similar to those of
an unmarried daughter. While she remains part of her husband's
household she is entitled to support, but cannot demand a separate
share of the estate. Nor can she choose to establish a separate household without her husband's permission. If a man takes a second wife,
however, the first then has the right to claim half his estate and to
establish a household for herself and her children, if she has any.
There is some disagreement about the pattern of inheritance following
on such a division. Some informants maintain that land would be
divided equally among all a man's sons, while others suggest that the
sons of each wife would inherit only that portion of the estate held by
their mother. Although the two contradictory ideals exist side by side,
what in fact appears to happen when a man has sons by more than one
wife is that the wife who establishes a separate household is allocated
an amount of property according to the number of her male heirs.
In one instance I was able to record, the four sons of a man by his first

wife each inherited an amount of property equal to that given to a fifth son born to his second wife.

The existence of contrary notions about inheritance is partly a a reflection of the lack of precedents in such matters, due to the low incidence of polygynous unions.[1] Men seldom marry for the second time while their first wife is still alive unless she has produced no sons, goes away with another man, or returns to live in her natal home because of failure to get along with her husband or other members of the household. Only eight Indreni men have two wives. In five cases a second wife was married either because the first was barren or had borne only daughters; in another case an only son had died after his mother was beyond the age of child-bearing; and in two cases because the first wives, neither of whom had had any children, returned to their natal homes shortly after marriage and had no intention of returning to their husbands.

An important reason inhibiting multiple marriages relates to their high costs.[2] Moreover, prestige does not attach to a man with more then one wife, and the wealthiest Limbus in the Cluster are mono-gamous. Indeed, a man with two wives is often regarded with a mixture of pathos and amusement. While co-wives remain together (two Indreni households contain both wives) disputes are considered inevitable, and a husband who must mollify his spouses is little envied. The quarrels almost invariably lead to separation, with one of the women, usually the senior wife, either leaving the Cluster and return-ing to her natal home – as did the wives of two men – or moving into a separate homestead within the Cluster and becoming custodian of part of her husband's estate. Such a division has been effected in two cases where first wives have moved away from their husbands. When a wife claims her rights to a part of her husband's lands, she becomes, in effect, the head of a separate household. She controls the income and expenditure of the unit, and directs the labour of its members. Although her husband continues to enjoy sexual rights, he does not command her labour or that of her household, and can assert no claims to its income. But he does retain a veto over the transmission of his lands by his wife to third parties. He also continues to take a strong interest in the affairs of her household, and a husband would be

1 It is probably due also to the fact that most kipat lands have been pledged away (see Chapter 4) so that half-brothers would in any case have only titles to quarrel about.
2 See Chapter 5.

considered remiss in his duties if he did not try to help in every way he could. The husband of one woman who had established a separate household with her daughters arranged a lucrative tenancy agreement for his wife and agreed to act as guarantor of the rent.

Some informants suggest that the division of a man's estate does not merely confer rights to a portion of his lands on the wife who separates, but leaves the remainder of the estate under the control of the other wife. Thus it is said that 'when a man has two wives he has nothing'. The husband in such a situation is viewed as a pauper dependent on the goodwill of his spouses for his subsistence, and discussions of polygyny often include a joke about 'the man who starved to death between the homesteads of his two wives'. In fact, a husband resides permanently with one of his wives, and is the effective household head, in control of its estate and in complete charge of its personnel.

The point has been stressed that the right to establish a separate household accrues to a woman only if her husband takes another wife. But it is also contingent upon her continued residence in her husband's settlement cluster. If a woman resides in her natal household she forfeits her claim, and if she leaves after having already established a separate unit her husband reassumes control of her portion of the estate. The fact that this usage is sanctioned by both custom and law, however, did not prevent one wife living in her natal home from pressing – successfully – for half her husband's lands. The case is worthwhile recounting because it presents a good example of norms being enunciated and clarified at the very time they are being disregarded.

In 1953 a wealthy and much-respected ex-army serviceman of Chitok arranged the marriage of his eldest son to the daughter of a man of similar status resident about fifteen miles west of the Indreni Cluster. About a year later the young woman came to live in the Cluster, but, unable to get along with her husband, returned to her natal home after a few months. Her husband made no attempt to persuade her to return, and in 1958 he married for the second time. In 1963 he established a separate household and received a partial property settlement. In January, 1965, the first wife and a number of her close kinsmen came to Chitok to demand a divorce. They accused the young man's father of allowing his son to marry another wife without first using every possible means of persuasion to have the first wife rejoin her husband. The boy's father and his supporters reminded the girl's family that it was not contrary to Limbu custom for a man to take a second wife, and that they still regarded the girl as their daughter-in-law. As such, she had every right to claim the prerogatives of a wife and demand a half-share of her husband's estate. The girl's representatives were adamant in their demands for a divorce, but the young man's side were equally firm in their refusal to grant one. Although the reasons were never made explicit, it was clear to everyone that to acquiesce in a divorce would mean waiving their rights to recover at least a portion of the marriage expenses in the form of compensation if and when the girl remarried. After about two days of conversations, the girl's family agreed to accept the offer of half the husband's estate, but on condition that the woman would continue to live in her natal home. This shocked the Indreni men (and the many women who had gathered to enjoy the spectacle) even more than the demand for a divorce. In the end, however, after protesting that such an arrangement was contrary to all custom, the young man, with the support of his father, agreed to the condition of their in-laws. An agreement was reached whereby the husband would cultivate those lands over which his wife now had usufruct, and pay her a fixed amount as rent.

Privately, the boy's father and other observers rationalized the decision by surmising that the girl's family had really come to 'raise their prestige' and that sooner or later the young woman would marry another man, whereupon her Indreni husband would receive compensation and at the same time resume full rights in his lands again.

Finally, the rights to land of widows without sons should be mentioned. Following the death of a man who leaves no male heirs, his property is inherited by his nearest agnatic kinsmen. Their claims, however, are held in abeyance during the lifetime of his widow. Like spinster daughters and wives who have separated, the widow enjoys rights to the usufruct of the land, but cannot alienate it or pledge it without the permission of the agnatic heirs.

Thus, we have seen that certain women have well-defined rights to land and its products during their lifetime, subject to specific restrictions on their freedom to dispose of these rights. The categories of women for whom these prerogatives are prescribed include those who for a limited phase of their lives are faced with a loss of economic support from their husbands or fathers and brothers. The rights granted these women thereby enable them to achieve a measure of security when it is most needed, yet maintain the patrilineal pattern of land ownership and inheritance practised by the Limbus.

Limbus without kipat

To this point the discussion has concerned only Limbus owning kipat land. The Indreni Cluster is also inhabited by a number of Limbus who are not members of kipat-owning kin groups, and so possess no ownership rights to this kind of land. The existence in the Cluster of non-kipat-owning (NKO) Limbus has created a situation in which two sections of the population enjoy unequal status on the basis of differential rights to land.

The presence of NKO Limbus urges us to consider the relationships between kipat-owning groups and Limbu 'outsiders'. Formerly, in conditions of land abundance, those owning land either absorbed outsiders into the group or enabled them to acquire land in other ways. More recently, however, outsiders have been denied access to kipat land ownership as qualifications for group membership have been more stringently defined. In the following paragraphs I consider how various outsiders were accommodated in the past and how the lineages and households owning kipat became less willing, indeed less able, to do so when land shortages reached acute proportions about the turn of the century.

I have already alluded to the uncertain origins of the Kambos.[1] Perhaps due to these uncertainties, or because of their small numbers and high ratio of land to population, the Kambos tended in the past to absorb outsiders into their ranks. Prior to the turn of the century kipat paddy lands were granted to outsiders by the incumbent Subba of Kambo lineage 1. It is not certain if or how the outsiders were related to the grantors, but in any event the genealogy was arranged to accommodate the new lineage members (see Fig. 2 overleaf).

Today their descendants cultivate these lands as Kambos and pay taxes to the present Subba. They also observe pollution on the death of a lineage mate and in every way act as members of the lineage. The only diacritical evidence of their uncertain pedigree is the fact that they possess no dry plots as part of their kipat estates. Only their paddy fields on the ridge-slopes below the residential areas are under kipat tenure.

No one attempts to deny the fact that two branches of Kambo lineage 1 are accretions to the original lineage. Nor do 'real' members of the lineage seek to isolate or in any way embarrass the absorbed

1 See pp. 25–6.

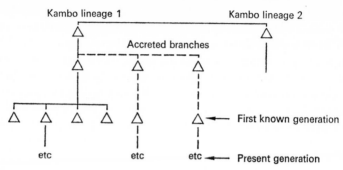

Figure 2

branches. One reason may be that, due to death and migration, the senior branch of the lineage is now outnumbered by the two accretions. Another reason may relate to the severe impoverishment of the entire lineage, so that no crisis has arisen which might test the structural cleavage. Such a crisis, however, did arise among the Nembekes. A dispute erupted in 1944 when the consequences of a similar (alleged) absorption threatened the land-holdings of several Nembeke households.

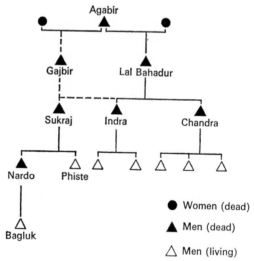

Figure 3

In that year Phiste, the son of Sukraj (see Fig. 3) returned to the Indreni settlements after spending twenty-three years in India. He claimed that his father's lands had been registered at the time of the 1936 revenue settlement in the names of his father's brothers Indra and Chandra and their sons. He demanded the return of the lands. He then went on to argue that since his father had been the only son of Gajbir, who in turn had been the only son of the first wife of Agabir, the lineage founder, his (Phiste's) branch of the lineage was entitled to one-half of all lineage lands. He claimed that Sukraj had not inherited his due share because a final division of property had still not been made at the time of his death. Phiste demanded the lands which he claimed were rightfully his.

Since Indra and Chandra had both died, their five sons came together to defend their interests against the interloper. Their lands together represented the great majority of lineage holdings, and Phiste's claim to half, if successful, would have constituted a blow of the severest kind. They did not attempt to deny that Phiste had a right to the lands of Sukraj. They claimed that these lands had not been registered by Indra and Chandra, as Phiste insisted, but were in fact in the name of Phiste's brother's son, Bagluk. The problem with which the defendants concerned themselves was Phiste's claim to half of Agabir's lands. They argued as follows: that, indeed, Agabir had two wives. But that the first was barren. The second then had a son, Lal Bahadur, and they are his descendants. Lal Bahadur died before the revenue settlement of 1890, which recorded his lands in the names of Chandra and Indra, and the headmanship in the latter's name. About this time, they then stated, Sukraj had come from Sikkim and, in searching for a place to settle, had come to Dorumba in the Indreni Cluster, since he was probably related consanguineally to the Nembekes there. Sukraj had pleaded with Indra to give him some land to cultivate. Indra did grant him some kipat and 'made him a Nembeke'. But even so, they concluded, neither Sukraj nor his son Phiste could now claim to be the co-heir to all the lands of Agabir. 'They are not real (*pakka*) Nembekes.'

After a number of attempts to settle the matter within the Indreni settlements had failed, the plaintiff (Phiste) took the matter to court. There he was faulted on a technicality, and when he appealed the case the higher court threw it back to the lower court and asked for a decision on the vital question of descent. Litigation costs prevented Phiste from pursuing the matter, and shortly thereafter he returned to India.

It would have been folly for the defendants to concede the point that

Phiste was a lineage member by descent (even if he had been one), and then seek to avoid his claim to a full share of lineage lands. They were constrained to attack the very basis of his status in the group. Only in this way could they hope to deny him the rights which would have accrued to him as a *bona fide* member. They could not deny him membership of the lineage, since they had observed pollution on the death of Sukraj and acted in every way as lineage mates to the accreted branch. But they could suggest (or remind him, whichever it was) that he was a lineage member by absorption and not by descent.

A different way of accommodating outsiders was to grant them kipat lands without attempting to incorporate the recipients into the kipat-giving group. In the 1890s the Syelings and Phatras, who now possess kipat land in the Indreni Cluster, were given grants in this way. The Syelings received theirs when the sister of the Subba of Chongbung lineage 2 married a Syeling man, who then settled uxori-locally. The original Phatra recipient came to the Indreni settlements as a boy with his mother, a widow, who married the Subba of Chong-bung lineage 4. In both cases these lands have been registered in the names of the recipients and are inherited through the male line. The grantees recognize the Subbas of the grantor lineages as their headmen and pay taxes to them.[1]

It is impossible to presume a single attitude by kipat-owning groups to requests for land from outsiders. Decisions would undoubtedly have depended on such factors as the need for labourers or supporters, the nature of kinship ties between the host and the outsider, and perhaps on the need for capital, since some of these grants might in fact have been made for financial gain. But the chief determining factor would have been the availability of land.

In the Indreni Cluster the grantors were most often Subbas. This is not unusual, in view of the fact that the Subba, because of the rights attached to headmanship, was able to accumulate more lands than other households in his lineage.[2] Nevertheless, because all lineage households were potential co-parceners, no household could alienate kipat lands in this way without the consent of the entire lineage. Prior

---

1 Informants were uncertain about what would happen if the groups which received these grants were to die out. Some suggested that the grantors could then resume the lands; others said this latter course would only be possible if no patrilineal kinsmen of the grantees were to come forward to claim the land.
2 See Chapter 5.

1 View of the Indreni settlement area
2 A poor man's house—of bamboo and mud

3 Planting paddy in terraces
4 Transplanting rice seedlings

to the turn of the century, when land was relatively plentiful, a decision to grant land to an outsider would have met with little opposition on the part of other lineage households. During the past seventy years no lineage in the Cluster has been in a position to make such grants. Land-shortage has led to a more stringent definition of criteria for lineage membership and restricted the group's ability to alienate kipat to outsiders.[1]

The result is that there exists in the Indreni settlements today a category of Limbus without ownership rights to kipat. There are fifty-eight persons in the NKO category,[2] comprising 12.7% of the Limbu population. Four household heads are the agnatic descendants of a man of Angu lineage who came to Bharapa to marry the sister of the Chongbung lineage 2 Subba. The father of another household head married the grand-daughter of the same Subba. In Dorumba, the Nembeke Subba's daughter was married to a Limbu, who, after a decade of virilocal residence, accepted the invitation of his father-in-law to settle in the Cluster. His sons are another of the NKO groups.

Not all NKO Limbus in the Indreni settlements are the patrilineal descendants of men who came to reside in their wives' natal settlements. Two are the offspring of women who married Indreni men and brought their sons by previous marriages with them. One example will illustrate how reluctant kipat-owners have become since the turn of the century to alienate land to outsiders. The case is especially interesting, since it involves a Kambo man who was himself the descendant of an outsider absorbed by the Kambos into their lineage and given a kipat grant.

While Gabe, whose father was accreted to Kambo lineage 1, was in the army during the First World War, his wife went away with another man and bore him a son. When Gabe came home on leave and learned that his wife had gone away he went to her natal settlement to claim compensation. After some pressure by the woman's kinsmen, Gabe agreed to waive his claim and instead to take the woman back with him. He agreed also to allow her to bring with her the son she had had by the other man. In the ensuing years she produced two more sons for Gabe.

1 In a somewhat analogous situation, Colson (1953, 80) notes that the Makah have become concerned to define membership in the tribe more rigidly since membership now brings with it economic benefits and political privileges.

2 This figure includes eleven persons temporarily attached to kipat-owning households.

Although the son of his wife by the other man became a part of Gabe's household and was addressed by the kinship reference for eldest son or brother, he was not absorbed into the Kambo lineage. The lineage affiliation of the boy's genitor was remembered and his rights to kipat land were considered to exist where those of his genitor did, but not in the Indreni settlements. When the boy grew up he chose to remain in the Cluster and not to return to his kipat. Today his son, Dhanman, is head of a household in the Cluster, but, like his father, has no ownership rights to kipat land in the Indreni settlements. The position was dramatized when a member of Kambo lineage 1 died in 1964. Dhanman took as full a part as any lineage member in the various activities consequent upon the death of an agnate. But when it came time for the purification rite to be performed Dhanman had to stand aside. Lineage members bunched together facing the ritual specialist and, at a particular time, came forward to touch salt and oil which rendered them de-polluted. Dhanman could only stand close to the group, but not mingle with it; nor could he touch the holy foods. 'He is not polluted when one of us dies, and we will not be polluted when he dies. His own "brothers" would have to mourn him,' stated a Kambo spokesman.

Ideally, every Limbu should know where his kipat is situated. Several NKO households, only one generation removed from their kipat lands, still retain links with agnates and even visit these kinsmen on occasion to take advantage of financial benefits accruing to kipat-owners.[1] But links to kipat fade as prolonged residence away from ancestral lands leads to the severance of contact with agnatic kinsmen. Some NKO groups in the Indreni settlements have no precise knowledge of where their kipat land is located and have lost contact with patrilineal kin. The Angus, for example, are aware that their ancestral home is in a region some three or four days away from the Cluster, but have dropped all ties and probably could not exercise a claim to their kipat even if it could be located.

A person who resides in a settlement cluster where he owns no kipat land can never hope to enjoy the same prestige as a man who lives on his ancestral territory. During the early period of my field-work, when I was collecting genealogies, on several occasions heads of NKO households attempted to conceal their lineage affiliation. In every case they gave the names of one of the kipat-owning groups in the

1 See pp. 96 ff.

Cluster and only later admitted that they were members of NKO groups whose kipat lands were in fact somewhere else.

For a member of a NKO group there are two ways to obtain land for both a homestead and cultivation. The first is to purchase raikar land in the open market. Raikar land can be bought and sold in a manner akin to freehold. Unlike kipat, which can be owned only by Limbus, raikar can be owned by anyone, including Limbus.

None of the NKO residents in the Indreni settlements has been able to afford irrigated raikar fields, although several own small raikar plots on which homesteads have been built. Descendants of the first Angu settler, for example, now live on raikar land which he purchased with his earnings from service in the local militia in Ilam. One other NKO household, in Dorumba, lives on a tiny plot of raikar land purchased by the Nembeke Subba and given to the present household head's father when he came to settle in the Cluster after marrying the Subba's daughter. Several kipat-owning households also have, in addition to their kipat holdings, a few plots of raikar dry land. Those outsiders who were absorbed into Kambo lineage 1 and given kipat paddy lands but no dry fields have built homesteads on raikar plots purchased by their forefathers.

By and large, the high costs of raikar land place it out of the reach of the great majority of Limbus in the Indreni settlements. As a consequence, with the few minor exceptions noted above, raikar land tends to be associated only with non-Limbu sections of the population.

There is another way in which NKO Limbus can get access to land. This is to provide credit to an owner of kipat land in return for which rights to cultivate a plot of land are obtained. This kind of usufructuary mortgage is the most common method used by NKO inhabitants to gain access to land, especially irrigated fields for paddy. Five NKO homesteads have been built on kipat dry land taken under mortgage in this way. A certain degree of security attends the homestead on this kind of land, since once it has been built the owner[1] could not easily evict the inhabitant. But the security extends only to the area on which the homestead stands, and not to the cultivable plots which may surround it, so that both irrigated and unirrigated lands on which homesteads are not constructed can be repossessed at any time (after the harvest) by repayment of the loan. For the NKO Limbu this means an almost continual state of insecurity on the land. One Angu

1 Usually a descendant of the host household which enabled an outsider to settle initially on its land.

put it this way: 'They [referring to some Chongbungs] are owners of kipat [*kipatiya*], but I am only a Limbu. My kipat is in another place. Here I live with my *maoli* [mother's natal group]. I have no land of my own, only land taken under usufructuary mortgage. If my debtor returns the money to me and takes his land back I would have nothing.' This insecurity renders those without kipat land economically the most vulnerable section of the Limbu population.

One of the ways in which N K O groups have attempted to reinforce their position is by arranging marriages within the Cluster. Although unions with kipat-owning groups are of course preferable, the degrees of prohibited marriage and considerations of status do not always make such matches possible. As a result, many marriages are with similarly placed N K O groups in the Indreni settlements. Of seven extant intra-Cluster marriages, five involve partners who are of N K O status. Although the numbers are too small to be of any statistical use, they do point to the possibility that intra-N K O group marriage is one way of fortifying a shaky position in the settlements. Fig. 4 shows how one N K O group, the Angus, have married with other groups in the Cluster.

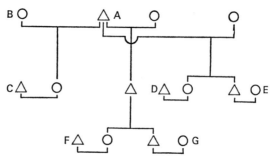

Figure 4

A married *B*, a Chongbung woman of Bharapa; settled uxorilocally in the Cluster.
C = a kipat-owning Phatra.
D = a kipat-owning Chongbung.
E = a Chongbung woman.
F = a NKO man of Chitok.
G = daughter of a NKO man of Angbung.

In the part genealogy shown above, within two Angu generations, excluding that of the first uxorilocal settler, the Angus have married within the Cluster five times. They have given women to kipat-owning groups twice, to a NKO group once, and have taken one woman from each kind of group themselves.

Conclusion

My aim in this chapter has been to examine the ways in which a Limbu obtains rights to kipat land. This required a consideration of the descent group system of local clan segment, lineage and household. For each group holds, in Gluckman's terms, an 'estate' consisting of a series of rights in land (1965). If I had been concerned to present an exhaustive account of the kipat system of land tenure, it would have been necessary to analyse the distribution of rights among these various groups. For the purposes of the present discussion, however, it is enough to make two main points. The first is that the household is the group with the strongest and most immediate rights in land. Questions regarding the use of land and its division are settled primarily within the household. Moreover, for the past seventy years or so the house-hold's prerogatives have been reinforced by the registration of titles. This has somewhat mitigated the individual's responsibility to re-affirm his membership in any group wider than the household. Despite its 'encapsulation' within a series of wider descent groups, the household is essentially an 'individuated' unit.[1] This means that the decisions Limbus make in the course of their daily lives are affected not so much by the interests of wider structural groupings as by those of the household itself.

The second point I want to make is that each of the kin groups discussed is corporate in the sense that land is transmitted within the group by and to those persons recognized as group members (Goody, 1961). At least this is the situation found today among the Limbus. I have suggested that it was not always so. It stands to reason that when and where land was plentiful it would have made little sense to deny Limbu outsiders their requests for plots to cultivate and settle. The outsider might have been absorbed into the group of the grantor or allowed to retain his own original clan affiliation. With land-shortage the policy altered. Restrictions on land-alienation were introduced

---

1 Individuation means that 'the elementary family is separated off, dif-ferentiated out as a distinct and to some extent autonomous social group . . .' (Bott, 1955, 375).

and 'true' agnation became the principal criterion for ownership rights to land. Outsiders were no longer given kipat land, although a few were allowed to settle on raikar plots or on kipat lands loaned or mortgaged to them by their hosts. But even these meagre pickings are no longer available. For the past twenty-five years no outsider has been integrated into the Indreni settlements, save as a temporary member of a kipat-owning household. Land-shortage has virtually obviated any possibility of accommodating outsiders.

To this point I have taken the Limbus out of their surroundings and discussed the problems of kipat land rights in isolation. It is now time to introduce the Brahmans: and to show how their presence has affected the social situation in the Indreni settlements. The next chapter will consider the cleavage between the two groups. It will be followed by an examination of their relationships of interdependence.

Chapter 4

Limbus and Brahmans: the cleavage

Changes in the methods of allocating property rights among the Limbus arose out of the transition from abundance to scarcity of kipat land. By scarcity of land three things are implied. Firstly, population growth has increased the pressure on land resources and led to the fragmentation of family estates (cf. Bailey, 1957). Although figures for the period prior to 1952 are based on unofficial estimates, they indicate that between 1920 and 1961 the population of Ilam increased by approximately 40%.[1] Between 1954 and 1961 alone the net increase in the district was 8%. Although no separate statistics are available for the Limbu sector, there is no reason to suspect that its rate of growth has not kept pace with that of the total population. Secondly, the amount of kipat land owned by Limbus has diminished over the past century. And, thirdly, Limbu access to the productive capacity of their remaining kipat lands has been reduced considerably, due to extensive mortgaging.

All three manifestations are, to a large extent, concomitants of contact between the Limbus and the Brahmans. More specifically, they are the outcome of the interaction of these two groups and a third protagonist – the government. To begin the present discussion I consider the role of the latter.

Government land policy

By confirming the rights of Limbus to hold land under kipat tenure, the government by no means abrogated its own privilege to determine the course of events in its easternmost region. Following the

---

1 The estimate of the 1920 population is from Landon (Vol. 2), 1928, 256–7. The 1961 figure is from the preliminary Census report of that year.

incorporation of Limbuan into the Kingdom the policy which came to be followed by successive administrations in Kathmandu was double-edged. On the one hand, they sought to placate the Limbus, ever jealous of their rights, by providing safeguards of their lands. On the other hand, they lost no opportunity to reduce the area under kipat tenure and at the same time convert these lands to raikar tenure. The results of this policy are evident in Ilam. In the district today only 39·7% of irrigated lands (*khet*)[1] are under kipat tenure, with the remaining 60·3% under raikar tenure.[2] In the Ilam-Darda subdivision of the district the figures are 40·5% under kipat and 59·5% under raikar.

The arrival of non-Limbu settlers was part of a policy instituted by Kathmandu encouraging the immigration of Hindus into Limbuan. Limbus, for their part, were urged to settle these immigrants on their lands. Since Limbu land-holdings were extensive and there was a need for settlers to provide both labour and a following, the Limbus conferred land grants called *soranni*[3] on the immigrants. Recipients of these holdings gave away sub-holdings to other immigrants out of the lands which they could not themselves cultivate. Until 1886 these lands continued to be regarded as belonging to the Limbus under kipat tenure. In that year the government introduced legislation which in effect allowed non-Limbu settlers to convert into raikar tenure all lands which had been or would in future be granted to non-Limbus by their Limbu owners (Regmi, 1965, 97–8). Thus at a time when land-shortages were beginning to be felt in east Nepal the government effectively dissolved whatever rights still remained to the Limbus in the *soranni* holdings they had given away. These conversions were regarded by the government as immutable. Once registered as raikar, land formerly held under kipat tenure could not be made kipat again. On several occasions the Limbus petitioned the government suggesting that any kipat lands which had been converted into raikar and later repurchased by Limbus should be occupied again under kipat tenure.[4] The argument

1 Since dry lands are not measured, there is no way of knowing whether the proportions are the same as on irrigated lands. There is no reason to believe that they are any different.
2 The proportion under kipat is probably higher in other areas of Limbuan.
3 The term *soranni* is a contraction of *sora anna*, meaning 16 annas or one Indian rupee. Most Limbu informants insist that their forefathers gave their lands to immigrant settlers for this meagre sum.
4 See, for example, the 1951 petition of the Subbas of Ilam, p. 185.

was that in any case the land had once been kipat.[1] These requests were turned aside by the authorities, who would entertain no reversal of the kipat-into-raikar trend they had initiated.

Other aspects of government policy designed to reduce the area under kipat tenure concerned the appointment of Subbas and the registration of land titles. An official Subba, on appointment by royal decree (*lalmohar*) was required to pay an initial fee of Rs 52,[2] which represented a considerable sum in the past. He was also required to surrender 60 muris[3] of paddy land to the government as raikar. If the claimant could not afford this amount, he could choose a lesser title (*rai*), which would be granted after the surrender of half the amount taken from a Subba. Although these regulations still exist, the dearth of land to convert in this way makes the creation of new Subbas an extremely rare thing. In the Indreni settlements the only Subbas who surrendered land in this way (and are thus 'official' headmen) were the three original grantees of royal decrees in the first quarter of the nineteenth century.[4]

Government insistence on documentary evidence of title to kipat land provided the climate for further conversions of kipat into raikar tenure. At first the government allowed that actual possession and the concurrance of local dignitaries would suffice for proof of ownership in the absence of documentation. But in the 1888 edition of the Legal Code and, indeed, in all subsequent legislation, failure to produce evidence of title was decreed tantamount to an admission that the kipat-owner had encroached on raikar land. The kipat land would then have to be converted into raikar. This led to further losses, since in most instances documentary evidence was either totally lacking or at best vague and open to conflicting interpretations. Although in some cases Subbas had received royal decrees stipulating the exact boundaries of their domains, in most cases, certainly in Ilam, the decrees merely confirmed that the Subbas could go on using the lands of their forefathers. In one such decree given to the Kambo Subba in the Indreni Cluster, for example, it is stated that '. . . you may use your ancestral property, whatever your forefathers

1 For a discussion of Limbu activities to defend their lands against encroachments see Chapter 7.

2 In 1964–5 one Nepalese rupee was equal to approximately 1s. or (U.S.) $0·14.

3 About 2 acres. A *muri* is also a volumetric measurement equal to 2·40 bushels.

4 See previous chapter, pp. 28–9.

used.' . . . With such manner of title, it is obvious that kipat-owners have always been vulnerable to accusations of encroachment on raikar land.

In other ways, too, government policies led to a retreat of kipat boundaries. Revenue settlements, postal services and army maintenance were partially financed by the surrender of kipat lands, but the subsequent reliance on alternatives for raising such revenues did not result in the restoration of the kipat lands. Their conversion to raikar was judged to be irrevocable (cf. Regmi, 1965).

The courts and administrative offices in Limbuan apparently did little to redress the balance in favour of the kipat-owners. On the contrary, they tended to find against the Limbus even when the law appeared to be on the side of the latter. When the owner of a plot of kipat land dies without heirs his nearest agnates are entitled to claim the land. If this has been pledged to a non-Limbu creditor, the death of the kipat-owner confers no special privilege on the person holding the usufruct as against the co-heirs. Nevertheless, in cases where the non-Limbu creditor sued for full ownership rights, the courts often found in his favour, and, of course, the land became raikar.[1]

In addition, the basis of the taxation system for kipat is that any homesteads built or lands brought under cultivation by the Limbus need not be reported to the revenue authorities until a revenue settlement is held. But complaints of land or homestead concealment were continuously being entertained by the courts and government offices between the holding of such settlements, and the 'guilty' party would have his land confiscated and converted to raikar tenure.[2]

A certain amount of kipat land was also finding its way into Hindu possession through direct alienation, a practice forbidden by Limbu custom, but apparently countenanced in law. Non-Limbus insisted on the outright alienation of kipat lands in response to growing Limbu demands for mortgage credit.

By the turn of the century the rate of kipat conversions into raikar had reached alarming proportions. The government therefore executed a partial reversal of its policy, and in 1901 banned the permanent alienation of kipat lands to members of other groups. Thereafter, no Limbu could give his kipat land by grant or sale to a

1 Report of the Muluki Office, 1947 (cf. Regmi, 1965).
2 Ibid.

non-Limbu. The legislation had the effect of freezing the distribution of land in Limbuan. Kipat lands ceased to come under raikar tenure through contractual arrangements between Limbus and members of other groups. Conversions did occur on a small scale, however, as a result of court decisions or by occasional government directives aimed at specific areas of Limbuan.

Fiscal considerations were undoubtedly an important motive underlying the government's kipat policy. By increasing the amount of land under raikar tenure, income could be substantially enhanced. At the same time, because of the peculiar characteristics of the taxation system as it applies to kipat, a decrease in the proportion of kipat lands brings no corresponding decline in revenues from kipat-owners. The government had more than once made explicit its concern that whatever moves it made in regard to kipat should not result in any loss of revenue. When the Limbus suggested that raikar land purchases by a tribesman should be convertible into kipat tenure, the government refused on the grounds of the decreased income from taxes which would result. The need for funds to finance administration in the Limbu areas of the country was a constant problem. And taxation from kipat land contributed little to the general income. It is possible that Kirkpatrick had this problem in mind when he wrote that the Nepal government 'derives little or no advantage from [the Limbus] in any respect' (1811, 281). In Ilam, although 39·7% of all paddy lands in the district are under kipat tenure, tax revenues from kipat-owners constitute only 10·6% of the total land revenue.

Still, despite the obvious importance of fiscal considerations, it is doubtful if they were of paramount importance in determining the government's kipat policy. It would appear that the main concern of the authorities all along has been to establish their own hegemony in east Nepal, and the control and decrease, not to say abolition, of kipat tenure was a priority in effecting such a goal. In addition, the growing numbers of non-Limbus in the region demanded land to cultivate, and would obviously not be content to hold this land only at the pleasure of the Limbus. This led to strong pressures on the government for conversion of kipat areas to raikar tenure.

Successive governments felt themselves compelled to reverse those policies adopted by the early Shah kings granting Limbus a large measure of autonomy and security on their lands. The initial policy of support for the kipat system soon changed to one of encouraging a reduction of land under this kind of tenure and a corresponding increase in raikar lands. But the process was gradual and characterized by a series of seemingly petty encroachments, often accompanied by minor concessions to the Limbus (Regmi, 1965, 123–5). Generally speaking, kipat was nibbled at, not swallowed whole. Even the prohibition on the permanent alienation of kipat land must be seen as an attempt to check the too rapid loss of kipat lands which had resulted from the government's earlier course. Kathmandu had to take into account Limbuan's strategic location on the borders of Tibet, Sikkim and India. The government's policy, therefore, while clear and consistent, was continually subject to the mitigating considerations of a volatile area which, because of its location and distance from Kathmandu, could prove difficult to control.[1] The authorities were aware that, in their own words, 'Far Kirat [i.e. Limbuan], a distant and extensive territory, must be governed through a conciliatory policy'.[2]

Brahman manipulation of government land policy

For the Limbus, the land struggle has two aspects. Firstly, they must strive to preserve their lands under the kipat form of tenure and, alternatively, keep them from being converted to raikar, which ultimately means alienation to non-Limbus. Secondly, it also demands from the Limbus a continuous effort to prevent the usufruct of their remaining kipat lands from passing to members of other groups. The struggle, then, must be waged on two fronts. On one front, they must engage the government which makes land policy, and I will return in the penultimate chapter to a discussion of how this has been done. On another front, they must oppose the Hindus – especially the Brahmans – in their midst, because it is mainly through the Brahmans that Kathmandu has been able to realize its goals in Limbuan. The Brahmans have derived the greatest advantages from government kipat policy, and so are seen as the prime instruments of that policy. At the expense of the Limbus, they have become the most powerful ethnic group in east Nepal society.

1 In some parts of Limbuan the government has been unable to hold a revenue settlement since 1893 because of the intransigence of the Limbu population.
2 Order to the Dhankutta District Court, 1880 (cf. Regmi, 1965).

In a number of ways catalogued above more and more lands came into their hands. The holdings granted by Indreni Limbus were converted to raikar and the latter lost all rights in these lands. Limbus are adamant about what they allege to be the deception perpetrated on them by their erstwhile dependents, whom they accuse of responsibility for conversion of their lands to raikar. Since over 70% of those who received land-holdings granted by Indreni Limbus were Brahmans, the latter receive the brunt of Limbu hostility. When discussing Brahman 'treachery' (*jal*) one Limbu informant summarized his views in the following rhyme:

> Tip of the sugar-cane, root of the radish,
>   Keeping a servant is the ruin of a house.
> Left in the barn he drinks the cream,
>   Left in the home, he takes your spouse.

The Brahman is regarded as an 'ungrateful servant' who, trusted to watch over the land he was made custodian of, 'stole' it by converting it to raikar tenure. The fact that the government provided the legislation necessary to enable the Brahmans to effect the transfer is disregarded in the face-to-face situation. On the local level of interaction, the cleavage which arises from the land-confrontation is between Limbus and Brahmans.

Why were the latter able to benefit more than other non-Limbus from the government's land policy? Three factors would seem to suggest possible explanations: numbers, literacy and government service. In the village area under the jurisdiction of the Syawa Panchayat Committee the Brahmans constitute the single largest group with 32·5% of the population. They are 39·8% of the non-Limbu population in the village and 50% of this category within the Indreni settlements. Thus, by weight of numbers alone Brahmans would be expected to be favoured by any legislation designed to benefit non-Limbus.

Literacy is another factor which has worked to their advantage. Most Brahmans were able to acquire the ability to read and write, despite the almost total lack of formal educational facilities in Ilam until the 1940s. Traditionally, young Brahmans were instructed by religious teachers individually, or attended informal 'schools' (*patshala*) organized by learned men in the area where, through the medium of Sanskrit, they became literate in the Devanagari script, in which the Nepali language is written. Some of the wealthier men sent their sons to Benares, Darjeeling or Kathmandu for schooling. A few Indreni Limbus were able to acquire a modicum of literacy through friendships established with Brahman tutors, but on the whole, until they began serving in the army, Limbus remained illiterate. In consequence, they were forced to rely on Brahmans, as were most other groups, to prepare the documents required at the time of property-division, land-transactions, disputes, etc. And only a few Brahmans, with a high degree of literacy, could manage the skills required in drafting petitions to various branches of the administration and the courts. With their knowledge of Sanskrit, they alone were able to cope with written and spoken Nepali 'officialese', which contains a considerable amount of Sanskrit words.

Ability to read and write was also one of the qualities demanded for government service. Although the top posts in the district administration tended to be filled by Kathmandu appointees, some senior and most intermediate and junior positions were open to local candidates. As a result, Brahmans were able to play a key role in the local administration in Ilam. Wealthy men were able to widen their range of contacts and to use their positions to secure for themselves and their kinsmen some personal advantage. For men without means, service in the administration was perhaps the only avenue of advancement, and on their return to their settlements they were able to utilize the prestige and more concrete benefits of service to enhance their wealth and status. Some of the most prominent Brahman families in Syawa village have a history of government service. The father of the Chairman of the Panchayat Committee was a senior official in the Ilam administration for many years.

These factors, then, undoubtedly provided the wherewithal for Brahmans to attain ascendancy in the politico-economic life of the area.

Brahmans in the area of the Cluster took advantage of legislation to improve their economic position at the expense of the Limbus. A government ruling that possession of kipat land had to be supported by documentary evidence of title proved lucrative ground for ambitious Brahmans. Since the government did not possess the apparatus to enforce this ruling, it relied on – indeed, encouraged – informants (*polaha*) to bring these matters to the attention of the local authorities. The reward to these informants for successful prosecutions of land 'concealment' was the land itself. Immigrant settlers and their descendants were thereby encouraged to contest the flimsy evidence of ownership rights held by their Limbu neighbours. Residents of the Indreni settlements did not escape these challenges to their rights to occupy kipat land in the Cluster.

In 1913, for example, a Brahman from a settlement one mile south of the Cluster petitioned in court in Ilam to be awarded about 4,000 units of paddy land[1] registered as kipat in the names of five members of Chongbung lineage 4. He argued that the Limbus did not possess proper documentary evidence of ownership rights to these lands. The defendants cited a number of written assurances given by the government that uncultivated lands converted into paddy fields and brought under cultivation by the Limbus could be held as kipat. They also produced copies of several documents attesting to Chongbung rights to cultivate their ancestral lands as kipat. But the court agreed with the petitioner that the documents presented as evidence by the Limbus did not in fact prove sufficient title, since for one thing there was no mention of boundaries and, for another, they were granted by local officials and not by the Crown. The defendants were fined Rs 1,570 for 'false registration', and the lands, representing approximately one-half of the total paddy area of the lineage, were converted into raikar tenure and given to the Brahman.[2]

Another facet of the relations between the two groups concerns the need for Limbus to rely on Brahmans for the bulk of their credit.[3] This has given rise to the notion, backed to an extent by readily cited experiences, that all Brahman creditors engage in sharp practices to the detriment of the Limbu debtors. At the turn of the century creditors were, for the first time, required to share in the tax burden of those Limbu kipat-owners whose lands they had taken under pledge. Shortly after the regulation was introduced the Limbus began complaining that many creditors were attempting to claim ownership of the lands on the grounds of having paid the required tax share (*damasahi*). The government was obliged to assure the Limbus and their creditors that it did not intend this to happen.

Another ruse was employed in land-pledging transactions whereby the creditor would provide a small loan and after obtaining the

---

1 For the definition of 'unit' see Appendix A.
2 Another Brahman, encouraged by this case, brought a petition in 1929 against *all* the Subbas of Ilam, contesting their rights to hold kipat. The case was thrown out on the grounds that the petitioner did not specify which lands were involved.
3 See Chapter 5.

signature – or, more likely, the thumbprint – of the kipat-owner, would then add 'a few zeros' to the amount, thus making it impossible for the kipat-owner ever to raise the required amount to repay the loan and resume his lands. One old Limbu, referring to a Brahman with whom he had had such an experience, related how the latter

would invite me to his house and offer me rice and meat. Then he made me put my thumbprints on papers. He would give me a few rupees and when I came some months later to return the money and take back my land, he would say: 'This is not enough. Why do you bring me a few rupees and ask for your land back? The document says the amount of the mortgage is five hundred and you bring me five! What am I, a fool?' What can you do to such a man? They are all like that, the Brahmans. They are treacherous.[1]

When the registration of land-transactions became widespread after 1945, such abuses were less frequently perpetrated. Even so, according to one Brahman informant, clerks in the treasury office could usually be bribed to register amounts which had not in fact been transferred to the kipat-owner.[2] It is worthwhile noting that on the whole only land-transactions involving Indreni Limbus with members of other groups are registered. Treasury office records list only four cases where land-transactions in kipat between Indreni Limbus were recorded. The explanation offered by Limbus and Brahmans alike is that 'Limbus trust one another; they do not have their transactions registered at the office'.

Although the numbers of Brahmans with whom the Limbus have any kind of face-to-face links represent only a small proportion of the total in the area, the attitudes and stereotypes are generalized and applied to the whole group. A legend related by a Limbu ritual specialist expresses the nature of the antagonism:

A Brahman and his wife came from the west and arrived at the Mai River. They told the River Goddess that they had nothing and were hungry. She gave them rice, lentils, vegetables and spices. She gave them fire, and some vessels in which to cook. They ate and rested, and when it became dark they went away, taking everything with them. When she saw what

1 At first I was under the impression that this was only a local habit of a few unscrupulous men. But the practice is mentioned in several references as being common throughout Limbuan. Cf., for example, Bhandari, 1959.

2 In one survey of agricultural conditions in the eastern hills the author blames petty officials for their complicity in aggravating the problems of indebtedness: '... one can say that government officials are the worst exploiters of farmers in the hills' (Gurung, 1949, 9).

5 Musicians entertain at a paddy planting.
6 Limbu lights a Brahman's '*kankat*' (Nepalese cigarette)

7 Brahman joint family
8 A meeting of the village assembly

they had done the River Goddess thought it would have been better not to give such people anything. So she cursed them and said that she would produce no more fish. Since that time men cannot fish in the river and harvests have also been reduced.

The hostility felt towards the Brahmans is overtly expressed in the legend. The themes of theft and deceit which occur here follow the stereotypes held of the Brahmans by the Limbus. The River Goddess, worshipped by all groups, echoes the antagonism and gives it supernatural sanction. The Brahmans, who have abused the kindness and generosity of the River Goddess, have behaved in like fashion towards their erstwhile Limbu benefactors.

This hostility is not one-way. The Brahmans, for their part, regard the Limbus as 'simple' (*lato*) and their ways as 'jungalee'. The Limbus are thought to be concerned only for the present. A Brahman informant observed that if Limbus had thought of the future, the Brahmans would never have been allowed to remain in Ilam, since they would have had no lands on which to settle. At the same time, the Brahmans are resentful of the fact that their economic position is largely dependent on holding the usufruct to kipat lands which they cannot own, which predicament renders them vulnerable to Limbu 'blackmail', as I show in Chapter 5.

Cultural differences

The cleavage which has grown out of the land-struggle is reinforced by differences in the cultural practices of the two groups. The distinctions are evident in matters pertaining to religion. To the extent that we can speak of two religious traditions, it should nevertheless be stressed that the boundaries are not clear-cut. For one thing, there is an awareness by members of each group of the beliefs and customs of the other. Members of one group may profess belief in the efficacy of certain deities associated with the other. Thus, for example, many Brahmans placate Limbu household goddesses, although the form of worship is adapted to the Brahmanic pattern. Limbus, in turn, often rationalize their own religious customs in terms of Hindu beliefs (Benedict, 1962, 1,237). Both groups also enjoy a set of convictions regarding certain forms of divination associated mainly with illness, and share a common pool of ritual specialists for this purpose. Finally, along with the rest of the

6

population, Limbus observe the principal Hindu festivals, such as
Dasein and Tiwar, since these have become national holy days.

Nevertheless, despite the overlap, we can distinguish, as do the
Limbus and Brahmans, between two distinct sets of religious customs.
Whereas Brahmans worship the universal Hindu pantheon, Limbus
worship, by means of blood sacrifice, a host of deities which have no
place in traditional Hindu belief. These are of two main types:
domestic and forest gods. The former are associated with women.
'Men have no gods', say the Limbus. 'Just as a man inherits his
father's lands, a woman inherits her mother's gods.' When a woman
marries and comes to live with her husband she brings her deities
along, and these become recognized as the gods of the household in
which she resides. Certain important deities will be common to all
women, but each will have a more or less unique set.

Although the household worships as an independent unit, it must
take account of its place in a wider agnatic group. Harmonious relations among members of a lineage are deemed necessary to ensure the
efficacy of household worship. If a man has caused ill-feeling to exist,
whether intentionally or otherwise, it is said that he is considered by
the domestic deities to be in a state of impurity (*jutto*), and until he is
purified he cannot properly effect their propitiation. For this reason,
each occasion for the placation of domestic gods is preceded by a rite
to 'wash away bad feelings' (*sarap bagaunu*) in the lineage.

In addition to domestic gods there is also a complex of forest deities
who require propitiation. These are thought to inhabit the area
permanently and to have no special relationship with women. Nevertheless, their appetites are similar, and the manner of their worship
is the same as for domestic gods, except that the rites are conducted
in a field away from the dwelling.

Some of the differences between the forms of worship of Limbus
and Brahmans are immediately apparent in certain diacritical features
surrounding their respective houses. The courtyard of a Limbu
house will not contain a shrine for the worship of a Hindu deity. Nor
do Limbus follow the Brahmanic practice of propitiating an ancestor
god (*kul deota*) which requires the setting aside of a special place of
worship within the Brahman home.

The differences in the ritual significance attached to the taking of
meals is expressed in the kinds of kitchen constructed by each. The
Brahman kitchen consists of a platform of mud raised several inches
above the floor and to which only ritually qualified members of the

household or their Brahman guests have access. The cooking stove, too, is of special mud-and-stone construction, and both stove and platform (which individually and jointly are called *chulo*) are required to be replastered with a mixture of mud and cow dung after each meal. Brahman men take their meals only after ritual bathing and while wearing a special white loincloth (*dhoti*), which replaces their ordinary clothes. Limbus, on the other hand, cook on a simple stove consisting of several stones or an iron tripod. They eat in their ordinary clothes after washing only their hands and face, and no special platform is built inside the house for eating purposes.

Distinct dietary practices are associated with each group. Although some Brahmans are strict vegetarians by choice, most eat the meat of goats and sheep. Limbus also eat buffalo, chicken and pig meat, which are forbidden to Brahmans.[1]

Limbu mourning practices also differ from those of the Brahmans. To mention only two features: the Limbus bury their dead, whereas the Brahmans cremate theirs. Limbus observe a period of three or four days of pollution (depending on whether the deceased is female or male), while Brahmans consider pollution to extend for thirteen days after death.

Marriage practices, too, are distinct. Limbu marriages are performed by Limbu ritual specialists and require a blood sacrifice. Costs of marriage are borne by the bridegroom's family, and the ceremony itself takes place at the home of the bridegroom, before and after which a series of payments are transferred from the groom's to the bride's family. Limbu widows are remarried in essentially the same ceremony as are new brides. Brahman women, by contrast, are married at their natal homes in ceremonies conducted by Brahman family priests, and the marriages thereby made are considered indissoluble. The costs of the marriage are borne by the bride's family. Brahman widows are not remarried.

Finally, a word might be said about differences in the 'pleasure complex' of the two groups (Orans, 1965, 8). The most important aspects of this complex among the Limbus are drinking and dancing. Millet beer (*jar*) and liquor distilled from millet (*raksi*), the two main kinds of intoxicating beverage made and consumed in the settlements, constitute an integral part of Limbu social life. Obeisance to headmen is expressed in the presentation of liquor; the request for a girl's hand

1 All informants claim that beef was eaten by Limbus prior to the Hindu invasion.

in marriage is preceded by the offering of liquor; marriage payments include large quantities of liquor; the settlement of a dispute is symbolized by the sharing of liquor. Indeed, there is hardly a social event which does not in some way involve the sharing of drink. The importance of drink is especially evident during rituals which bring together large numbers of people. Weddings and funerary rites are characterized by the consumption of vast quantities of beer. The norms of hospitality, too, demand the serving of beer. A visiting kinsman or other guest is made welcome by offering beer in a bamboo container (*tongba*). I have heard one old Limbu remark: '*Tongba* is the Limbu god.'

Another form of recreation which marks off the Limbus from the Brahmans is the former's enjoyment of dancing. The Limbu 'paddy dance' (*dhan nac*) involves a line of men and women, hand to hand, in a series of musical challenges and rebuttals, danced and sung in lugubrious rhythm over many hours. Since certain categories of kin – especially agnates of the opposite sex – are barred from dancing together, dances are usually held when visitors arrive from another settlement cluster. Limbu weddings and other occasions for large gatherings invariably include dances for the young men and women.

A number of major Hindu festivals provide additional opportunities for Limbus to indulge their delight in dancing. One such occasion is a large four-day fair which takes place at the confluence of the Mai and Jogmai rivers, beginning on the first day of the Nepalese month of *magh* (January/February). The distinction in 'pleasure complex' between the Brahmans and Limbus is made manifest in the various ways in which the two groups regard the fair. Although the main purpose of the festival is sacred – viz. the worship of the Mai River – the Limbus gather in one section of the fair-ground and spend the better part of the time dancing and drinking. For the Limbus this is primarily a secular event, enabling the young people to meet others from every part of the district at the dances, which continue for days.

For the Brahmans the festival's importance is in its sacred content: the ritual purification obtained by bathing in the holy river, and the spiritual duty discharged by propitiation of the River Goddess. Consequently, the pleasure value of the festival is inseparable from the sacred value. This sacred aspect is the focus of all recreational activities in which Brahmans participate. Informal groups organized by wealthy Brahmans gather occasionally to sing religious songs.

Brahman weddings feature stylized singing competitions (called *silok*) – usually recitations of passages from the sacred literature – between the camps of the bride and groom. Women from the groom's settlement gather on the night of his wedding (which takes place at the bride's home) to indulge in songs and play (*ratauli*) – mostly of a lewd nature – at the expense of the bride's relatives. These and other ritual occasions provide the framework for the Brahman 'pleasure complex'. The dearth of secular occasions for recreational activity and the prohibition on drinking and mixed dancing set the Brahmans apart from their Limbu neighbours.

Despite their sharing of a common environment and their fusion into a single social system, each group maintains a distinct 'style of life'.

The feature most often stressed by members of both groups as symbolizing the distinction is the fact that the 'religion of the Brahmans' is a written tradition, while the indigenous religion of the Limbus is not. The following legend, which I heard repeated on several occasions by Limbus, illustrates the relative value they assign to the two systems:

Some ancient sages wrote the scriptures and covered the books with deer-skin for their protection, and floated them in the rivers so that men would find them. Many Brahmans and Limbus found these books. The Brahmans kept them safely, but the Limbus ate the skin and used the pages for their fires. So the Brahmans learned how to marry and mourn and conduct their daily lives from these books. But the Limbus who didn't obey these scriptures made their own customs, which are not written down, but are handed on by their forefathers.[1]

This legend suggests the fact, expressed in other contexts as well, that Limbus concede the superiority of the written tradition of Hinduism adhered to by the Brahmans. This is not surprising, considering that Nepal is officially a Hindu state and remembering the super-ordinate status enjoyed by the Brahmans in Limbuan.

To sum up the argument to this point: the cleavage between Limbus and Brahmans has emerged mainly as a result of a historical confrontation over land. This confrontation has given rise to stereotyped attitudes held by each group about the other. These are both related directly to historical experiences and reinforced by cultural

1 This myth has much in common with some found in societies where there are cargo cults (see p. 190).

differences between the two groups. Moreover, the differences are conceptualized as hierarchic in order. In other words, Brahmans and Limbus are not merely distinct and opposed groups, but opposed in a hierarchy based on ritually assessed attributes. This requires a word about the caste framework[1] in which their relations are set.

The caste hierarchy

Each caste in Nepal is associated with one of three main levels in the hierarchy.[2] These are objective divisions in the sense that until 1963 the law was applied differentially on the basis of castes which were for the most part classified into three tiers. In the old legal code the Brahmans, along with Jaisis[3] and Chetris, were designated *tagadhari jat*, which implied that they were high Hindu or 'twice-born' castes. In common parlance, Brahmans and Jaisis are referred to as *bahun*, while the three groups together are termed *khas-bahun*. However, whereas Jaisis will generally refer to themselves as *bahun*, Brahmans normally prefix the term *upadiya*, denoting a status superior to the Jaisis. All three groups wear the scared thread, a symbol of their high ritual status. Brahmans serve as priests to the three groups, but aside from this no specific occupation is associated with any group: all are cultivators.[4]

Below the twice-born castes in the ritual hierarchy come the various tribal groups. Limbus, like the Rais, Gurungs, Magars, Sunwars and Tamangs, are termed (both in the old legal code and in everyday conversation) 'drinking castes' (*matwali jat*). Each of these castes assigns to itself a position in the middle stratum of the hierarchy not always in accord with the position it is assigned by other groups. So

1 Since it is not my purpose in this book to discuss the nature of caste in Limbuan, I have not tried to be precise when using the term. It translates the term *jat*, which is employed in reference to all ethnic groups in Nepal. If by a caste system we mean that ties between groups are organic (Leach, 1962), then it is doubtful if such a system can be said to exist, or ever to have existed, in east Nepal. The struggle for land between Limbus and Brahmans has meant that their relations have all along been 'segmentary' (Bailey, 1961).

2 The Newars are generally classified separately, since they are internally ranked (cf. Fürer-Haimendorf, 1956).

3 These are the issue of unions between Brahman men and Brahman widows, or their intermarrying descendants.

4 Brahmans in east Nepal, unlike those in some parts of the country, plough.

that although it is generally accepted that drinking castes rank below the twice-born groups in the ritual hierarchy, how the former are arranged is a matter of some uncertainty. None of these groups in the middle tier wears the sacred thread. Nor does any follow a specific occupation with which it is associated by tradition. Like those in the top stratum, the 'drinking castes' are primarily cultivators.

Finally come the menial castes – from whom others will accept no water (*pani na calne*). These 'untouchables' rank lowest in the hierarchy. Although some Blacksmiths, Tailors[1] and Cobblers perform traditional services for the higher-ranked groups, the majority depend mainly on agriculture for a livelihood.

The law protected the interests of the Brahmans by making an infringement of their exalted status a crime. Thus, for example, it was considered a criminal offence for a man of lower caste to have sexual relations with a Brahman woman. Moreover, a member of a lower caste who was cuckolded by a Brahman was prohibited from killing the latter, a right which he could exercise under certain conditions against members of any other caste. Brahmans, too, were exempted from compulsory labour for the government and from paying certain kinds of taxes, which obligations others, including Limbus, were required to meet.

The special position of the Brahmans was protected in local conditions as well. In 1957 a quarrel ensued between a Brahman and a Limbu when the former diverted an irrigation channel into his own paddy field after the Limbu had already begun flooding his terraces situated below. The Limbu struck the Brahman and the matter was brought to the Panchayat Court. At three separate points in his petition the Brahman repeated the words: 'I, a Brahman, was beaten by a Limbu.' When the Court, whose members were all Brahmans, fined the Limbu, they too concentrated, not on the morality of physical violence, but on the contravention of a ritual code embodied in the caste hierarchy: 'You should not have beaten him, because he is a Brahman.'

The hierarchical basis of relations between Limbus and Brahmans is also reflected in the pattern of deference which symbolizes their respective statuses. The manner in which greetings are exchanged mirrors the relative statuses of the persons meeting. Unless they are kinsmen, when specific forms are called for, it is usual for a subordinate to incline his forehead to be 'tapped' by the superordinate.

1 Tailors are also musicians.

The criteria of relative status are not easy to isolate. Between members of the same caste they are usually a combination of wealth and age. Across caste lines, however, ritual rank becomes an important criterion, so that Limbus are almost always the subordinate greeting-partners of Brahmans. I have seen a sixty-year-old Subba go along a row of Brahmans to be 'tapped', and only a small percentage of these were his seniors in age, although most were his economic betters.

The same pattern applies to verbal forms of address. Brahmans use the lowest honorific grade, which an elder generally uses to a junior, when addressing Limbus, regardless of their relative ages.[1]

The cleavage in Limbu-Brahman relations is also expressed in and reinforced by certain forms of social segregation. Although the overall caste structure provides for the accommodation of offspring of hypergamous marriages into the Khatri-Chetri caste (Fürer-Haimendorf, 1960) both Brahmans and Limbus express distaste for such intermarriages. The union of a Limbu woman and a Brahman male would place the former outside the matrix of her natal group. On economic grounds alone, her marriage could not be welcomed, since her group would receive no bridewealth. Her kinsmen would take no interest in her well-being and would not offer the protection and support usually given a daughter or sister after marriage. Such unions, in any case, are a statistical rarity. In one instance which I have recorded, the widow of a Kambo man married a Brahman from a neighbouring settlement. In another a Brahman of Bharapa who spent ten years as a policeman in a town about five miles west of the Cluster took a Limbu wife resident in the town. On his return to the Cluster – where he has a Brahman wife – he did not bring the Limbu woman, although he continues to visit her occasionally and provides for her support. The marriage drew wry comments from Brahmans and Limbus alike, and the husband himself admitted that such unions are regarded with disdain, and pointed out that if he had brought her to live in the Cluster both he and the woman would have been scorned by everyone.

Since hypogamous unions until recently were violations not only of caste, but of the law, they cannot be considered as instances of intermarriage. A Brahman woman who forms a liaison with a Limbu

---

1 In all these manifestations of hierarchy, significant exceptions are made for the category of wealthy Limbus, usually ex-army pensioners. See pp. 170ff.

automatically forfeits her caste status and assumes that of her partner. But despite the fact that she is regarded as a Limbu in the eyes of the Brahmans and the law, she is not considered as such by the Limbus themselves. The only circumstance in which such a relationship could survive would be if both partners fled to a town where they were unknown or, as is usually the case for hypogamous couples, if they settled in India. In the only case of this nature involving an Indreni Limbu, which occurred about forty years ago, the couple fled to Assam, severing all ties with their kinsmen. The man, who was a Kambo, forfeited his share of the household property, since he never returned to the Cluster. That the stigma falls most heavily on the woman is illustrated by another example involving a Limbu from a settlement a few miles from the Cluster. After the seduction of a Brahman widow from the same settlement, both went to the Darjeeling area, where they remained for several months. The Limbu then returned alone to Ilam. He was accepted back by his kinsmen and his Limbu wife as a matter of course, but it was clear that the Brahman woman could never join him. The Limbu's prestige was not at all compromised, and as long as he made no attempt to introduce the union into the settlement he suffered no personal disadvantage. The Brahman woman, however, was forced to remain in exile.

The virtual absence of intermarriage between members of the two groups provides what is perhaps the most important measure of social separation. There are other contexts in which interaction is minimal. Attendance at marriage and mourning rites tends to be restricted to members of a single ethnic group. Co-operative labour gangs recruited by Limbus from among their neighbours on the basis of mutual exchange do not normally include Brahmans. Differences of wealth and status and the pattern of residence obviously help to explain this segregation. But these factors are supported by the over-riding opposition of the two groups, which, though partly a function of these very factors, assumes a reality *sui generis*. The result is a virtual absence of interaction in most of the important social contexts.

Commensal relations reflect both the ritual and secular statuses of the two groups. Ritually defined norms proscribe the acceptance by Brahmans of certain foods prepared by Limbus. Thus foods labelled *bhat* (rice, maize or millet), *dal* (lentils) or *tarkari* (curried vegetables or meat), which are cooked in water by Limbus, cannot be eaten by Brahmans. Moreover, such foods, even when prepared by Brahman cooks, must not be eaten unless members of the two groups are seated in separate lines. A Brahman who willingly disregards commensal regulations would cease to be welcome in the kitchens of other Brahmans, would not be able to offer any hospitality to fellow caste members, and would not be likely to find a Brahman spouse for his child.

Considerations of secular status, however, can lead to a widening of commensal rules such that acceptance of even ritually unimportant foods from Limbus is not countenanced. Some Brahmans, for example, in seeking to validate high secular status, insist that commensal prohibitions extend to all types of food. Such attempts to restrict all commensal interaction are often the cause of bitterness and resentment among Limbus. They argue, as indeed do poor Brahmans, that foods prepared in oil or clarified butter, or beverages such as tea, are ritually neutral and can be shared by all, save untouchables. When I asked several Limbus who make an annual Satya Narayan rite why they prefer a particular Brahman priest, the reply was that he willingly accepts tea and the doughnut-shaped breads (*sel roti*), prepared in clarified butter for the occasion. One Limbu changed his Brahman priest because the latter refused to accept even tea. Such Brahmans try to justify their behaviour by reference to ritual interdictions. But in the context of Limbu-Brahman relations the extension of commensal restrictions becomes a means of validating in ritual terms the existence of status differentials based on economic and political criteria.

Conclusion

To understand the origin and nature of the cleavage between Limbus and Brahmans in the Indreni settlements it was necessary to consider, on the one hand, the kipat-land policy of the government and, on the other, the conditions which made it possible for the Brahmans to manipulate this policy to their best advantage. Thus, the analysis has had to take account of factors both external and indigenous to the local setting.

The cleavage itself, which has arisen essentially from a confrontation over land, has a number of aspects. It is expressed, first of all, in the attitudes held by members of each group towards the other. The Limbus, who have seen their lands pass into Brahman hands, are bitter and resentful of the latter, whom they regard as deceitful and dishonest. The Brahmans, for their part, are full of contempt for those who, they suggest, were too simple to protect their own interests. Their view of the Limbus is coloured, too, by the cultural differences between them, which represent yet another manifestation of the cleavage. Despite a certain degree of overlap, the cultural practices of the two groups are separate enough to enable us to identify two distinct 'styles of life'. And because of the high value placed on Brahmanic Hinduism, Limbu practices are regarded as inferior; at the same time, the culture associated with the Brahmans, who are also secularly dominant, is recognized as superior by the Limbus themselves. This cultural cleavage is reinforced by the existence of a hierarchic caste framework which confers on the contrasting 'styles of life' and on the groups which are identified with them a differential ritual evaluation. The stringent rules of caste also prevent intermarriage, restrict commensality and generally reduce certain types of social interaction between members of the two groups to a minimum.

But cleavage is only one facet of Limbu-Brahman relations; interdependence is the other. This will be evident from a consideration of their economic links, which is the subject of the next chapter.

Chapter 5

Interdependence: the economic context

The economic interdependence of Limbus and Brahmans arises, like the cleavage dividing them, out of the confrontation over land. Since the turn of the century the majority of Limbus have found it impossible to maintain their level of consumption and meet minimal social obligations without resort to borrowing from Brahmans and, to a lesser extent, other non-Limbus. The creditors, whose numbers have increased, are in need of additional areas to cultivate and demand, as security for their loans, that the kipat lands of the Limbus be given them under usufructuary mortgage. In other words, the creditors assume the rights of usufruct pending repayment of the loan. The circle is as cumulative as it is vicious. As they go further into debt, the Limbus are forced to mortgage more and more land; and as they lose access to their lands, they cannot earn enough to repay the mortgages.

Why must the Limbus borrow? Loans are taken almost exclusively for consumption purposes, because income from all available sources is insufficient to meet the household's various cash needs. In the following paragraphs these needs are considered.

The food gap

By and large, the Limbus do not have adequate agricultural production to meet their food requirements. By this latter term is not meant an objective measure of minimal demands of nutrition. Instead, it emerges from the estimates given by household heads of the quantities of grain needed daily to feed their families.[1] The eighty-five

1 These estimates vary little from one informant to the next. Those aged fourteen and over consume one unit per day (see footnote 1, p. 77).

Limbu households in the Indreni settlements require approximately 102,500 units of grain annually, or an average of slightly more than 1,200 units per household.[1] Kipat lands in the Cluster have a productive capacity of about 137,000 units, more than enough to meet aggregate food requirements. In addition, Limbus own raikar land with a productive capacity of 8,300 units. However, a large proportion of kipat lands have been mortgaged and the usufruct of these lands is held by others.[2] Agricultural income thus amounts to approximately 87,000 units, or just under 85% of the food requirements of Limbu households.[3] But this is a total figure for the whole Limbu population in the Cluster. The degree to which each household produces its own food needs varies considerably. Twenty-two (25·9%) households produce more than their minimal requirements. Another eight households (9·5%) produce just enough to meet these requirements, while the remaining fifty-five households (64·6%) produce less than they require. Table 7 gives the breakdown of households in the latter category.

TABLE 7
Production of food requirements by 'deficit' households

Percentage of food requirements produced	No. of households	Percentage of households
Under 25	5	5·9
25–49	19	22·3
50–74	22	25·9
75 plus	9	10·5
	—	—
	55	64·6

By way of comparison, of the non-Limbus in the Cluster, all six

Children from ten to thirteen years are half-consumers, while those between two and nine years are quarter-consumers. The requirements of children under two years are insignificant and can be ignored. These figures accord almost exactly with those given by Bailey (1957, 277–8) for an Orissan village.

1 For the definition of a 'unit' see Appendix A.
2 The circularity of the process is here evident. The food-gap arises partly because of mortgaging; further mortgaging occurs because of the food-gap.
3 For the details of how the total agricultural income is arrived at see Appendix B.

Brahman and one Jaisi households produce more than their requirements. The four Magar and three Blacksmith households, on the
other hand, like the majority of Limbus, produce less than their
minimal needs. Cash is therefore required to purchase grains to fill
the gap.

Recurrent expenditures

Despite a substantial production deficit, all household budgets
regularly include expenditures on a number of consumer goods.
Kerosene, cooking oil, tobacco and paper, spices, soap, tea, salt and
meat – the latter the most expensive item in the food budgets of most
households – are normally purchased on market day in Ilam Bazaar.[1]

For those with children at school there are fees and other school
expenses to pay. Fifteen Limbu children from twelve households –
about one-third of Limbu boys aged from six to thirteen years –
were enrolled at the primary school in the Cluster. No Limbu girls
have as yet attended school. Most boys who were registered in fact
attended sporadically, when they were not required to mind cattle
or work in the fields. During March, 1964, when maize was being
planted, only ten of these children appeared at all at the school and
only half that number attended with regularity. Still, enrolment
requires the payment of fees which range from Rs 0·80 per month for
students in their first year to Rs 1·60 for those in the fifth (and
highest) class. Additional expenses for the parents of schoolchildren
are for copy-books and pencils, and the contribution of a bundle of
thatch and a day's labour for re-roofing the school house each year.

Households require cash to pay taxes. Limbus in the Indreni
settlements pay a total of Rs 327 in kipat taxes each year, which means
an average of Rs 43·5 per kipat-owning household. Nine households
pay Rs 29 on raikar lands owned, an average of Rs 3·25. Kipat owners
who have mortgaged some of their lands, however, are entitled to
claim a proportion of their taxes from those who have taken the lands
under mortgage. The greater the amount of land pledged and the

1 Much of the quantitative data on household budgets were collected during
   the course of a comprehensive census of the Cluster. To check the statements I received, I occasionally accompanied people to the market and
   recorded their purchases. In addition, I made a point of visiting a sample
   number of household heads and their wives immediately they returned
   from the market, to ask about the day's transactions.

more numerous the mortgagees the larger their tax share (*damasahi*). Many Limbus with lands mortgaged have thus not only had their tax burden eased, but have in fact been able to turn a profit from this regulation. Eight households with taxes of up to Rs 5 to pay receive more than Rs 10 in *damasahi* payments from the creditors. With total taxes assessed at Rs 327, Limbus collect approximately Rs 380 in this way. On an aggregate basis, then, taxes do not constitute an expense. But not all households receive *damasahi*, and the amounts received by those who do are not equally distributed. In all, 35% of Limbu households must set aside cash to meet annual tax obligations.

Budgets allow for substantial expenditure on clothing. Each member of the household expects to be provided with a new set of clothing at least once a year, generally at the time of the Dasein festival in autumn. Indreni Limbus purchase Indian-made cloth in Ilam Bazaar. To sew their clothes they engage members of the Tailor caste.

Traditionally, the Tailor's service was supplied within the context of an ongoing relationship between client and craftsman. The latter received a fixed amount of grain (*bali*) at harvest-time in return for the services he provided. Moreover, the tie was permanent in that it was transmitted from one generation to the next. Nowadays, all but two Limbu households engage Tailors from settlements in the surrounding area or Ilam Bazaar on a piece-work basis, and pay in cash for the services received. Even in the case of the two households who prefer to pay their Tailors annually in grain the relationship between client and craftsman is unlike the traditional one, in that it must be renewed each year and the payments determined anew on the basis of the estimated needs of the client.

Households also require constant repairs to and replacement of a variety of farming implements and other metal wares. This work is reserved for members of the Blacksmith caste. Like Tailors, most Blacksmiths are hired on a contractual basis.[1] But whereas only two households retain tailoring services in return for a fixed amount of grain, ten households enter this kind of arrangement with Blacksmiths. The reasons given by these Limbus for preferring an annual payment in grain vary. Some state that payment in a lump sum at harvest-time precludes the necessity of finding ready cash which

1 Relationships with service castes are similar to those described by Harper (1959) for the Malnad area, viz. the alliances are easily broken; payments are mainly in cash; and the prices of services fluctuate.

may not be available on each of the occasions when a Blacksmith's services may be required. One informant insisted that it was less expensive to pay a fixed quantity of grain, while several others admitted that the expense was probably greater, but that it was worthwhile if the craftsman gave good service. The insistence of some Blacksmiths on this form of payment and the dictates of tradition were other reasons offered.

It is the wealthiest households which tend to maintain a relationship based on payment in grain. This is to be expected, since only these households are able to commit in advance a fixed quantity of agricultural income. There is, too, a question of prestige involved in maintaining the traditional type of relationship. It does not escape the Limbus that all Brahman and Jaisi households in the Cluster prefer this kind of arrangement with both Tailors and Blacksmiths.[1] Why more Limbus have such ties with the latter than with the former, however, is difficult to explain. It may be that the Tailors

TABLE 8
Two annual household budgets[2]

	Household A	Household B
	Rs	Rs
Kerosene	20	52
Salt	10	16
Cooking oil	34	80
Soap	3	4
Tobacco and paper	20	36
Spices	10	16
Tea	40	52
Meat	75	150
Cloth	60	160
Tailor services	6 (cash)	16 (cash)
Metals	10	12
Blacksmith services	15 (cash)	32 (grains)
School expenses	–	6
Taxes	1	2
	314	634

1 Gould (1964, 18) points out that 'the capacity to retain traditional ties with [service castes] marks a household as socially important'.
2 In order to view these figures in perspective, see the estimates of average annual income per household on pp. 89–90.

themselves prefer to be paid in cash, for I have heard that Tailors who accept an annual grain allotment are difficult to find.

The budgets of two households are given in Table 8. Household A contains two adults and produces only 57% of its food requirements. Household B contains three adults and six children aged from one to fourteen years. It produces 152% of its annual requirements of food.

Contingent expenditures: mortuary rites

There are a number of contingencies which arise, inevitably, in the lifetime of a household, and impose a temporary but considerable financial burden. Those which involve the greatest expenditures are mortuary rites and marriages.

The death of a Limbu renders lineage members ritually polluted for a period of three days if the deceased is a woman, or four if a man. During this period they are required to refrain from eating foods cooked in oil or seasoned with salt. At the end of the period a ritual of 'touching oil and salt' (*nun-tel chunu*) is performed to remove the pollution. At this time the principal mourner (*kiriya putra*) must give a feast for those who assisted in the burial rites. However, neither the mourning sequence nor the expense ends there. Lineage members are prevented from propitiating household deities or making marriages until a second ritual is held to signify the cessation of further intercourse between the living members of the lineage and the deceased, and to indicate the return to normal relations between the lineage and the rest of the community. This latter ritual, which is also accompanied by a feast, may be held at any time from nine days to a year following the death. To avoid the costs and inconvenience of holding two rituals, some Limbus prefer to combine them by refraining from eating prohibited foods for only one meal following the death and then observing the period of pollution from the seventh to the ninth day after burial. Both rites are then held at one time.

The quality and variety of food served at mortuary feasts varies little, being confined to buffalo meat, rice and millet beer. Thus the precise costs depend mainly on the number of guests. Participation in these rites is a function of spatial, kinship and status distance between the principal mourner or host and his potential guests. Persons resident in the same neighbourhood as the host are invariably invited to attend mortuary rites and feasts. The host of a

7

rite to be held in Angbung, for example, would expect other residents of the settlement to attend, as well as some from the adjoining settlement of Bharapa. Inhabitants of the two northernmost settlements in the Cluster would not be invited on grounds of propinquity.

The spatial factor, however, is mitigated by kinship ties. Since lineage members are required to be present for ritual reasons the degree of their spatial separation from the host is irrelevant. Ties of agnation outside the lineage are also of some importance in determining the range of invitees. Other than lineage mates, those who share membership of a local clan segment are not ritually affected by a death. Nevertheless, many recognize the loss of an agnate by refraining from ritually relevant foods for a single meal. This tie is often acknowledged by the invitation of at least some agnates who live beyond the immediate neighbourhood of the host, provided, of course, he can afford it. A wealthy Chongbung man of Angbung, for example, extended invitations to a mortuary rite as far as Chitok, the northernmost limits of Chongbung residence in the Cluster.

Other kinds of ties may be acknowledged as well. These result from the practice of taking wives from descent groups with which affinal ties have already been established.[1] The result is that few women marrying into the Indreni Cluster are not already related agnatically to at least some wives of Indreni men. The death of an Indreni woman, therefore, obliges the host to invite the dead woman's agnates resident in the Indreni settlements, even if ties of agnation do not already exist between the host and the husbands of these women.

The participation of affinal relatives is essential for both prestige and ritual reasons. The consent of affines is required to remove the pollution of death from a lineage. In addition, whereas no other Limbu ritual enjoins the officiating priest to be related in any special way to the host, rites following a death are thought to be more efficacious if the person officiating is an affine. The Limbus say that 'with an affine we are certain that the mourners will be rid of pollution'.

I have already pointed out that Brahmans do not normally attend Limbu mortuary rites unless the Limbu host is a man of high status. Do distinctions of status similarly affect relationships within the

---

1 Of the 145 women married into the Indreni Cluster, ninety-one belong to thirty local clan segments from nineteen settlement clusters within a radius of six miles.

Limbu community? Wealth differences alone have little bearing on social ties among Limbus. These differences are irrelevant to the formation of work-gangs for cultivation, or friendships, or attendance at one another's rites. This may be due to the realization that wealth differences are ephemeral and that the fortunes of a household can change, figuratively speaking, overnight. But it also accords well with the Limbu view of themselves as an egalitarian people. However, where wealth is seen to be more than temporary, and, moreover, where it is accompanied by other qualities which are universally hailed and which lead to recognition of the wealthy person as a 'Notable' (*bhaladmi*),[1] the status differences which emerge can produce a 'discontinuity' in social ties.

Status distinctions are expressed in the absence of a social superior from the mortuary rites of his inferiors. Attendance implies recognition of the superiority or equality of the host. The conflict of this principle with that of egalitarianism is resolved by excluding women from the conceptual hierarchy. Thus, one Limbu who would not attend any of the feasts to which he was invited because the hosts were 'small men' would allow his wife and daughters-in-law to participate while he remained away with his sons. In sum, the greater a man's status the higher the numbers likely to attend the rites he sponsors.

The total expenditure on one mourning rite which about 125 people attended was in the region of Rs 250. Another rite, attended by half that number of guests cost the host Rs 200, while a third, which attracted the same number of guests as the first, cost Rs 300, mainly because the host did not have time to search around for a smaller buffalo and so ended up buying one larger than he in fact needed. In the latter two instances the entire costs were borne by the household head whose daughter-in-law, in one case, and wife, in another, had died. The expenses in the first instance were shared among three brothers whose classificatory sister, a spinster, had died.

Since the pattern of mortuary rites is standard, costs tend to vary only moderately in accordance with the number of guests attending. This is apparent from the examples above, where the cost of the second rite was only 17% less than the first, despite the fact that half the number of guests attended. Expenditures on marriages, on the other hand, display a much wider range, due to variations in the kinds of marital unions effected.

1 See pp. 139ff.

Contingent expenditures: marriage

Limbus marry in three ways: by arrangement (*magi biha*); by the 'theft' of an unmarried girl (*chori biha*); or by absconding with another man's wife (*jari*). No stigma is attached to the latter two forms. Children of arranged, theft or *jari* marriages inherit equally. Nevertheless, arranged marriages are the most prestigious and consequently the most frequent. Of 172 virilocal marriages in the Indreni settlements, 58·7% were by arrangement, 21·5% were by theft, and 19·8% were *jari* marriages.[1] Two-thirds of all married men in the Cluster have been married only once. Their marriages, shown in Table 9, are compared with those of men married more than once.

TABLE 9
Distribution of marriages

	Men married once	Men married more than once	
		First marriage	Subsequent
	%	%	%
By arrangement	66·6	68·4	44·0
By theft	20·0	18·4	25·5
By *jari*	13·3	13·2	30·5

Clearly, what emerges from these figures is that a significant majority of Limbus marry their first wives by arrangement,[2] but that subsequent marriages are more frequently effected by theft or *jari*.[3]

Arranged marriage is the most expensive of the three forms. Traditionally, because marriage took place at an early age, the task of

1 I count here only those marriages of which at least one spouse is still alive.
2 There is no indication that the proportion of first marriages by arrangement is higher among eldest sons than among their junior siblings. Of thirty-three eldest brothers (excluding only sons) 63·7% married their first wives by arrangement, while of thirty-nine younger brothers the proportion is 64·1%.
3 Altogether, of 113 married men in the Cluster, twenty-two have married twice, eleven men have had three wives and five men have married four times.

finding a wife had been the responsibility of the boy's guardian, usually his father. However, during the lifetime of a single generation the average age at which young men tend to marry has increased by about four years – to eighteen. This has resulted in greater pressure by the young men on their elders to negotiate for partners they have already seen and chosen for themselves. Young men frequently have occasion to visit the settlements of their relatives and at such times mix freely at dances with the local girls. In 1964 a young Chongbung man was married to a girl he had first seen in 1962 when he attended the wedding of his father's brother's wife's brother. Since that time he had made a number of visits to her settlement in the company of other Indreni boys. When it came time for him to marry he informed his father of his choice. The latter agreed and set in motion the machinery for negotiations. The elders tend not to disagree with the preferences of the young men so long as the household of the prospective bride is of approximately equal status to that of the groom. According to the wealthiest Limbu in the Cluster:

The character of a big [i.e. rich] household differs from that of a small one, since there is much housework to do, many guests to feed, visitors who must be given tea, and so on. For these reasons the people of a big household do not like to take a daughter-in-law from a small household. And a boy from a very poor family does not come to ask for the daughter of a rich man, since he could not make the necessary payments or provide for her in the way she has known before. She would soon run away.

Bridewealth (*sunauli*) is paid to the girl's household immediately the marriage proposal made by the groom's representatives has been accepted. The size of the payment depends on two main factors. The first pertains to the wealth and status of the groups being united. The average of bridewealth payments made during the past decade by households in the lower half of the economic scale amounts to Rs 110, which is approximately 68% of the average payments – Rs 160 – made during the same period by those in the top half of the scale.[1]

1 Although I could not bear this out statistically, it appears that if a young man succeeds in his proposals of marriage to a girl from a household which is far better off economically than his own the bridewealth he will be obliged to pay will be at least as high as that demanded of a household on the same economic level as the girl's. In the only two instances of this nature which I was able to document the bridewealth payments were above the average paid by households in the highest bracket (Rs 190 and Rs 225). This would suggest that payments are related to the wealth of the bride's household and not the groom's.

The second determinant of the size of bridewealth payments relates to whether or not the bride has already been married. Limbus allow widow remarriage and there is no difference in status within the household or community between a wife married for the first time and one taken in widowhood. The natal household of a widow, however, receives a smaller bridewealth. One wealthy Indreni resident paid Rs 130 in bridewealth for a widow who four years earlier had been given as a virgin to her first husband for Rs 175. Another was married for the first time to a nubile girl for whom bridewealth of Rs 150 was paid. Later the same year he was married again, this time to a widow, for whom Rs 80 were asked.

A widow may, but is not obliged to, marry her late husband's younger brother. If she does, no bridewealth need be paid by the second husband, although certain other marriage payments (*rit*) would be demanded (see following pages). There were two such cases of widow inheritance in the Indreni settlements. The rule applies only to real and not classificatory younger brothers, who would have to pay bridewealth anew.

Marrying a dead wife's younger sister is also permitted. However, there is no obligation on the part of the woman's group to provide another wife following the death of the first. The marriage of a Chongbung man came to a rapid end when his wife died only a month after he had paid bridewealth to her father. He could neither claim the return of the money nor her replacement by another woman from her natal household. Still, some groups seek to reinforce their fledgling relations by arranging for the provision of a younger sister of the dead woman as a new wife. In such cases, bridewealth is paid for the second wife as well, although the amount demanded by the woman's household would be less than for the first wife.

Apart from paying bridewealth, the groom is required to make a number of other payments (*rit*) in cash, meat and liquor. Some of the *rit* payments, like bridewealth, are retained entirely by the household of the bride. The remainder is shared among her lineage mates and their wives, and the tie to her mother's brother is also recognized. These payments are sent to the bride's home the day following the wedding festivities. The quantities transported require three or four young men to carry them and the journey can take up to two days. To present the payments, an elder must accompany the party and act as its spokesman on its arrival at the bride's home. The groom's father must undertake to pay the road expenses of the entire party.

Table 10 records the *rit* payments made by an Indreni groom in 1965.

TABLE 10
Rit payments at one marriage[1]

		Rs
(a)	Fee to bride's father on arrival at his home	1·60
(b)	Whole pig for bride's father, plus Rs 1·60	81·60
(c)	One thigh of buffalo for bride's paternal grandfather	10·00
(d)	One thigh of buffalo for bride's father	10·00
(e)	For bride's father's brother	1·40
(f)	For bride's father's mother	1·40
(g)	For bride's grandfather's sister	1·40
(h)	For bride's mother's brother	1·40
(i)	For Subba of bride's lineage	2·00
(j)	For four other lineage agnates	4·00
(k)	For wives of above lineage agnates	1·60
(l)	Fee to bride's father on entry of groom into house	2·40
(m)	Costs of meat (*perengo*)	12·00
(n)	Costs of liquor	40·00
(o)	Costs of transporting *rit* payments	15·00
	Costs of *rit*	185·00

Note : The *rit* payments recorded in the above table are about average. The range is from Rs 150 to Rs 225.

Marriage payments extend over a period of three years. The Limbu husband returns to the bride's natal settlement each year during the festival of Dasein to make obeisance to his wife's father and the latter's lineage mates. On each of these occasions he brings meat – a whole pig plus *perengo* – and liquor on a scale equal to the initial *rit* payments made at the time of the marriage. The fees to the bride's lineage agnates and their wives need not be paid again, although these relatives continue to receive *perengo* and liquor. The costs for each of these three annual payments for the husband whose

1 Each of payments (c)–(k) is accompanied by a small wicker purse (*perengo*) containing about ½ lb. of pig-meat. The equivalent of about 1 pint of liquor (*raksi*) would also be added to each payment. The bride's household received 20 pints. The cost of meat and liquor appear as separate items (m) and (n).

expenses are listed in Table 10 would thus amount to Rs 168·60 (items (*b*), (*c*), (*d*), (*m*), (*n*), (*o*)) or a total of about Rs 500 over the three-year period.

Bridewealth and *rit* payments for a theft marriage follow the same pattern as those in arranged marriages and amount to approximately the same. The husband of a woman married without the prior consent of her guardian also continues payments over a three-year period. One additional and non-recurring payment is made to the bride's household at the time bridewealth is transferred. Theft of a wife calls for a fine of Rs 10–20 because, say the girl's kinsmen, 'our roof has been broken'.

Marriage by theft eludes the costs of wedding festivities, which constitute the heaviest item of expenditure in arranged unions.[1] As with mortuary rites, attendance, and hence costs, are related to factors of residence, kinship and status. Members of other castes do not, as a rule, attend Limbu weddings.

Only at the wedding of the grandson of the Cluster's richest Limbu were members of other castes, including the area's most distinguished Brahmans, in attendance. Their presence attested to the prominence of the host, who is recognized as a Notable in the area. Because of his status, the number of guests (300) attending was far higher than the average for Indreni weddings. Consequently, the costs of the festivities (Rs 800) were about 20% higher than the average expended on such celebrations. Still, once an arranged marriage has been decided upon, there is a minimum standard of largesse expected from the host, however humble his means or status. The lowest cost I have recorded for wedding festivities during the past decade is Rs 325 for the marriage of an Angu of less than average wealth and with a narrow range of kin ties, thus making possible a comparatively low attendance figure of just under 100 guests.

To help meet the costs of wedding feasts, guests bring contributions of cash (*chanda*). The amounts are recorded and reciprocal donations are expected from the host when he is invited to attend the weddings of his guests' sons and brothers. Eighty-three households contributed Rs 240 to the costs of the wedding feast given by the Limbu Notable. This is slightly higher than the average volume of contributions, which normally cover about 15% of the expenses.

---

1 Almost without exception, men give as their reason for 'stealing' a bride the high cost of wedding festivities.

The least expensive way of obtaining a marriage partner is by absconding with another man's wife. The costs of a *jari* marriage are, by and large, confined to the amount of compensation (*jarikal*) the new husband pays to the cuckold. Compensation must be paid for violation of a man's monopoly of sexual rights to his wife.[1] The amount is to a large degree determined by the negotiating skills of those representing the offended and offending husbands.[2] The former try to recoup as large a proportion of the marriage costs as they can. A Limbu who had spent a total of Rs 1,300 on his marriage was able to get only Rs 500 when his wife went off with another man three years later. In another instance a woman married by *jari* left her Indreni husband two years later to live with yet another man. The Indreni husband, who had paid compensation of Rs 650 in 1959, collected Rs 400 when she left him in 1961. This process of 'devaluation' of women is recognized in compensation claims. The greater the number of men with whom a woman absconds the lower the compensation that need be paid for her. Indeed, the old law code stipulated that a woman who absconds for the third time is considered a whore (*besya*) and no compensation can legally be claimed by the last cuckold. The average amount of compensation paid by Indreni men for their *jari* marriages during the past ten years amounts to Rs 450.

After compensation has been paid, the new husband makes token obeisance to his father-in-law by presenting the latter and his lineage mates with some meat and liquor, the costs of which seldom amount to more than Rs 50. He does not pay bridewealth or other *rit* payments. Nor are visits to his in-laws during Dasein obligatory for a three-year period, although most Indreni Limbus do make the trip along with small offerings at least once.

In sum, then, *jari* is the least expensive form of Limbu marriage. Roughly, its costs amount to one-third of those for arranged marriages and half those of theft marriages (see Table 11 overleaf). The considerable costs of marriage are made evident when we note that the average annual income per Limbu household from all sources can

---

1 A husband can, of his own accord, dispose of these rights by taking part in a ceremony in which he symbolically removes the red powder (*sidur*) from the forehead of his wife, signifying an end to the marriage. He forfeits at the same time his rights to claim compensation if she forms a union with another man.

2 See Chapter 6.

TABLE II
Comparative marriage costs

Type of marriage	Range of costs
	Rs
Arranged	950–1,400
Theft	650–950
Jari	300–500

be estimated at Rs 1,650. Thirty out of the eighty-five Limbu house-holds in the Cluster earn under Rs 1,000, and only twenty-three households have an income in excess of Rs 2,000.

The new law code, introduced in 1963 in an attempt to discourage *jari* practices, sets a compensation figure of up to Rs 1,000 or five years' imprisonment if the cuckold chooses to bring charges. So far Limbu reluctance to use the courts in dealing with compensation claims has left unaffected the amounts transferred. But this law is one of the few in the new code with which the Limbus are conversant and the threat of court action could yet become a potent weapon in the hands of the aggrieved husband.

One other kind of marriage expenditure, the dowry given married daughters, should be mentioned. A dowry (*daijo*) is usually given several years following a marriage, after all the marriage payments have been completed and when one or two children have been born. In the case of a wealthy household, several hundred rupees or their equivalent in cattle and jewellery may be given. Mostly, however, dowries to Indreni women are small, consisting of some household utensils and between Rs 25 and 50 in cash. Since lineage mates receive a share of marriage payments given for a girl, they also contribute to the cost of her dowry, thus relieving what little burden there is on a girl's household. In consequence, the marriage of a daughter is regarded not as an economic disaster, but as an event bringing the household temporary but much welcome gains. 'We Limbus,' they say, 'sell our daughters in order to eat'.[1]

The costs of a son's marriage, on the other hand, must be borne entirely by the household in which the boy resides. Only the contribu-

---

1 In contradistinction, a Brahman with many daughters is a much-pitied man.

tions of wedding guests relieve the burden slightly.[1] The lineage, or even the sibling group – unless it constitutes a single household – does not share in the expenditure. As with mortuary rites, marriages of sons emphasize the independence of the household as an economic unit.

I have asked why Limbus mortgage their lands, and it is apparent that they do so because their recurrent and contingent expenditures are high, and because their income from agriculture is insufficient to fulfil their normal food and household requirements, let alone meet their social obligations. There are a variety of opportunities for earning cash now available to Limbus – which I examine at the end of this chapter – and to the extent that they are exploited the need for credit is proportionately reduced. By and large, however, they are of fairly recent origin and have not, as yet, substantially altered the pattern of land-mortgaging begun at the turn of the century. I now inquire about the types and extent of this mortgaging.

Mortgages

There are two kinds of mortgage. The first – *bhog bandhaki* – leaves unchanged the amount of principal and enables the Limbu mortgagor to repossess the land upon repayment of the amount. The second type – *masikatta*[2] – reduces the mortgage by a specific sum each year. This latter type, which applies to 85% of all mortgage transactions in kipat land, enables the kipat-owner to repossess the land at any time upon repayment of the original loan, less the fixed

---

1 It is considered proper for the marriage of a young man to be made by his agnates. This is not always what in fact happens. Circumstances may lead to a boy being brought up in his mother's natal home. In such cases the costs of the marriage will be met by his mother's brother, although this tends to compromise the prestige of the young man and his agnates. Occasionally, a boy raised in his mother's natal home will strive in every way possible to find the cash needed for the marriage himself. In one instance, outside sources of income enabled an Indreni man raised by his mother's brother to provide the costs of his own marriage, a fact he was most anxious to stress.

2 *Masikatta* has certain features in common with the *kanam* system prevalent in Malabar (cf. Mayer, 1952, 79–81; Kumar, 1965, 23–5).

annual reductions.[1] In both kinds of mortgage agreement the creditor (mortgagee) exercises rights of usufruct in the land as long as the loan is outstanding, although he may not charge interest on the loan. If the mortgagor repays the loan after the seed has been sown, he must allow the mortgagee to take the harvest of the land. The former is prevented from taking the land back piecemeal by repaying the loan in instalments. Once pledged, a field is regarded as a unit, which can only be returned as a unit when the entire principal is repaid as a lump sum.[2] Only when the field has been subdivided among the heirs of the Limbu mortgagor can each repossess his own share individually.

Of the kipat owned by the Limbus in the Indreni settlements, 68·2% is under mortgage. The percentage of irrigated lands pledged is much higher than that of dry lands – 82·8% of the former as against only 38·6% of the latter. This is due mainly to the fact that a fair proportion of dry lands are homestead plots, which are not mortgaged.

Limbus in the Indreni settlements therefore have unrestricted rights of usufruct to just under one-third of their kipat lands. The extent of mortaging varies from one household to another.[3]

Table 12 shows us that almost two-thirds of kipat-owning Limbu households have pledged more than half their lands. The figure of only one household having mortgaged all its kipat land stresses the tendency for Limbus to hold on to homestead sites. Since the figures are for both dry and irrigated fields, they obscure the fact that thirty-nine households (57·3%) have pledged all their irrigated lands.

---

1 *Masikatta* derives from a kind of mortgage, no longer extant, which enabled the contracting parties to stipulate a period of time during which the amount of the mortgage would be reduced by an agreed sum annually, and at the end of which the kipat-owner would resume his land without further payment. Such agreements did not allow the mortgagor to re-possess the land before the end of the stipulated period, which sometimes was set at 100 or more years. This type of mortgage was abolished in 1914 in response to Limbu complaints to government.
2 This practice does not derive from any mystical notion about the unity of a field, but relates to the increasing costs of cultivating a field which is diminishing in size as a result of piecemeal repossession.
3 Unlike the situation in most other agricultural communities, wealth among the Limbus is not so much a question of the amount of land owned, but of the amount unmortgaged.

TABLE 12
Kipat mortgages by household[1]

Percentage of kipat lands mortgaged	Number of kipat-owning households	Percentage of kipat-owning households
		%
None	7	10·3
1– 9	1	1·4
10–24	–	–
25–49	16	23·5
50–74	19	28·0
75–89	16	23·5
90–99	8	11·7
100	1	1·4
	68	99·8

Other kinds of credit

Is the pledging of land the only means whereby Limbus can obtain credit? It is necessary to consider this question in order to discern the range of credit choices available, and the relative importance of mortgages as compared with other kinds of credit.

Loans can be obtained by offering as security land or other property which is retained by the borrower and only forfeited (if *kipat*, its usufruct) if he defaults on the payment. Loans (*rin*) of this sort bear interest at anywhere from 15 to 35%.[2] A fair proportion of loans are made in grain, and both interest and principal would

1 I include here only households which are potential mortgagors of kipat. This excludes by definition households which own no kipat land. But also excluded are households which, though potentially kipat-owning, are not in a position to mortgage these lands. Two household heads have received only a partial property settlement, and this does not include kipat lands which they own and therefore can mortgage. Three other households are headed by women who have been granted the use of kipat during the course of their lifetime, but cannot transfer these rights to others. I have excluded these households from the table.

2 Short-term, non-interest-bearing loans of small amounts (*sapat*) are occasionally given to close kinsmen or neighbours. They require no security. These loans account for only a minute proportion of credit transactions and can be ignored.

generally be paid in kind. Even where cash loans are made, creditors almost always state the interest and require its payment in quantities of grain. This has tended to work against the interests of the debtor, since grain prices have been rising steadily, so that, for example, a loan negotiated ten years ago at 20% interest on the basis of a stipulated quantity of grain would now bear from 30 to 35% interest at the present price of the same grain.

The amount of this kind of credit available is limited by the property which Limbus can put up as security. Where land is offered, potential creditors tend to insist on taking the usufruct, unless the borrower puts up his homestead plot. Other than land, only jewellery and cattle are available to secure loans. Jewellery usually enters a house as part of a woman's dowry. If the husband can afford it, he may give his wife an additional gift of gold or silver ornaments. But any jewellery given a woman by her natal household remains her personal possession and her husband exercises no claim to this property. The rights of the husband to gifts given by him to his wife are less clear. Most informants suggest that, once given, a gift of jewellery could not be taken back during the wife's lifetime. But they add that a good wife would allow the jewellery to be put up as security if the household were in serious economic difficulty. Moreover, a man's prestige would suffer if it were known that he offered his wife's ornaments to secure a loan.

In any case, few Limbu households manage to store any substantial wealth in the form of jewellery. All women possess silver bracelets; a few have silver anklets; but only the wealthiest are able to afford a splendidly carved silver charm-box. The value of silver ornaments amounts to an average of approximately Rs 80 per household. Ownership of gold jewellery averages somewhat more, although perhaps half of all Limbu women have no more than a gold nose-ring and a nostril-piece worth about Rs 50 together.

Loans are also obtained by offering cattle as security. A fully-grown pair of draught animals can fetch up to Rs 500 on sale, and a milch cow is worth in the region of Rs 350. The paucity of cattle, partly a function of the dearth of grazing land in the area of the Indreni settlements, limits the amount of credit available on such security. Despite the fact that draught cattle are essential for farming, only fifty-six out of eight-five households possess a pair of bullocks. Sixty-one additional head of cattle are distributed among thirty-five households, while eight households share nineteen buffaloes. Thus a total of 192 head of cattle are available in the Limbu community, the majority of them already offered as security.

The Limbus in the Indreni Cluster have interest-bearing loans owing of approximately Rs 28,000. When compared with the cumulative total borrowed by pledging land – approximately Rs 318,400 – it is seen that the former kind of credit is a very small proportion (8%) of the total outstanding debt.[1]

TABLE 13[2]
Comparison of mortgages and interest-bearing loans

	Interest-bearing loans (average per household)	Mortgages (average per household)
	Rs	*Rs*
Chongbung		
Lineage 1	750	6,150
Lineage 2	500	4,300
Lineage 3	200	2,100
Lineage 4	150	2,350
Lineage 5	500	6,000
Kambo		
Lineage 1	500	10,000
Lineage 2	350	15,500
Nembeke	550	5,400
Syeling	50	3,300
Phatra	150	25

Table 13 compares average mortgages with interest-bearing loans outstanding by Limbu households in each lineage. In no case is this kind of loan more than 11% of the household's total debt. The exception is the single Phatra household, which has only a small plot of kipat land which it has not had to pledge. It is clear that mortgages are by far the primary means of raising money in the Indreni settlements. I have suggested that a scarcity of security other than land

1 The estimate of interest-bearing loans is based on verbal statements taken from Limbu debtor households and verified, wherever possible, by the creditors. Mortgage figures were checked against land documents held by the mortgagees (cf. footnote, p. 98).
2 Ten households of non-kipat-owning Limbus have outstanding debts of Rs 3,000, but since, by definition, they have no land to mortgage, I have omitted these figures for the purposes of comparison.

may be one reason for this disparity. The reluctance of creditors to accept land as security unless they can obtain its usufruct may be another. But there is a third factor of great importance. Once land has been mortgaged a Limbu can obtain additional loans on the security of the same land, thus obviating the pressures to seek credit elsewhere. This process involves the exploitation of ownership rights to kipat lands.

The exploitation of kipat ownership

Since 1901 kipat land has not been alienable by sale or permanent transfer. Members of non-Limbu groups with money to invest in land can purchase only raikar, which is in short supply. As a result, its costs have been driven to almost prohibitive heights. For many, taking kipat under pledge is the only practical alternative. But since most kipat land is already pledged, the potential landholder[1] is forced to offer the kipat-owner a higher mortgage than that given by the existing landholder. 'Kipat is like a goat,' landholders say; 'it goes to the highest bidder.' Since the kipat-owner can repossess his lands upon repayment of the loan, the new landholder supplies this amount, and an increment (*bard*) to the owner. This increment is not a gift, but is added to the mortgage principal. Rights of usufruct are then transferred to the new landholder, where they remain until the process is repeated. In this way, many kipat lands change hands every few years, so that the security of kipat landholders can be tenuous. This process can be documented by two examples:

(*a*) In 1954, Loftane pledged a kipat paddy field to a Brahman in a nearby settlement outside the Indreni Cluster. The amount borrowed was Rs 950. In 1958, the land was repossessed by the Limbu and re-pledged to a Rai landholder who had added another Rs 960 *bard*, bringing the mortgage to Rs 1,910. In 1963, the first Brahman landholder offered to let Loftane have another Rs 960 *bard* for the right to the usufruct on the same land. The latter took the field back and re-pledged it to the Brahman. The mortgage principal is now Rs 2,870.

1 Henceforth, I use 'landholder' to refer to the mortgagee or creditor and distinguish this person from the landowner, i.e. the Limbu with primary rights, and the tenant, or person who cultivates the land for a share of the crops.

(*b*) In 1926 a Kambo mortgaged a paddy field for Rs 80 to a Cobbler. Six years later the younger brother's widow of the deceased Kambo repossessed the land and transferred it to a Brahman, who gave her *bard* of Rs 50, bringing the principal to Rs 130. Five years later the usufruct was again transferred to a Chongbung Limbu, who offered Rs 70 *bard*, thus bringing the principal to Rs 200. The present landholder, a Jaisi, took possession fifteen years later by adding Rs 200 to the principal in the form of *bard* given to the original Kambo owner's heirs. The mortgage now totals Rs 400.

The decision to transfer kipat from one landholder to another is taken only after the kipat-owner is satisfied that the existing landholder will not meet the new offer. Since all mortgage holders recognize the potential threat to their security of tenure, the practice has taken root in the Cluster whereby landholders accede to Limbu requests for *bard* on a regular basis, without waiting until another potential landholder forces their hand.

The Limbus are thus able to use the ownership of land and their rights of repossession as a wedge to obtain interest-free loans. The Limbu who owns kipat long since mortgaged relies on periodic visits to his landholders for *bard* to meet a variety of regular and contingent expenses. We might follow the history of one mortgage on land given to a Brahman in 1938 for Rs 128 to cover household expenses. For the next ten years the two Limbu brothers who owned the land took an average of Rs 90 per year for similar expenses. In 1948 the elder brother died and an additional Rs 80 were borrowed to help meet the costs of his mortuary rites. During each of the five years following an average of Rs 40 was added to the mortgage for household expenses. In 1953 the son of the younger brother was married and Rs 144 were borrowed, the amount added to the principal. An average of only Rs 32 were taken each of the following five years for the household food budget and in 1959 the widow of the elder brother died. For her mortuary expenses Rs 80 were borrowed. During the next five years, until 1964, an annual average of Rs 63 were taken for the household. The total value of the mortgage is now Rs 2,009.

Limbus attempting to keep mortgages to a minimum in the hope of repossessing their kipat, of course do everything they can to avoid running up the debt. In such cases the mortgage may remain level for years, and no attempt is made to play off landholders for the purpose of obtaining *bard*. But these Limbus represent a very small minority of the Indreni population. For most, *bard* represents an important

8

source of credit. It bespeaks a despairing attitude on the part of the majority of kipat-owners towards ever reclaiming their lands. Few entertain the hope of repaying their mortgages, but realize that in their ownership rights lies the only opportunity to benefit from kipat. A variety of practices have been devised to exploit these rights.

Limbus with more than one field pledged to a single landholder might request one of these fields as *bard*, and distribute the principal on this field among the mortgages on the remaining fields. Some who are tenants on kipat lands which they own themselves will withhold the rent owed the landholder and regard it as *bard* to be added to the loan. Others desirous of becoming tenants on their mortgaged fields will use the threat of repossession and transfer in order to pressure an otherwise reluctant landholder.

Placed in such a position, landholders must balance the demands of the kipat-owner against the benefits they derive from continuing to hold the land under mortgage. Unlike the owners, many of whom are unaware of the extent of their indebtedness[1] and hence unable to establish a rational basis for their continued demands for *bard*, most landholders determine approximate limits beyond which additional loans would bring diminishing returns. Even so, the 'cut-off' point is constantly changing as pressures on land increase. In a sense, *bard* can be seen as a built-in cost index for kipat land. For as its value rises the landholders recognize the increase by giving the kipat-owner these additional loans against security of the land they have already taken under mortgage. An analysis of seventy-five kipat histories based on land documents reveals the pattern of increases in mortgage principal due to *bard* increments (see Table 14).

Taking the initial mortgage as index 100, twelve histories show that during the first five years the principal increases by an average of 25%. Another eleven histories of land held between six and ten years indicate that by this period the loan has risen to an average index of 145. Eighteen histories indicate that the mortgage will have risen to just over double the initial amount between eleven and fifteen years after the land was mortgaged. Between sixteen and twenty years after the initial mortgage the average index will be 315 – based on thirteen histories. Twenty-one histories of land held for the unusually long

1 This is partially due to the traditional practice of making only one document, which is kept by the landholder. Since 1962 both parties have been
required to keep a copy of the mortgage agreement, but *bard* receipts are
still kept only by the landholder.

TABLE 14
Mortgage principal increases over time

Period after initial mortgage	Average index
Up to 5 years	125
6–10 years	145
11–15 years	205
16–20 years	315
Over 20 years	475

Initial mortgage – index 100

period of over twenty years show *bard* to have driven the principal up to an average index of 475.

The practice of *bard* is made possible by the nature of the kipat system of land tenure. Because kipat land is inalienable by sale, the Limbu owners retain the final right of repossession of lands however transferred to others. By retention of this right the kipat-owner is able to play off competing interests for scarce lands to his own advantage in a kind of institutionalized extortion. It is not surprising that on more than one occasion I was told that if it were not for *bard* the Limbus would have to emigrate to India.

I do not want to create the impression of the Indreni settlements as a market-place where land is freely bid for and continuously transferred. There are, of course, restrictions on the kipat-owner's freedom of choice to sever existing and form new mortgage ties. The most obvious of these limitations is the fact that the Limbus are an economically depressed group and, as such, depend for a large part of their subsistence on these relationships. A second limiting factor pertains to the pattern of linkages created by mortgage and tenancy arrangements. I proceed now to examine each in turn.

Distribution of mortgages

To whom do the Limbus pledge their kipat? By far the great majority of mortgaged lands (72%)[1] are held by non-Limbus. Thus, kipat landholders and landowners are, to a large extent, members of different groups. Table 15 gives the distribution of mortgaged lands among non-Limbus.

1 I am here referring to the percentage of units pledged. See Appendix A.

TABLE 15
Distribution of mortgages among non-Limbu landholders

Non-Limbu landholders	Percentage of kipat land held
Brahmans resident in Cluster	11·3
Jaisis resident in Cluster	2·9
Others resident in Cluster	–
Brahmans resident outside Cluster	33·0
Jaisis resident outside Cluster	2·6
Others resident outside Cluster	22·6
All non-Limbus	72·4

These figures illustrate several points. The first is that members of the two highest castes – particularly the Brahmans – have taken by far the largest proportion of kipat lands under mortgage. Brahmans and Jaisis between them hold half of these lands, while members of other non-Limbu castes hold slightly over one-fifth. Secondly, Brahmans and Jaisis resident in the Cluster have a much higher proportion of landholdings in relation to their numbers than those resident outside the Cluster. Whereas members of these two castes in the Cluster represent only 3% of the total number of Brahman and Jaisi households in the village of Syawa, they have 14·2% of the kipat landholdings. Finally, none of the other non-Limbu households in the Cluster – there are seven: four Magar and three Blacksmith – have taken any kipat land under mortgage.

The majority of kipat lands pledged are concentrated in the hands of less than a score of landholders (see Table 16). These nineteen 'Main Landholders', most of whom are Brahmans, have taken 68·8% of all lands mortgaged. They are resident mainly in the Cluster or its immediate environs. Only a few live beyond a radius of two miles of the mortgaging household.[1] I have given the residential location of each of the Main Landholders because geographical propinquity appears to be an important factor in the formation of mortgage ties. The kipat-owning households tied to three Dorumba landholders (Brahmans A and B and Jaisi G), for example, are confined to Dorumba and that area of Chitok adjacent to Dorumba. Similarly,

---

1 These are Limbus Q and R, who are kinsmen of Indreni Limbus, and S, who is a wealthy man from the district of Panchthar with interests throughout Limbuan.

the landholders resident to the east and south of Angbung have mortgage ties almost exclusively with Limbu households in that settlement and Bharapa, its neighbour to the north. Only two landholders (Limbu H and Gurung O) have links to kipat-owning households in all four Indreni settlements, while another four (Brahmans E, F, and L and Limbu I) are linked to households in three settlements. The majority of thirteen hold land in one or two (adjacent) settlements.

TABLE 16

Distribution of mortgages among 'Main Landholders'

Landholders	Residence	Percentage of land held	Number of linkages to landowners
In Cluster:			
Brahman A	Dorumba	1·6	2
Brahman B	Dorumba	1·1	2
Brahman C	Chitok	2·9	3
Brahman D	Bharapa	1·0	2
Brahman E	Chitok	2·6	6
Brahman F	Chitok	2·3	5
Jaisi G	Dorumba	2·6	7
Limbu H	Chitok	6·2	16
Limbu I	Chitok	3·9	8
Outside Cluster:			
Brahman J	1 ml E of Angbung	2·7	3
Brahman K	1 ml E of Angbung	3·6	13
Brahman L	½ ml S of Angbung	4·7	13
Brahman M	1½ ml S of Angbung	9·6	17
Brahman N	½ ml W of Chitok	2·4	4
Gurung O	1 ml W of Dorumba	10·6	17
Newar P	1 ml S of Angbung	3·6	9
Limbu Q	Ilam Bazaar	3·2	4
Limbu R	3 ml W of Cluster	1·8	3
Limbu S	Panchthar district	2·4	3
		68·8	

The table also shows that the Main Landholders are linked in mortgage relationships with an average of 7·2 Limbu households,[1]

1 I am forced to ignore what might be called the relative weight of each linkage. A landowner may give one field or several to a landholder; the mortgage may be great or small. 'Linkage' obscures these differences.

although the range extends from a minimum of two to a maximum of seventeen. Landholders with the greatest amount of pledged land tend to be tied to the largest number of kipat-owning households. Limbu landowners, for their part, disperse their mortgages, especially if they are heavy, among several landholders. Households which are linked to only one landholder are those which have pledged few lands or, conversely, have only few lands to pledge. Taking the total number of linkages (137) between Limbu households and the Main Landholders only, we find that seventy-seven (56·2%) are with Brahmans and Jaisis, thirty-four (24·8%) are with Limbus,[1] and twenty-six (19%) are with members of other groups. Out of fifty linkages between Limbu households and non-Limbu creditors who (*a*) live outside the Cluster and (*b*) are not included among the Main Landholders, thirty-six are with Brahmans, four are with Jaisis, and ten are with members of other groups. The average Limbu household is linked to four landholders; this includes linkages to others as well as to the Main Landholders.

The picture, then, is of a series of prongs emanating out from Limbu kipat-owning households, linking them to an assortment of landholders, the majority of whom are Brahmans. Most households have ties to several landholders, others to a single one. Some have links to Limbu landholders who are themselves mortgagors of kipat.

Tenancy

Mortgages transfer rights of usufruct from the landowner to the landholder. But there still remains the question of who cultivates the land? The person to whom land is pledged may choose to cultivate the land himself, or transfer the rights of cultivation to a tenant in return for a share of the crops. Two kinds of tenancy arrangement can be made. The first is an agreement to share equally all the production of a field, including any subsidiary crops. On an irrigated field, for example, the contracting parties would divide not only the paddy crop, but the lentils which are usually grown in the levees of the terraces. They would even share the straw of the paddy. With such an arrangement, the landlord[2] provides at least half the seed.

---

1 This category of Limbu landholders is examined in greater detail in the next chapter.
2 I use 'landlord' as a generic term for the person who transfers the rights of cultivation to a tenant. He may be the landowner or the landholder.

The second kind of tenancy, which is more commonly practised, stipulates a fixed rent to be paid by the tenant at the time of harvest. The rent is generally a part of the main crop, but where a tenant cultivates a dry field the agreement may specify payment in either maize or millet. The landlord has no claim on subsidiary crops or straw, although he has first right to the produce of the land, so that he has a measure of insurance against a poor harvest. The landlord does not provide the seed, but he normally pays the costs of transporting the rent from the field to his home.

Whether or not a landholder cultivates a field he takes under mortgage depends on a variety of factors. If the land is near his homestead, the time saved in going to and from the field, and the ease with which manure can be transported to and the harvest brought from the field will likely make it worthwhile for the land-holder to cultivate the land himself.[1] Furthermore, if the land is adjacent to a field he is already cultivating he will almost certainly work it himself. The additional expenditure of resources required to encompass the adjacent field is considerably less than the commensurate gains he can expect. One factor likely to weigh in favour of giving the land to a tenant is a shortage of labour in the household. But even with adequate labour resources at his command, a wealthy man, especially a Brahman, is reluctant to send the women in his household to the fields. And rather than hire agricultural labourers he might decide to transfer the cultivation rights to a tenant.

If a landholder chooses to give the kipat land he has taken under mortgage to a tenant, the Limbu kipat-owner is considered to have the right of first refusal. The latter may waive this right or accept the tenancy and then transfer cultivation rights to a sub-tenant. This practice is rare, however, and I have recorded only a dozen instances involving such double tenancy.[2]

Rents vary considerably from as 'little' as one-quarter of gross production to as much as one-half. No single reason can explain the variation. Some landholders consistently charge high rents; others are content to accept less than the going rate. When it is found that a Limbu kipat-owner is paying a low rent as tenant on his own land the

1 There is also the problem of guarding dry fields against monkeys, who sometimes destroy a substantial portion of the maize crop.
2 To avoid confusion, in any figures on tenancy the person actually cultivating the land will be regarded as the tenant.

explanation may lie in the size of the mortgage.[1] A Limbu may be forced to pledge a field to meet an unexpected obligation, and accepts far less than the normal rate in the hope of repaying the loan quickly and resuming his land. In such cases the rent would probably be a comparatively small proportion of the harvest. The relationship between the landlord and the tenant can affect the rent as well. In three instances where the contracting parties were close agnates (siblings, father and son), the rents were in the range of 25%.

Over half the lands mortgaged by Indreni Limbus are being cultivated by the landholders themselves, while the remainder have been let to tenants. The majority of these lands are worked by Indreni Limbus; just under 15% by their owners. Table 17 gives the distribution of cultivation rights.

TABLE 17
Distribution of cultivation rights on mortgaged lands

Cultivators	Percentage of mortgaged land being cultivated
(a) Limbu landholders	15·1
(b) Non-Limbu landholders	37·4
(c) The kipat-owners as tenants	14·3
(d) Other kipat-owning Limbus as tenants	15·1
(e) Non-kipat-owning Limbus as tenants	1·3
(f) Non-Limbus resident in Cluster as tenants	1·8
(g) Non-Limbus resident outside Cluster as tenants	15·0
	100·0

Fifty kipat-owning households cultivate kipat land as tenants. They are linked to an average of 1·5 landlords. Here again the greatest proportion of linkages between tenants and landlords are with Main Landholders (76·4%) while 12·9% are with other kipat-owning Limbus in the Cluster and 10·7% with other non-Limbus. These

1 Some informants state that kipat-owners pay less rent as tenants on their own land than they do when cultivating land belonging to someone else. My own data on rents do not bear this out. The evidence also indicates that rents will have the same variation whether the contracting parties are both Limbus or members of different groups.

figures can be compared with those of linkages formed on the basis of mortgages.

TABLE 18
Comparison of the distribution of mortgage and tenancy linkages

Linkage type	Percentage with Main Landholders	Percentage with other Limbus	Percentage with other non-Limbus
Mortgage	59·4	19·0	21·6
Tenancy	76·4	12·9	10·7

The comparatively low figure for tenancy linkages with landlords other than the Main Landholders suggests, on the one hand, that the latter, who are by definition the wealthiest landlords, cannot cultivate themselves all the lands they have taken under mortgage. On the other hand, the remaining landlords, to a much greater extent, take lands under mortgage in order to cultivate these lands themselves, and so are not as able to transfer cultivation rights to Limbu tenants.

Another kind of linkage might also be mentioned. It is that between a kipat-owner and the tenant on his land which has been pledged to a landholder. Table 17 shows that 33·2% of mortgaged kipat is cultivated by tenants other than the kipat-owner himself.[1] In such cases a tie is created between the kipat-owner and the tenant working the land. The tie is not a direct one in the sense that no payments are made by one to the other. The relationship is based only on different interests in the same land. For one thing, since the kipat-owner is considered to have prior claims to tenancy, the rights of a tenant who is not the owner are dependent to some extent on the kipat-owner's desire and ability to exercise his claims. For another, any change of landholder can influence the security of a tenant and, as I have shown, the Limbu landowner is in a position to effect such a change.

When examining the ways in which Limbus raise credit, I suggested that they are able to manipulate rights of kipat ownership to obtain from landholders incremental loans (*bard*) against lands already pledged. I then pointed out that this freedom is not unrestricted. An examination of mortgage distribution and tenancy arrangements has

1 Categories (*d*), (*e*), (*f*) and (*g*) in Table 17.

shown why. A complex pattern of economic relationships binds Limbu households both to one another and to members of other groups in the Cluster and surrounding area. Many of these linkages are concentrated within a small wealthy class, most of whom are Brahmans. This means that many of the links overlap, so as to make it difficult for the Limbu kipat-owner to withdraw from one link without affecting the others in which he is involved with the same person.

The Limbu household, in other words, can be viewed as the central point from which emanate several series of linkages. Each series relates to a specific sphere or purpose. Mortgage relationships are established with one or more landholders; this is one series. Another is formed on the basis of tenancy arrangements, and perhaps a third when the household obtains interest-bearing loans. When superimposed on one another, these linkages give a picture – at one moment in time – of the range of a household's relationships in, say, an economic context. The superimposition reveals a certain amount of convergence in the linkages, so that some kipat-owners are not merely mortgagors of several fields to particular landholders, but tenants of and borrowers from these same individuals as well. Thus thirty-three households are linked to their landholders as mortgagors of kipat and as tenants, while eleven are further tied to these same persons as borrowers of interest-bearing loans. In such instances we might speak of double and triple convergences. When these ties are compounded by such factors as neighbourhood and political dependence the Limbu household becomes further 'hemmed in' by its relationships, and its capacity for choice is curtailed even more. It might be suggested that the more convergent the linkages, the less freedom of action for the kipat-owner to manipulate relationships based on land.[1]

---

1 There is no difference of kind, only of emphasis, between what Gluckman calls 'multiplex' relationships and what I have here termed 'convergent' linkages. I have thought it necessary, first of all, to indicate not only that the same persons interact in a number of different contexts, but that within any single (in this case, economic) context, there will be convergent links. Secondly, it is important to appreciate that there are different degrees of overlap in any social situation. By indicating what these are we may better understand the boundaries of choice.

The 'commercial' economy: local sources

The configuration of economic ties which I have been discussing rests essentially on subsistence agriculture. This is the kind of economy which traditionally was, and to a large extent still is, found in Ilam. Even so, for many years a number of opportunities for earning cash have been available within the region of the Cluster. A literate young man may hope to teach in a primary school. An assiduous fisherman can trap up to 10 lb. a week in the Pua River and sell the fish at Rs 2 per pound in the settlements or in Ilam Bazaar. There is, too, a market for scarce dairy products, such as curd or clarified butter. And there are other, more substantial sources of cash.

(*a*) Most Limbu households contribute to a pool of agricultural labour for the better-off Brahmans and a few of the wealthiest Indreni Limbus. To determine the need for and availability of this kind of labour it is necessary to examine the pattern of cultivation.

The household can handle most stages of maize and millet cultivation on its own. Since the fields are usually within reach of the cultivator's homestead, the work can be done at a leisurely pace. The growing of maize and millet is further simplified by the fact that men and women can perform the same labour, except ploughing. Only if the household possesses no bullocks for ploughing or if it works many lands does it require more than a few outside hands to help in the various tasks. The typical scene between March and June, when maize is planted and weeded, and again in late August and early September, during the maize-harvesting and millet-planting season, is of household groups working with only a minimum of assistance in their separate fields.

The picture changes radically in June and July, and again in November, for the cycle of paddy cultivation. Because of the pressures of a limited planting and harvesting season, a great many tasks must be performed in a short span of time. During the days prior to a planting, the field has to be ploughed and the terrace walls cleared of grasses and weeds so that they will attract no insects or mice, and so that the grasses act as fertilizer, since no other is used. The latter work is performed mainly by women. When it is completed the terraces are flooded. On the day prior to the planting, women remove the paddy seedlings from the seed bed and tie them in bundles which can be easily carried or thrown to the planters.

At planting time the ploughmen first turn and level the flooded terraces. They are followed by men whose job it is to complete the levelling of the mudded terraces with hand-hoes and repair and reinforce the levees broken by the ploughs and levellers. Women then plant the seedlings, working in clusters of two or three to a terrace. Several other women are required to keep them supplied with seedlings.

At harvest-time, a fairly rigid division of labour is again evident. Members of both sexes share the job of cutting the paddy stalks, which are left to dry in the sun for about four days. The stalks are then bundled by men and carried, mainly by women, to a terrace which has been levelled for threshing. The stalks are piled in a mound and left to dry for about a week. The job of threshing and winnowing is left to the men, who are assisted by the women in bringing the grain to the houses. Transporting the bundles of straw is left mainly to the women.

In view of this elaborate division of tasks and the pressures of time, the household requires a labour force which it is unable to provide from its own resources.[1] To produce the 790 units of paddy which is the average for the sixty-three Limbu households cultivating this crop requires approximately forty-six male and fifty female labour days for planting and harvesting alone. The household obtains the assistance it needs to cultivate its fields through the recruitment of labour gangs. Each of the gangs is formed for the performance of a particular task and dissolves upon its completion. Planning in advance is necessary, because commitments to join a gang on a specific date are on a 'first come, first served' principle, and no man can claim prior rights to command the labour resources of any other household than his own. Since there is a potential Limbu work force of only 257 persons (twelve to sixty years old) the need for co-ordination is evident.

The great majority of these gangs are recruited on the basis of mutual exchange of labour (*pareli*). The system is preferred by all who have labour to exchange, since it obviates the need to transfer scarce cash. Labour exchanges are strictly reciprocal, however, and each household keeps its account of the number of labour days it is owed and owes.[2] There is a recognized scale of job equivalents, so

1 Limbu households contain an average of 3·02 adults (twelve to sixty years).
2 In times of illness or other crisis, neighbours will help one another without expectation of a return. But the practice (*guhar*) occurs infrequently.

that, for example, a household without draught animals will have to exchange three days of planting for one day of ploughing. These equivalents, however, relate only to jobs and not to the ability of the individuals performing them, so that a young girl can be sent to repay the labour given by a strong young man, as long as the jobs are considered on a par with one another. Labour exchanges need not be immediate: a labour debt incurred at the time of paddy-planting may be repaid at harvest-time. The sanctions for fulfilling labour obligations are the need to depend on others for similar assistance, and failure to meet labour debts would mean no further help for the recalcitrant houshold.

Despite the fact that paddy fields are scattered and situated at some distance from homestead sites, labour is exchanged not with those who cultivate adjoining fields, but with settlement neighbours. Only seldom are the two coincidental. Bonds among households exchanging labour only occasionally extend far beyond the boundaries of settlement, so that labour gangs formed in Angbung are recruited mainly from households in the settlement and partly from adjacent households in Bharapa. The restricted radius of recruitment also tends to exclude members of other castes from Limbu work gangs. Only a handful of households in Bharapa exchange labour with Magars and a few poor Brahmans living in an adjacent settlement. Labour is never exchanged with wealthy Brahmans in the Cluster. This is due mainly to the reluctance of the latter, for reasons of prestige, to send members of their households to work on the fields cultivated by others.

Seventeen Limbu households do not partake of mutual labour exchanges because they cultivate insufficient lands to require help from other households. The work they have to offer, therefore, is for payment only. Along with fifty-seven other households which combine exchanges with labour for wages, they form a reservoir of agricultural labourers. The eight Limbu households regularly hiring labour are compelled to do so because the hands they require to cultivate their lands are not obtainable through mutual exchanges alone. The labour gangs recruited by these households, then, are apt to contain both paid and exchange labour. But whereas the recruitment of the latter type is confined to neighbourhoods, agricultural labour for wages is sought from within a wider circumference. Residents of Angbung, for example, who never exchange labour with Chitok Limbus, do work for wages on the fields of the latter. Agricultural labourers can earn more by working for Brahmans in settlements to the south of the Cluster than by labouring for Limbus or Brahmans in the Indreni settlements. For hoe work the daily rate in the Cluster is Rs 0·80, while Brahmans outside offer up to Rs 1·20. Similarly, a ploughman receives Rs 1·60 if he works on Indreni fields, and up to Rs 2·40 if he ploughs for outside Brahmans. Limbus, of course, do work for the latter, but not at the expense of the former. Here again explanation must be sought in the multiple linkages within the Cluster which bind labourers and those who hire them.

It is impossible to estimate the amount of income earned by Limbu households from agricultural labour. Of seventy-four households engaged in casual labour of this sort, six rely only on this source to supplement income from the fields they cultivate. Most other households do not offer their labour regularly, but only as specific cash needs may arise.

(*b*) A few households have mandarin groves. The fruit are transported to Sanisare, a market town about twenty-five miles away in the Terai where they fetch up to Rs 2 per dozen, which is about double the price in Ilam Bazaar.

(*c*) Limbu ritual specialists (*phedangma*) earn a regular income in the Cluster. A *phedangma* discovers his powers through dreams or, as is more often the case, by becoming possessed. He then seeks the guidance of a teacher from whom he learns the secrets of his calling. Households choose their *phedangma* on the basis of utility. Some try and discard several before finding one they believe to be efficacious. Others alternate between two or more *phedangma*.

Fewer than one-third of all Limbu households ever utilize the services of a Brahman priest. For those that do – and they are mostly the better-off households – the occasion is an annual Satya Narayan ritual. Limbus choose this particular rite because it is brief and relatively inexpensive.

The *phedangma* officiates at the important Limbu *rites de passage* at the time of birth, marriage and death. He is also required to conduct the worship of domestic deities and is one of a variety of specialists who may be called upon to treat illness. The fee generally paid for the performance of a ritual is Rs 1·60, a pint of liquor (Rs 1) and enough rice for a meal (Rs 0·60). The *phedangma* can expect to earn a minimum of about Rs 10 per client per year.

(*d*) Extremely poor households earn small incomes by providing more affluent Limbus with 'domestic service'. The most common practice is for young boys from poor families to live in wealthier homes. They are treated like members of the household and, as with other members, their labour is at the disposal of the household head. They are referred to as 'herdboys' (*gothalo*) although they work in the fields and around the homestead as well as tend cattle. For these services they are fed and clothed, and paid an annual salary of from Rs 15–50. The relationship seldom persists over a lengthy period, the herdboys generally returning to their homes after a year or two.

(*e*) The government has been a potential source of income almost since the establishment of an administration in Ilam. Indreni Limbus have been employed for many years as minor functionaries in government offices in Ilam Bazaar. A number of military and para-military units stationed in Ilam also provide opportunities for earning a regular cash income, although in some cases it may involve residence away from the Cluster for short periods of time.

(*f*) Opportunities for petty trading have grown apace with the commercial development of Ilam Bazaar. At the turn of the century, the Bazaar contained only half a dozen shops, enough to cater for the few resident government employees as well as others visiting the town on market day. By 1964 there were ninety shops[1] and a resident population of approximately 5,000.[2] The size of the market, too, has grown. On any Thursday upwards of 2,000 inhabitants of the surrounding area make their way to the Bazaar, and provide a substantial buying public for the permanent shopkeepers and the petty traders who set up shop in the main square.

Women of the Indreni settlements regularly bring for sale in the market a kind of yeast loaf (*marca*) used in the preparation of liquor. In addition, they distil liquor from millet and sell this to 'tea'-stall-owners in the town, who retail it on market day. Some of the women also sell liquor on the main road through the Cluster to persons going to or returning from the market. Households situated beside the main road occasionally offer hospitality to trading expeditions, providing cooking utensils and sleeping arrangements free of charge, and profiting from sales of spirits. Despite a government ban – never

1 See Table 3.
2 Under the Panchayat regulations, to qualify as a 'town' there must be a population of 10,000. Ilam Bazaar has thus absorbed a number of surrounding settlements to make up the difference.

enforced – on the sale of liquor without a licence, this is the most important commercial income earned locally by Indreni Limbus.

(*g*) Another source of income is casual labour in the Terai or in bordering areas of India, such as the Darjeeling district of West Bengal. The agricultural lull around January and February, before the maize is planted, finds a number of Indreni Limbus working as unskilled labourers on a variety of building projects out of the district.

(*h*) Since the revolution of 1951 Ilam Bazaar has enjoyed an unprecedented growth. The expansion of existing and the establishment of new government services (including two secondary schools and a college) and a growing population have led to a surge of building activity. Since road communications in the district, as in most hilly areas of east Nepal, are extremely primitive, goods can only be transported by horse caravans or on the backs of men. For residents of the Indreni settlements, this has meant new opportunities to porter the increasing volume of raw materials required for building. Chief among these is wood.

Over the past five years alone the amount of wood coming into the district capital has increased fourfold. During the dry season from November to May porters carry planks from the forests south of Ilam Bazaar, where the wood is cut and trimmed, to the capital. Indreni men usually work in teams, contracting to carry a specific number of feet at an average rate of just under Rs 200 per 1,000 feet. Several Limbus who are skilled sawyers contract to cut some of the timber carried by the porters.

Portering wood is confined to households in the two southernmost Indreni settlements, Angbung and Bharapa. This is partly because these settlements are closest to the forests. By leaving their homes in the early morning, the porters are able to return, after carrying a timber load, the same evening. But the confinement of this enterprise to households from one section of the Cluster also attests to the strength of neighbourhood ties. Porters like to travel in company with others, and neighbours are preferred company.

Tin sheets for roofing, water-pipes, cement, kerosene – indeed, a whole range of capital and consumer goods needed to sustain Ilam Bazaar's growth – are also carried by porters. For these items, however, the men must go to Sanisare in the Terai. But unless they can carry a load both ways the journey is not worthwhile. Porters therefore transport mandarins to Sanisare from groves north of the Cluster.

Some accept a fixed rate – about Rs 3.20 per 100 – to porter the fruit. Others assume the roll of middlemen. They purchase the mandarins from the orchard-owners and transport them to Sanisare, where they can fetch from two to three times the hill price. The capital required is small and the profits earned can be reinvested in consumer and capital goods needed in Ilam Bazaar.

The existence of commercial opportunities in the region does not alter the fact that the Indreni economy is based on subsistence agriculture. Earnings from these commercial sources amount to approximately 18% of net agricultural income.[1] By and large, these injections of cash are only palliatives for the Limbu household. They reduce its need to rely on mortgages for raising cash. They enable the household which does not have sufficient agricultural production to fill the gap, and allow another with adequate agricultural resources to sustain a viable position. But this cash income is not enough to bring about any lasting improvement in the overall economic position of the Limbu household. In this sense, the participation by Limbus in the 'commercial' economy of the region does not substantially alter the pattern of interdependence between themselves and the Brahmans.

The opportunity offered by employment in the 'Gurkhas', however, can and does affect these relationships in two ways. In the first place, it has given rise to a small class of wealthy Limbus who, to the extent that they invest this wealth in land, are displacing Brahmans and members of other groups as landholders. Secondly, the exploitation of this source of earning adds a significant amount to the income from sources outside the agricultural system. And as the importance of the subsistence sector recedes in the overall economic picture, the dependence of the Limbus on those who dominate access to the land is correspondingly reduced.

The 'commercial' economy: military service

The most lucrative source of income for Limbu households is service in foreign armies. The history of military service by Indreni men goes back to the establishment, in the first decade of this century, of two Gurkha regiments composed exclusively of Rais and Limbus. Prior

1 See Table 19.

9

to this time, members of the two groups had been admitted to various para-military forces stationed in Burma and Assam. But their service in the Gurkhas, created a century and a half ago, had been limited. The Limbus, particularly, were considered to be inferior soldiers, apparently having acquired a reputation for lack of discipline (Jackson, 1940, 434). Following the creation of the two eastern regiments, however, an average of 221 Limbus were recruited annually from east Nepal. As the prejudice against them gradually fell away, their numbers rose. During the next decade an average of 283 were recruited each year (Vansittart, 1915, 8).

The acceptance of Limbus into the Gurkha forces coincided with the growth of large-scale mortgaging of kipat lands in the Cluster. The Limbus were compelled to find other sources of income. Possibilities were limited, since Ilam Bazaar was still in its infancy and could not offer opportunities for trading and portering described above. After the first two Indreni men were enlisted in the Gurkhas prior to the First World War military service was seen to be a viable means of earning income lost as a result of land-mortgaging. During the First World War, when recruiting was intensified and standards of induction relaxed, eleven Indreni men were accepted into the army. Since then a substantial proportion of the Cluster's male inhabitants has served in the Gurkhas.[1]

The reason most often cited for joining the army is the need to earn money because of economic hardship (*dukha*). Linked to the financial inducements is the respect accorded a returning soldier, especially one who manages to rise above the ranks. Prospective volunteers speak of 'making a name' (*nam kamaunu*), and each of the recruiting forces is graded according to how it is believed to allow for promotion.[2] Young men also admit to an urge to travel and, occasionally, to the fact that personal squabbles within the household may drive them away from the Cluster. Still, economic motives must be seen to underlie the widespread attachment to military service. Despite the fact that Ilam district has never been a prime source of

1 By and large, Brahmans and Jaisis do not serve in the Gurkhas. Although members of other groups, especially the 'drinking castes', such as Magars, are recruited, none resident in the Indreni Cluster is in the army.
2 In 1947 the Gurkha regiments were divided between the Indian and British armies, each of which now recruits separately. There is also the Assam Rifles, whose recruiting efforts are closely co-ordinated with those of the Indian Gurkhas. For convenience I include the Assam Rifles with the latter.

recruits,[1] 43·8% of all living Indreni Limbu males over eighteen years of age either have served or are at present serving in the army. Those in the forces at present constitute 11·5% of the adult male population.

As might be expected, the more depressed sections of the community turn most frequently to Gurkha service. Members of groups without ownership rights to kipat in the Cluster are a case in point. In Chapter 3 it was shown how the accommodation of 'outsiders' by Indreni kipat-owners varied in accordance with the availability of land. Once the shortage had reached a critical stage, affinal or cognatic kinsmen who settled in the Cluster could not expect to receive kipat grants. At best, they were able to occupy small plots of kipat belonging to their hosts or, as in some instances, to purchase a small piece of raikar land. But these lands were invariably insufficient to support their descendants. Whereas impoverished Limbus with ownership rights to kipat lands had first refusal on tenancy offers, in addition to rights of *bard*, those without kipat could claim no such prerogatives. In consequence, males of the first succeeding generation of outsiders tended to join the army. A few examples will illustrate the pattern which repeated itself almost without exception.

A man from the district of Panchthar settled in the Cluster after marrying the sister of a Chongbung man. During his lifetime he cultivated a small piece of kipat land taken under mortgage from his father-in-law. The land was not adequate to support two additional families which his sons would soon create. On reaching adulthood, both joined the army. In a replica of this instance, all four sons of a man who married the daughter of the Nembeke Subba joined the army.

Sometimes the process is delayed a generation. The first Indreni Angu settled in the Cluster after marrying a Chongbung woman. Since he was a government employee, he had an income with which he was able to purchase some raikar land in Bharapa. There was sufficient land to divide among his three sons, although one fell on bad times and enlisted in the Gurkhas. When the lands were divided again amongst the grandsons, the estates proved too small. Four of his six grandsons served in the army.

The army is still the most important income source for Limbus

---

1 Apparently, it still is not. Out of approximately 180 Limbus inducted in 1964 at Dharan, the British recruiting depot for eastern regiments, only sixteen were from Ilam district.

without ownership rights to kipat land. Six of the twelve men in the army at present are members of households which have no kipat of their own. They account for about 45% of Limbu males between eighteen and forty years. The six who own kipat, on the other hand, represent just over 11% of kipat-owning males in the same age bracket.

Military service, of course, is not entirely a matter of the individual's own choosing. Firstly, acceptance into the army depends on physical and intellectual criteria over which the volunteer has no control. Secondly, his chances vary in accordance with the annual quotas accepted by the various forces. Hundreds of hopeful candidates are turned away each year at the recruiting camps or by special recruiting agents in the hills. But once accepted into the army, a number of factors may still militate against long service. During both world wars, for example, standards were lowered to allow for maximum enlistment. But at the conclusion of hostilities most of the wartime recruits were discharged. Sixteen of the thirty Indreni men who have completed their service were wartime volunteers who spent an average of 5·4 years in the military. Most were released; others chose not to re-enlist. Some, like four men who were in the Gurkhas between the wars, came home on leave and never returned.

The need to return home to manage an estate is a common reason for the failure of Indreni men to complete the minimum service required for a pension.[1] Those who are away rely on fathers and brothers to protect their interests. The death of such a person, then, might require a man to leave the service. Quarrels over division of property are also causes of premature resignation from the army. But personal inability to adjust to army life also counts as an important reason for leaving. The early years are the most difficult, and desertions or resignations occur most frequently in the formative years. None of the Indreni servicemen left the army after serving eight years without first qualifying for a pension. The investment of so much time is thought to be worthwhile only if it leads to a pension, so that during the latter half of the period of service, the pressures of obligations at home are resisted more assiduously than during the first years.

Eight of the thirty ex-servicemen in the Cluster are receiving pensions for long service, two are receiving theirs for medical dis-

---

1 The period of service required to receive a pension varies. By and large, to receive a private's pension, fifteen years of service is mandatory.

abilities received while in the army, and three persons receive pensions paid to immediate descendants of servicemen killed in action. The total income from pensions amounts to over Rs 8,000 each year.

Service salaries account for a substantial proportion of current income. Twelve soldiers earn a total of Rs 14,250 annually in pay. Based on past remittances and on estimates of average savings, it can be assumed that about 60% of a soldier's pay eventually reaches the Indreni settlements. Not all this money enters the Cluster on a regular basis. No arrangements exist for the transfer of funds to homes in the hills. Remittances can be sent to the recruiting centres and fetched from there, much as pensions are collected. Servicemen returning on leave often bring money for the families of soldiers with whom they are serving.

There is little pressure on unmarried sons or brothers to send money. Even when they return on leave they are not expected to hand over all their savings to the household head. Even though the service-man who is not formally separated is a part of his father's or brother's household, and recognizes his membership by token remittances, his position is somewhat ambiguous. Throughout his army career he enjoys a special status, not entirely consistent with membership of a household. This is best understood by considering the typical sequence of goals to which his army savings are applied.

The young man who enters the Gurkhas as a bachelor first of all saves for his marriage. Following this, for as long as he remains part of a joint-type household, he contributes to it a part of his savings, but holds back the greater proportion for the time he decides to establish a separate household. This usually comes several years later, when he has saved enough for a small estate. Occasionally, he puts off separa-tion until completion of his service. One Gurkha soldier who was pensioned off in late 1963 separated from his father's household three months later. He used savings accumulated over a number of years to obtain land, build a house, purchase cattle, and so on. The money, strictly speaking, should have been turned over to his father while he was a part of the latter's household. In fact, the extent of remittances will depend somewhat on the size of the soldier's nuclear family. As its numbers grow the greater the obligation to aid in their support. There is also the matter of residence. If they are a part of his father's or brother's household, or remain in the wife's natal settle-ment as part of his father-in-law's household, the serviceman is expected to contribute accordingly. On the other hand, now that facilities exist for wives to join their husbands for at least part of the period of service, some soldiers do bring their families with them, and correspondingly reduce their remittances. Clearly, the service-man who remains part of a joint-type household retains a special status unlike that of other household members. He tends to act as if he is the head of an independent household even if he is in fact nominally part of a larger unit. Just as clearly, members of the latter unit have little power to coerce him into placing his entire earnings at their disposal.

When a soldier becomes the head of a household, the situation changes drastically. He assumes not only the responsibility for his own wife and children, but for younger siblings as well. Here, too, there is discernible a set pattern of priorities in the allocation of army savings. Firstly, food-shortages must be made up and recurrent or contingent expenses met. For example, in 1965 a soldier returned on leave with Rs 1,500 designated for the marriage of a younger brother. Following his own marriage, his savings had been deployed towards the repay-ment of interest-bearing loans and the purchase of food. When his brother approached the age of marriage money was set aside to meet these costs.

Investment in land generally occurs only after these initial obliga-tions are met. For this reason, short-term service seldom has any real effect on the overall economic position of a household. It is only the cumulative effect of long service which allows for an alleviation of the poverty which may have driven the Limbu to enlist in the first place. Those who remain in the army for longer periods stand a better chance of promotion, with its attendant pay increases, and of course derive the financial security provided by a lifelong pension.[1] With these opportunities to accumulate savings investment in land is then possible. The following examples will illustrate the process.

(*a*) In 1962 a Chongbung of Bharapa with eight years of service in the army returned on leave from the Assam Rifles with Rs 960 which he had saved to repay a mortgage on a paddy field. The land, his own, had been pledged by his grandfather to the father of a Newar resident in a neighbouring settlement. The members of his household, which included his mother, brother and sister, repossessed the field and

1 Pignède (1966, 145), writing about a Gurung village in west central Nepal, makes a similar observation: '*Seuls, les sous-officiers et officiers servant quinze ans et plus . . . ont une chance d'améliorer sensiblement le statut économique de leur famille.*'

resumed its cultivation, which added 400 units to their paddy income.

(*b*) In 1964 a resident of Bharapa, without ownership rights to kipat, in his tenth year with the Gurkhas, came home on leave and took under mortgage a paddy field which had previously been pledged to and worked by a Brahman from outside the Cluster. The mortgage principal was Rs 1,300, which he had saved during the previous two years. Since his household contained only his wife and a young daughter, he gave the land to his mother's brother on tenancy for an annual rent of 190 units.

(*c*) An Angu of Bharapa, without ownership rights to kipat, completed fifteen years of service in the army. With Rs 3,200 of his savings over the previous three years, he paid *bard* to the kipat-owner and took under mortgage a field producing 1,200 units of paddy. The field had previously been pledged to a Brahman, who had cultivated it himself.

These cases, although only random samples, demonstrate two important effects of Gurkha service. First, during the past twenty years or so there have emerged a number of Limbus with sufficient savings and pensions to obtain and regain landholding rights to their kipat. And, second, virtually all the lands repossessed or taken under mortgage with these funds had previously been pledged to members of other castes, mostly to Brahmans resident outside the Cluster.

From the point of view of the owners of kipat who do not serve in the army, the inflow of cash earned by Limbus in military service provides added opportunities for them to obtain *bard* in the course of transferring landholding rights. But, as I have pointed out, the freedom to manipulate rights of landownership can be restricted by the pattern of convergent ties. This is certainly true when the parties concerned are all Limbus. A dispute which arose following the transfer of a kipat mortgage from one Limbu to an ex-soldier neighbour suggests the kind of reaction forthcoming upon an attempt to disregard these ties:

In 1960 Kabir Hang borrowed Rs 600 from his classificatory brother's son, Ram. Kabir Hang in return gave the latter a small plot of unirrigated land to cultivate under mortgage until the loan could be repaid. The plot adjoined one of Ram's own fields near his house, so he could cultivate the entire stretch at one time. In 1964 Kul

Bahadur, an Angu, and a recently retired soldier, offered Kabir Hang
the mortgage 'price' and an additional increment of Rs 350. The
landholding rights to the plot which Ram had been cultivating were
then transferred. The maize was sown by Kul Bahadur in March,
but Ram said nothing at the time. In August, shortly after Kul
Bahadur had transplanted his millet seedlings, Ram confronted Kabir
Hang in a rage and demanded to know why the latter had allowed
Kul Bahadur to plant his millet on Ram's land. A boundary dispute
then ensued, and was eventually composed with the disputed section
being divided into equal parts.

When I asked Ram about the quarrel, he did not refer to the disagreement over the boundary, but instead was vexed about the fact
that Kul Bahadur had offered Kabir Hang *bard*. He was annoyed with
Kabir Hang for taking the land away from a neighbour and an agnate
and giving it to Kul Bahadur, an affine who owns no kipat (but who
is also a neighbour). Ram then went on to say how being in the army
and earning a lot of money had gone to Kul Bahadur's head. He
brought up a number of examples of the latter's impertinent and
haughty behaviour. What had seemed only a boundary dispute was in
fact a grievance over having lost landholding rights to a plot of land. It
was also a general statement about the fact that servicemen are at a
distinct advantage in bidding for lands pledged to others. Ram was
giving vent to his anger, and since Kul Bahadur is not only an ex-
serviceman but a member of a group without rights to kipat as well,
Ram chose to attack along the lines of an already existing structural
cleavage.

Such a dispute is atypical in so far as the great majority of lands
recently taken under mortgage by soldiers and pensioners were previously pledged, not to Limbus, but to Brahmans. But I did not learn
of any instance where a soldier or ex-serviceman attempted to bid for
lands held by a Brahman with whom either he or the landowner is
tied in a variety of linkages. No Brahman in the Cluster, for example,
has had to give up usufructuary rights to kipat in this way. The people
most affected by the growth of this formidable source of income are
those landholders – mainly Brahmans – whose ties with their Limbu
mortgagors are single-purpose, and can be severed with impunity by
the latter.

How much of this movement of kipat lands away from members of
other castes and into Limbu hands can be attributed to Gurkha
service? Of all kipat lands mortgaged, 21·3% is in the hands of Limbus

resident in the Cluster. Of this amount, 14·8% has been pledged to ten ex-army pensioners. This represents an investment of Rs 37,800 during the past fifteen years and a transfer of just under 14,000 units – almost all of it from Brahmans – to Limbu landholders. These figures do not represent the entire picture since they exclude money expended by kipat-owning soldiers and pensioners to repay mortgages and repossess their *own* lands. Thus, six of the seven Limbu households which today enjoy the unimpeded usufruct of their own kipat lands can attribute their position to cash earned from service in the Gurkhas.[1] In addition, men serving in the army at present have invested close to Rs 8,000 to take over 1,000 units of kipat land under mortgage and purchase 500 units of raikar land.

In some measure, this tendency for funds earned in the army to be reinvested in land is to be explained by reference to alternative opportunities. There is no industry in Ilam which might attract these funds. Nor is there any other outlet which could offer the prestige and security that land provides. The only likely alternative is the provision of interest-bearing loans. This is in fact exploited, and four pensioners between them provide Rs 2,000 in loans of this kind, almost half of the credit provided by all Limbus in the Cluster.

But lack of alternatives is only part of the explanation. The system of kipat tenure, which ensures that rights to land can never be alienated, provides a strong incentive for men serving in the army to maintain their ties to home and land. For as long as they are away, ownership rights remain intact. The system, moreover, benefits not only those who own kipat. The fact that kipat is inalienable means that Limbus without ownership rights themselves, but with sufficient funds, can always obtain lands through mortgage, by employing their ties of kinship and neighbourhood to keep open this avenue of investment, and of course by their ability to provide *bard* to the owners.

The effect of the inflow of pensions and salaries, therefore, has been to improve the agricultural economy of those households benefiting from external sources of income. It is worth noting that four of the seven Limbu households with the largest income from agriculture are headed by ex-servicemen receiving the largest pensions in the Cluster.

How do earnings from all commercial sources compare with income from subsistence agriculture? Translating production figures into monetary terms at the current rate of Rs 1·20 per unit of paddy and

1 See Table 12.

maize, and Rs 0.80 per unit of millet, the value of net agricultural income is approximately Rs 99,500. Earnings from commercial sources are detailed in Table 19. The number of households engaged in each activity appears in the column on the left. About half of all Limbu households earn income from more than one of these sources.

TABLE 19
Earnings from commercial sources, 1964–5[1]

Local sources	No. of households engaged	Annual income[2] Rs
Domestic service	4	150
Fishing	3	400
Teaching	1	400
Sales of mandarins, dairy products	3	750
Ritual services	5	800
Trading, portering mandarins, etc.	8	900
Labour in Terai, India	9	1,100
Government service	2	1,300
Sales of yeast bread	11	3,100
Portering wood, wood-cutting	23	5,700
Sales of liquor	39	6,100
		18,200
Gurkha service		
Pensions	13	8,050
Army salaries, remittances[3]	12	8,550
		16,600
Total		37,300

The table above shows that commercial sources provide an income equal to approximately 38% of net agricultural income. Seventy-four

1 Income from agricultural labour proved impossible to estimate and is omitted here.
2 After initial statements were taken from informants, a variety of means were used to cross-check the information. For example, since most people engaged in 'commercial' activities in the company of others, it was possible to verify an individual's estimates of his own earnings with his co-workers. Even so, it is necessary to stress that some of these figures are only approximations.
3 As I explained, remittances from servicemen are not made regularly or in full. The figures are for potential, not actual income.

households have some income from commercial sources. The majority (fifty-three households) earn funds amounting to less than half their income from agriculture, while another eleven households have commercial incomes which amount to between 50 and 99% of their earnings from agriculture. Approximately one-quarter of Limbu households earn more from commercial than from agricultural sources.

Table 20 compares actual earnings of households from agricultural and commercial sources.

TABLE 20
Comparison of agricultural and commercial income

Annual income	Agricultural	Commercial*
Under Rs 500	26 households	59 households†
Rs 500–999	21	15
Rs 1,000–1,999	23	8
Rs 2,000–2,999	8	2
Rs 3,000 and over	7	1
	85	85

* Excluding income from agricultural labour.
† Eleven households earn no commercial income.

Conclusion

The pattern of economic interdependence in the Indreni settlements is shaped, on the one hand, by Brahman land requirements and, on the other, by the credit needs of the Limbus. Loans are required for a variety of cash needs which the Limbu household is unable to meet from its income sources. Credit is obtained mainly by pledging land to Brahmans. As landholding rights pass to the creditors, Limbu kipat-owners are beholden to these same persons for cultivation privileges as tenants. But the relationship between Brahman and Limbu is not one in which economic power resides overwhelmingly with the former at the expense of the latter. Because land is scarce, kipat-ownership can be manipulated to obtain interest-free loans on fields already pledged, and the threat of transfer circumscribes the power of the individual creditor. The Limbu's freedom of action is curtailed, however, when the relationships in which he is involved become convergent, so that an attempt to withdraw from one tie endangers the others.

The growing commitment to commercial sources of income threatens to alter the existing configuration of economic inter-dependence. The agricultural system no longer represents the sole means of livelihood for the Limbus. To be sure, the origin of and, indeed, the motive sustaining their reliance on commercial activities turns on the insufficiency of agricultural resources. But as opportunities for earning wealth outside the agricultural system expand, the household continuously appraises its own alternatives and makes new choices based on self-interest. The effect, evidenced in the fact that already almost one-quarter of all Limbu households earn more from commercial than from agricultural sources, is to confer on the Limbu household yet a greater freedom to opt out of relationships of dependence on those who tend to dominate access to the land.

At the same time, wealth earned outside the agricultural economy which is reinvested in land redounds to the benefit of the Limbus and, conversely, to the detriment of the Brahmans, the chief landholding section of the population. Thus, Limbu exploitation of commercial income sources – especially Gurkha service – poses a threat to the economic ascendance of this group. The kipat system of land tenure, by guaranteeing Limbu ownership rights in perpetuity, keeps ajar the gateway to change. So that while agriculture is less important in the overall economy of the Limbus, land is still the basis of their security, and the Cluster still the focus of their social ties.

Chapter 6

Interdependence: the political context

The emergence of the Brahmans as the dominant economic section of the population has had important political consequences. Brahman leaders, once subordinates in a hierarchy based on land grants, have been, since the turn of the century, the most powerful men in the region of the Indreni settlements. Limbu headmen (the Subbas) have not only lost the bases of their traditional power, but must rely, like their lineage followers, on the support of influential Brahmans if their disputes are to be waged successfully. The latter, too, have come to dominate the new Panchayat Committee, which increasingly affects all people under its jurisdiction, including the Limbus.

In this chapter I consider the political configuration in the Indreni settlements. Any description of political life in the Cluster must, of course, take into account the factor of government presence. Since the absorption of Ilam into a national polity in 1774, Kathmandu, first through the militia, and later through the civil administration, has exercised a monopoly of coercive force. Settlements, however remote, have been encompassed within a wider political system and the influence of the central authorities is evident at the lowest levels.

I describe first the hierarchical framework of leadership which existed until the latter part of the nineteenth century, and show how this hierarchy collapsed as a result of changes in the system of land tenure discussed earlier. Contemporary contexts of leadership are then examined. Finally, the emergence of new Limbu leaders whose position is derived from wealth and status earned in military service is noted. Their presence mitigates somewhat the superordinate-subordinate nature of the interdependent ties which have, for more than half a century, linked Brahmans and Limbus.

The leadership hierarchy

I have already pointed out that Subbas gave grants of kipat land to non-Limbus immigrating into Limbuan from areas to the west. The recipients of these grants were at the same time appointed sub-headmen (Thari).[1] The latter were, in turn, encouraged to settle their own holdings by offering land to the immigrants who followed. In the region of the Indreni Cluster the extent of land grants was considerable. The Chongbung and Nembeke Subbas between them granted forty-four holdings,[2] out of which further allotments were made by the recipient Tharis. The holdings encompassed an area of some twelve square miles and included, by the time of the last revenue settlement in Ilam in 1936, approximately 1,000 registered households.[3]

Thus a political hierarchy was created which mirrored the hierarchy of land-holdings. This was symbolized in the annual payments of tribute made by dependents (*raiti*) to their Thari, and by the latter to his Subba. During the festival of Dasein Tharis were obliged to bring gifts of parched rice, curd and fruit, and in return received a ritual mark (*tika*) from their Subbas. Again, at the beginning of the Nepali year Tharis were constrained to bring further offerings of cash (Rs 1) as well as clarified butter and curd, at which time they would request the renewal of their land grants for the coming year.[4] Tharis were also expected to provide five days of unpaid labour or their equivalent in cash. This was usually obtained from among their own dependents, who owed their Thari a similar tribute. The Limbu dependents[5] of the Subbas, most of whom were his lineage mates, offered similar quantities of tribute.

Chief among the duties of the Subbas was tax-collection. This role

1 Limbu immigrants were given lands in the ways described in Chapter 3. None were made Tharis. All Tharis are non-Limbus.
2 Thirty-one of the Tharis on these holdings are Brahmans.
3 I was unable to ascertain the exact number of grants made by the Kambo Subbas, though they were probably fewer than either the Nembeke or the Chongbung grants.
4 It is unlikely, however, that Subbas could evict their Tharis without sufficient cause. See below.
5 The word most commonly used for what I call 'dependent' of a Subba is *bayad*, which connotes a kin tie and does not imply the same degree of subservience as the English term.

placed them in a position from which certain economic advantages could be derived. It has already been noted that under the system of tax-collection prevalent in Limbuan the number of taxable Limbu households are registered during the course of a periodic revenue settlement. But despite the fact that any households established between settlements are not liable for tax, Subbas were prone to collect taxes from these unregistered households and appropriate the revenue for themselves. The use of both Nepalese and Indian currency in Ilam also enabled Subbas to assess the taxes in Indian currency and pay the revenue in Nepalese coinage,[1] thereby pocketing the difference in exchange.

Other features of the system of land revenue accrued to the advantage of the Subbas. Once registered, a Limbu household was liable to the tax fixed at the time of the settlement. The tax was payable even if the kipat-owner died without heirs or emigrated. In such circumstances, if no other co-heir came forward to assume the liability of the vacant homestead – and most were prevented by what was formerly a heavy tax burden – the obligation fell on the Subba. But the law, by obligating the Subba to pay taxes for lands vacated by his lineage mates, also recognized his right to keep for himself or reallocate such vacated lands. Similarly, if a household defaulted on its tax obligation, the Subba could take its lands, since he would be held responsible by the authorities for the revenue. In fact, the defaulting household would usually be assisted by the Subba to pay its taxes. The government's tax policy, therefore, conferred on the Limbu headman rights which enabled him to accumulate more lands than his lineage agnates.[2] Table 21 overleaf contrasts land-ownership by the Subbas with the average land-ownership of households in his lineage.

The differences between the amount of land owned by the Subbas and the average for households in their lineages are evident in Table 21. These figures, of course, refer to present-day ownership and do not necessarily reflect with accuracy the ownership ratios almost a century ago, since they take no account of inheritance patterns. But the trend indicated by the figures seems more than coincidental.

1 The exchange ratio has fluctuated considerably over the years. In 1964–5, 1 Indian rupee was worth Nepalese Rs 1·60.
2 Since the Subbas were compelled to assume total responsibility for the tax liability on kipat land, the attitude grew up in many minds that kipat, as one Limbu phrased it, 'belongs not to a *thar* [clan segment or lineage] but to a Subba'.

TABLE 21
Ownership of kipat land by Subbas

Lineage[1]	Ownership of land by Subba*
Chongbung lineage	
1	270
2	299
3	378
4	239
5	174
Kambo lineage 1	435
Nembeke	213

* The average land ownership per lineage household is taken as index 100 in each case.

Moreover, it is likely that the differences in land ownership ratios between headman and lineage follower arose before the turn of the century, since after that time land shortages dissipated whatever advantages the Subba enjoyed. In the unusual case of land being abandoned nowadays, there is no question of its reverting to the Subba. Taxes are no longer an obstacle to potential co-heirs, so that these lands pass directly from one individual to another without any intervening authority. As a result land no longer accrues to the Subbas in this way unless they are related as co-heirs themselves.

Tharis collected taxes from the dependents on their holdings[2] and passed these on to the Subbas for submission to the land revenue office in Ilam Bazaar. If the Tharis attempted or, indeed, were implicated in attempts by their dependents to avoid taxes, the Subbas were entitled by the government to 'fine [the Thari] one year's production and eat [i.e. keep] the fine'. In cases of persistent attempts to avoid tax obligations, a Thari could be dismissed by a Subba, acting in council with other Limbu headmen.[3] By and large, however, as long as the Tharis submitted their taxes, behaved fairly to their dependents, and respected their Subbas, they enjoyed security of tenure and title

1 Phatras, Syelings and Kambo lineage 2 are omitted because in the first two instances they pay taxes to Chongbung Subbas, while in the latter case there are only two households in the lineage.
2 Holdings are revenue units.
3 Government of Nepal order regarding failure to register lands and homesteads in Far Kirat, 1868.

9 Ilam Bazaar on market day
10 Indreni Women sell vegetables and yeast cakes in Ilam bazaar

11 Portering timber to earn cash
12 Limbu girls

on their holdings. The Subbas could not arbitrarily evict either the Tharis or their dependents once they had been granted land.

The Subbas were the main channels of government control in the settlements. A judicial council of Subbas (*amal*) acted as a court of original jurisdiction, with rights to hear cases of a civil nature involving damages not exceeding Rs 100, and with authority to impose fines of up to Rs 25.[1] Their responsibility for the maintenance of law and order extended even beyond the boundaries of their holdings. When granted their titles, Subbas were instructed to 'arrest any person who crosses the border [into Ilam] without our [governmental] permission'.

Subbas were also held accountable for the maintenance of the main roads through their territory, and all dependents were required to contribute labour to keep the roads in good repair. They recruited the porters needed by the administration for the transport of essential foods and other materials. The Subbas were the earliest foresters and their permission had to be requested before anyone in the area under their jurisdiction could cut down heavy timber. They rounded up buffaloes and goats from the herds of their dependents for the Dasein sacrifice at military headquarters in Ilam. Obligatory contributions were imposed on the population at the time of such special occasions as the marriage of a princess or a royal coronation, and the Subbas were charged with the responsibility for administering the collections.[2]

The first chink in the political hierarchy which had evolved from the system of land grants appeared in 1886. In that year, the government decreed that all holdings granted to non-Limbus out of kipat land could be converted to raikar tenure by the Tharis. In consequence, the Subbas lost all rights in these lands. A dispute in 1954 illustrates the immutability of this regulation.

Shortly after 1912 the Nembeke Subba Indra granted some kipat land as a holding to a Jaisi and appointed him a Thari. At the time of the revenue settlement of 1936 the Jaisi registered the lands within the holding as raikar. In 1954 Jahare, the son of Indra, sent his son

1 The *amal* was not authorized to hear certain kinds of cases, called *panch-khat* – broadly speaking, those relating to caste offences or punishable by death or life imprisonment (cf. Regmi, 1965, 118).
2 Sometimes the Subbas were called upon for assistance of a more personal nature. Found among some old papers belonging to a resident in the Cluster was a note, written in 1876, and addressed to a Subba from a member of the administration in Ilam Bazaar. The correspondent, who was building a house, requested a few bundles of thatch for his roof, and suggested these might be forthcoming from the Subba's dependents.

Dharam to cut some leaves for their cattle from a nearby wood which was within the holding given by his father to the Jaisi. When the sister of the present Thari, Bhagi Rath (the son of the original grantee and one of the Main Landholders[1]) saw Dharam she became angry and told him he had no right to cut the leaves in this wood without her brother's permission. The young man cursed her and it is alleged that he struck her. When Bhagi Rath heard the commotion which ensued he came running and asked what had happened. Dharam told him that he was only a 'cowherd' (*gothalo*) on the land and did not own it, since it belonged to the Subba who had made the grant. As such, Dharam insisted that he had every right to cut the leaves of the trees. When the matter was brought before a mediation panel Jahare was held to be at fault for sending his son into another man's wood. Even if the land had once been kipat, they pointed out, it had become raikar and the descendants of the Subba who granted the land no longer had any rights in it. Jahare was made to promise that in future he would seek Bhagi Rath's permission if he wished to cut leaves from the wood.

Jahare had set out to test the immutability of the grant which his father had given the Jaisi. When Dharam used the term *gothalo* he was repeating a word used frequently by Limbus when referring to the relationship of the Tharis to the holdings granted them by the Subbas. A *gothalo* tends the cattle of his master, but does not own the cattle. Likewise, the Tharis were supposed only to mind the lands entrusted to them by the Limbus and take their products. The Limbus insist that the grants were given in good faith, and only the treachery (*jal*) of the recipients led to the conversion of these lands to raikar tenure.

Another development followed from the regulation of 1886: Tharis began to rely directly on the government for their security of title. The government, which had previously only guaranteed the Tharis a measure of security after appointment by the Subbas, began to take a direct hand in their assignment. Although succession to the title by primogeniture was usually accepted, the authorities reserved the right of confirmation. If a Thari died without sons or emigrated, leaving his holding without a headman, the government and not the Subba would make a new appointment, usually after consulting the dependents. For a brief period, Tharis were even allowed to sell their holdings, subject only to the approval of the new Thari by the government.[2]

The rights and responsibilities of the Tharis no longer devolved

1 See Table 16.
2 This right was abolished in 1911.

from the Subbas. Channels of communication led straight from the government to the Tharis. The final collapse of the leadership hierarchy came at the turn of the century, when the Tharis of Ilam began paying the taxes they collected from their dependents on raikar land to the revenue office instead of to the Subbas.[1] Thus the Subbas were left to collect only the taxes assessed on their own holdings of kipat. This rearrangement of the tax-collecting system relieved the Tharis of traditional financial obligations to the Subbas. They were no longer bound to pay tribute or make mandatory contributions of labour to the Subbas, even though they retained the right to demand these things from their own dependents. Such income bolstered their economic position, not only *vis-à-vis* their dependents, but *vis-à-vis* the Subbas as well.

Even so, these new advantages only strengthened the trend towards the economic ascendancy of the Tharis which had probably begun even before the conversion into raikar of holdings granted by the Subbas. I have already shown how government kipat policy, combined with population pressures and heavy Limbu social expenditures, brought about the large-scale mortgaging of kipat lands. The Tharis, because of the singular advantages gained through their position, were those best able to provide the loans and thereby become holders of kipat pledged by Limbus. Thus, all fourteen non-Limbus who are among the Main Landholders of mortgaged kipat are Tharis. It seems possible to project this correlation back to the last decades of the nineteenth century, and to infer that the leadership hierarchy initially based on the system of land grants was already on shaky economic foundations when the raikar regulations of 1886 were introduced. The lack of coincidence between the political status conferred on the Subbas by the hierarchy and their economic status is demonstrated by a consideration of their land mortgages. The figures have changed little since the turn of the century. (*See* Table 22 overleaf.)

These figures support the contention that the economic foundation on which the leadership hierarchy was originally built was eroded by the turn of the century. The government's restructuring of the tax-collecting system was fundamentally a recognition of this fact.

The Subba's role as government tax-collector on kipat holdings remains unaltered, and constitutes the basis of his formal authority.

1 I was unable to discover the exact year when this regulation came into effect. In some areas of Limbuan, Tharis still submit their taxes to the Subbas.

TABLE 22
Kipat mortgaged by Subbas

Lineage	Percentage of land mortgaged by Subba
	%
Chongbung lineages	
1 and 2	91
3	80
4	63
5	60
Kambo lineages	
1	98
2	97
Nembeke	87

But most of his other traditional duties have been usurped either by the Tharis or, more recently, by new administrative bodies, such as the Panchayat Committee (see below). Still, the Subba remains an important figure among the Limbus,[1] and the fact is recognized even by the Panchayat Committee, which channels many of its directives to the Limbus through the Subbas.[2]

The respect accorded the Subbas by other Limbus is evident, especially during the autumn festival of Dasein, when tributary payments are made and the Subba discharges certain ritual functions.[3] Although Subbas no longer have the authority to exact tribute, few Limbus make any attempt to avoid what they regard as obligations. In October, 1964, approximately 80% of kipat-owning Limbus visited their Subbas during Dasein, bringing gifts of liquor, meat and Rs 1·60, which latter, it was explained, replaced the traditional labour exaction to which Subbas were entitled. In one presentation I witnessed, the Subba sat in the middle of his room and as each lineage dependent approached, the gifts were placed on the floor beside the headman, following which the dependent bowed to the other's feet and

1 Headmanship apparently still carries sufficient prestige to have brought about a dispute over succession to the title between two Nembeke men. See pp. 153–4.

2 This is to some extent due to the failure to distinguish clearly between the jurisdictional boundaries of the Panchayat and the holding, the traditional revenue and political unit.

3 These rituals serve, in Leach's words, to remind the actors 'of the underlying order that is supposed to guide their social activities' (1954, 16).

received a *tika* on the forehead. The liquor was then shared among those assembled. Only members of Chongbung lineage 3 did not honour their Subba, since the latter was still a young man in his late teens. Even so, some gave their tribute to one of the other Chongbung Subbas, explaining that it was necessary to honour a Subba, and that it mattered little if he was the headman of another lineage.

This same attitude manifested itself on the ninth day (*naumi*) of the Dasein festival. This was the occasion for a display of the Subba's diacritical trappings of authority as well as of his generosity. Since each Subba is believed to hold his title by direct appointment of the King of Nepal, he is thought entitled to surround himself with the accoutrements of office. These are a post where sacrifices are performed, which stands in a fixed spot near the homestead of the Subba and attests to his 'rule' in the area; a drum, traditionally beaten to warn people in the area of impending danger; and a sword, which symbolizes the Subba's concern for the defence of his followers.

On the morning of *naumi* an animal was slaughtered at each Subba's 'sacrificial post' and the headman gave *tika* to those attending. The meat, provided by the Subba himself, was then cooked and eaten. Of particular interest was the pattern of attendance at these rites. Lineage was only an incidental criterion, despite the fact that the Subba is traditionally associated with a lineage. For example, a number of Chongbungs and members of groups who own no kipat land attended the rite of the Kambo Subba in Chitok and shared in the feast. One of his lineage mates from Bharapa also attended, but several Kambos resident in Dorumba attended the rite of the Nembeke Subba in that settlement. No division of followers took place at rites conducted by three Chongbung Subbas whose 'sacrificial posts' were situated in Bharapa and Angbung. There the three rites were held consecutively, enabling all participants, some of whom came from Chitok and some of whom were not owners of kipat land, to move from one rite to the next, thus honouring all three Subbas equally.

By cutting across lineage boundaries, these rites stress the point that the Subba has come to symbolize a wider collectivity. The nature of his position emerges more clearly in the context of the Limbu struggle to preserve the kipat system, to which I will turn in the next chapter. Here it is important to note a shift in emphasis away from the Subba as representative of a lineage towards the notion of him as a symbol of the unity of the Limbu people and, in the local setting, of the Limbu sector of the Indreni population.

This status, universally recognized by Limbus, enables the Subba to play an important part in composing disputes which involve people of different settlement clusters. Chief among these are quarrels over compensation claims arising out of the seduction of married women.

Disputes over compensation

In an earlier chapter I alluded to the high rate (almost 20%) of marriages by abducting the wives of other men. Such (*jari*) marriages precipitate crises on three counts. Firstly, they give rise to the possibility of violence. Secondly, they involve the severance of existing links between affinal groups, which is potentially disruptive, since the groups in question are often related in a number of ways. Finally, they require the settlement of compensation claims and so have economic consequences which seriously affect the fortunes of the households involved.

Although the use of force by a cuckolded husband is no longer recognized in law, attempts to employ violence to gain redress for extra-marital grievances are not unknown. When a Limbu of Bharapa abducted the wife of another man, the latter's attempts to take revenge on the adulterer led to an outbreak of fighting between supporters of both men, and resulted, in the words of one participant, in a number of 'broken heads'. Such occurrences are rare, since steps are taken to ensure that the new husband and the cuckold do not meet. Thus a Kambo man of Dorumba spent the better part of three days in hiding while the man he had cuckolded conducted negotiations for compensation with the former's representatives. The explanation for the disappearance was that 'if the cuckold meets the man who has seduced his wife he must "slaughter" him'.

However, in the great majority of cases compensation is sought directly from the new husband only if the woman has been abducted from her marital home. This is an uncommon eventuality, since both a husband and his kinsmen keep a close watch on the woman's activities and woebetide the man who is discovered attempting to seduce the woman under their very eyes. Most abductions take place while a woman is at her natal home. The ties between a woman and her natal group remain strong after marriage, with sisters and daughters visiting frequently and for long periods of time, and with many marital separations leading to the permanent residence of women in their natal settlements. This situation provides both the climate and the opportunities for the formation of liaisons with married women. When a woman is seduced while resident at her natal home, the aggrieved husband generally seeks compensation from her natal household, which then reclaims the amount from the new husband.

To negotiate the terms of compensation and, in general, to effect the severance of existing or the establishment of new marriage ties are the tasks of representatives chosen by the households directly involved. I have been told, though this is impossible to verify, that traditionally this role fell to lineage groups led by the Subbas. The latter continue to justify their claim to a special portion of marriage payments in terms of the obligations they are prepared to accept on behalf of lineage mates during the negotiations over compensation. The lineage group, if it ever was, is no longer a corporate unit in so far as these negotiations are concerned. The Subbas indeed play an essential part in the discussions, although more in their position as figures of influence within the wider Limbu community than in their capacity as lineage headmen. For one thing, they provide the channel through which discussions can be inaugurated. Since virtually all *jari* marriages are between partners in different settlement clusters, there are no universally recognized mediators, such as there would be in intra-cluster disagreements. To a large extent, then, the presence of Subbas and the common vocabulary of Limbu tradition of which they are seen to be the custodians provide a framework within which discussions can proceed. The residents from another settlement cluster who arrive to negotiate for compensation are expected to make the first formal statement of their intentions to a Subba. If this is neglected, as it sometimes is, the Subba could refuse to allow discussions to begin and certainly threaten to withhold his participation. By adhering to this custom, which includes the payment of a bottle of liquor to the Subba, the visitors ensure that the discussions will commence with haste and in an atmosphere of cordiality.

The households involved in these disputes must mobilize supporters on principles more varied than, although including, agnation. It is important to stress that the strength of a household's support depends not on the number of persons it is able to recruit, but on what might be called the strategic qualities of those enlisted. Although the numbers taking part in discussions vary from instance to instance, indeed, from hour to hour during a single case, the effective supporters of a household seldom number fewer than four or more than eight for any compensation dispute.

What are the chief criteria for recruitment? Of first importance is seniority. Although young men and women are invariably the partners in *jari* marriages the responsibility for dealing with the consequences of their actions falls on their elders. Young men may observe the deliberations of their representatives, or answer questions of fact if asked, but none would presume nor be invited to participate in the talks. Seniority implies a number of qualities. To wrangle over compensation and to handle the delicate task of severing affinal links requires patience, and a facility for self-expression, which latter suggests an ability to converse in the idiom of Limbu tradition and custom. Such qualities come only with age and experience. The importance of seniority is highlighted by an instance in which an Indreni Limbu found himself negotiating for compensation without the benefit of support from his elders. He had gone to fetch his wife, who had been visiting her natal settlement for a few months, and discovered that she had gone off with another man several days before his arrival. Instead of returning to the Cluster (a three-day walk) to muster support, he allowed himself to be persuaded by the girl's father to settle compensation immediately. His only supporter was another young man from the Cluster who had come along for the trip. He was able to collect Rs 300, but he would have received much more, he insisted, if there had been some older men with him. 'We were two babies [*balak*] against their elders [*burdo*].'

Not all elders possess the qualities usually associated with elderhood. In the Cluster men with the required talents are few and much sought after as supporters. From information obtained about twenty-eight cases of compensation disputes, the names of eight men appear constantly among the supporters recruited by households from every part of the Cluster. All but one – who is sixty-five years old – are between forty-five and sixty years, and possess the ability to present an argument forcefully and tactfully. They are all of above average wealth, although the richest Indreni Limbus are not among them. These men enjoy considerable prestige and influence among the Limbus.

During talks, one supporter on each side acts as chief spokesman, carrying the main burden of the discussion. Although any elder with oratorical talents can assume this role, ideally it should fall to a Subba, since it is felt his title alone commands respect. 'All men talk, but a Subba must be listened to.' In 70% of the cases recorded a Subba did act as spokesman, although in the majority of instances the household for which he spoke was not a part of his lineage. In those cases where households were, by virtue of owning kipat land, linked to Subbas as dependents, only 40% were actually represented by their own Subbas. Because most Limbu headmen were either too young or did not have the necessary qualifications to be spokesmen, another 40% of these households were represented by a Subba other than their own. In one case, for example, a Kambo man whose elder brother was a Subba, but still young and inexperienced, invited a Chongbung Subba to be his spokesman.

Neighbourhood is another important consideration when gathering support, since neighbours are first of all dependent on one another in a number of contexts and therefore thought to be reliable allies. Secondly, neighbours are expected to know the intimate details of the circumstances they are being called upon to discuss. Since most Limbus are neighbours to at least some of their lineage mates, we might distinguish between the latter and neighbours who belong to other lineage groups. Thus, 60% of the households in the cases recorded mobilized non-lineage neighbours to assist them, while 75% included lineage kinsmen. This latter figure is of some significance, since it indicates that one-quarter of the households did not muster their lineage mates, even though these were available in the same settlement. Most households recruited both categories of neighbour.

Great importance is attached to having among a household's supporters at least one person who is able to trace links in the opposing camp. If such a person cannot be found among lineage mates or neighbours, the household will turn to other neighbourhoods in the Cluster and even settlements outside the Cluster area. The importance assigned to the inclusion of supporters with ties to the opposition is illustrated by the following examples:

After Alahang, a Kambo of Chitok, had seduced the wife of another man and brought her to be his own wife, the woman's father and his supporters came to demand compensation.[1] Of the four persons recruited by Alahang one, another Kambo belonging to a different lineage, was related affinally, through his third wife, to the father of Alahang's new wife. A second supporter, a Chongbung of Bharapa, was also mobilized, partly because he had matrilateral ties in the same settlement cluster as the woman's father. By continually stressing the

---

1 It is not uncommon for the father of a woman who has gone off from her natal settlement to seek compensation from the new husband before the cuckold comes to claim from his ex-father-in-law.

importance of these ties, Alahang's supporters were able to dispel the initial hostility of the woman's father and his allies caused by Alahang's abrupt abduction of their daughter, and to reduce a first demand for Rs 1,500 compensation to a final figure of Rs 600.

In another instance, the married daughter of Sandu, a Chongbung, disappeared after a dancing party in Angbung which was attended by some young men from the district of Panchthar. Her husband, whose home was about four miles away, heard of her disappearance and came with his father and two other supporters to demand the payment of compensation. Here again two of Sandu's supporters traced affinal links to Sandu's in-laws. The first two wives of one had come from the same settlement cluster, and the present wife of the other was a lineage sister of the opposition's spokesman. Since Sandu could not pay the compensation, it was essential to postpone the discussions for as long as possible to give him the time to look for his daughter and her abductor, who had indeed disappeared, and to raise the compensation payments from his new in-laws. After a number of refusals, the husband's supporters agreed to a postponement of one month on the basis of a personal guarantee from the husband of their lineage sister (who was also a Subba) that at the end of the stipulated period the compensation would be paid.

Persons linked to both camps, even when not taking as crucial a part in the discussions as those in the two cases cited, do tend to bridge the gulf between the negotiators and so ameliorate the bad feelings which *jari* marriages can cause, while exerting a strong force for compromise.[1] Still, this is not the stated purpose for their recruitment. The household means to mobilize supporters and not mediators. One householder involved in such a dispute remarked: 'We want men who will carry us, not men who will compromise.' In this sense, the household musters an 'action set' to help it achieve a specific goal, viz. the settlement of compensation on terms favourable to itself.[2]

In the process of their confrontation, however, these sets are gradually transformed into a panel of mediation because of their interests in maintaining relationships which transcend in importance the immediate subject of their dispute. This becomes evident when it is noted that, once recruited, a set will negotiate without the direct guidance of the household it is meant to represent, and will reach

1 Both Gluckman (1956) and Colson (1953a) have shown how such 'divided loyalties' can bring about pressures for the settlement of disputes.
2 For a discussion of 'action set' see Mayer, 1966.

decisions which the members of both sets feel serve their own or the general interest. In the latter case cited above, for example, Sandu was entirely without control of his supporters, and did not wholly concur in the compromise they reached.

The inclusion in the household's set of Subbas and elders who are men of influence thus ensures that its case will be well represented, and at the same time guarantees that compromises reached will be respected. Even the most powerful Limbu households, although able to exert a greater measure of control over the sets they recruit and thus in a better position to influence the final decision of the mediation panel, would be reluctant to disregard this decision for fear of alienating the support of the Subbas and elders in future.[1]

Informal mediation of intra-Cluster disputes

The Subba's statutory authority no longer extends to the maintenance of law and order. The council of Subbas (*amal*) which existed until about fifty years ago, is now defunct.[2] In consequence, most disputes between Limbus within the Indreni Cluster are mediated informally by men who are regarded as Notables (*bhaladmi*). A man achieves notability with age, wealth and, increasingly, with literacy. He is expected to be fair and impartial when hearing disputes, and to possess an influence to make his decision acceptable to both parties. Still, the term is a vague one and depends not only on the context in which it is being used, but on the identity of the disputants. One man's Notable, so to speak, may not be another's. We might distinguish two categories of Notable. On the one hand there are the local variety, men who are regarded as Notables in each settlement or neighbourhood and who invariably help to compose minor quarrels between their neighbours. The Subbas and elders referred to above, for example, are regularly called upon to mediate in disputes involving individuals who recognize the higher status of the former.

1 These mediation panels are unlike the 'councils of reconciliation' described by Cohen (1965, 142–5) in that the mediators are not chosen by each side *because* they are neutral. In the sense that the sets which ultimately reach agreement regard themselves, at least in the initial stages of the discussions, as opponents representing different sides of a dispute, they resemble what Bailey refers to as an 'arena council' (1965, 9–15).

2 This is due mainly to the spread of government courts, which usurped many of the functions of the *amal*, and, of course, partly to the fact that Subbas have lost much of their traditional power.

To deserve the appellation of Notable on a Cluster-wide basis, however, demands validation by a status recognized in a wider context than the neighbourhood and even the Cluster. It accrues only to individuals with high status in the wider society. For reasons mainly connected with their economic impoverishment, none of the Subbas today enjoys the status of Notable in this sense; and, to avoid ambiguity, it is in this latter sense only that I will employ the term.

In the Cluster at present those regarded universally as Notables are army pensioners, more particularly pensioners who managed to rise above the ranks and who combine wealth with age and literacy. Of these qualities it is only wealth, of course, which, once attained, can be dissipated and lead to a loss of Notable status. To sustain a viable economic position over the years requires a combination of skill in managing a farmstead and a favourable balance of good fortune. That this is not always achievable can be illustrated by reference to one Chongbung ex-serviceman. As a result of the eighteen years he spent in the army he was able to repay a number of debts incurred prior to enlistment, to repossess his own mortgaged kipat lands and to take some other lands under mortgage. During the first few years following his return to the Cluster with the rank and pension of a havildar[1] (Rs 40 per month), he maintained a viable economic position. Within ten years, however, due to a series of unfortunate circumstances, chief among which were eight young children and a penchant for drink, the havildar's household was among the poorest in the Cluster. The status he imported from the Gurkhas is irrelevant in the context of Indreni leadership because of his present economic condition.

Another ex-soldier (Jahare), who attained the same rank and pension, has been able to maintain a viable estate, although with increasing difficulty because of his involvement in expensive litigation.[2] Nevertheless, now in his early sixties, he is recognized as a Notable in the Cluster, and disputes are frequently taken to him for mediation. Thus, a quarrel between two brothers over the division of some property retained by their widowed mother prior to her death was brought before Jahare, even though he was a Nembeke of Dorumba and the disputants Chongbungs of Bharapa. The brothers threatened to take the matter to court, but were assured by the havildar that a fair solution could be found which would be satisfactory to both and which would save them undue time and money. The procedure, as in most

1 A havildar is roughly equivalent to sergeant.
2 See pp. 153–4.

instances of mediation, was informal, with each disputant presenting his argument in turn and answering questions put to him by the mediator. Others joined freely in the talks and witnessed the signatures on the document setting out the terms which were finally agreed upon – the division of the land into equal shares. The return of harmonious relations was signified when everyone present was invited to share a bottle of liquor.

The dispute did not require the attention of a gifted mediator. The solution was obvious at the outset and could have been foretold by any Indreni man with an average amount of experience in these matters. Why, then, was it brought to a Notable and not to a Subba? When the question was put to one of the disputants, he replied: 'Why should we bring it to a Subba? He is no bigger than we are. If there is any dis-agreement about the decision in future, then others will tell us: "This is the work [decision] of a Notable; why do you quarrel about it?" '

The acceptance of mediation by men who are universally recognized as Notables thus ensures that the decision is not likely to be disregarded.

The most widely acknowledged Notables in the Indreni Cluster are two ex-soldier brothers of Chitok. Both are known and addressed by their army ranks: the elder, Lajahang, was a lieutenant; the younger, Parsade, a subedar.[1] Their pensions amount jointly to about Rs 2,300 annually. Between them they have taken under mortgage 10·1% of all kipat lands pledged by Indreni Limbus.[2] Lajahang also owns raikar lands in the Terai, purchased with his earnings during service, and from which he derives an income of approximately Rs 2,500 per year. Both are considered to be among the wealthiest men in the area. Since their return from army service in the early 1950s their assumption of leadership has seemed both inevitable and welcome. As the most important Notables, they have to mediate in the greatest number of disputes. One quarrel, involving a Subba's son, is worth recounting, since it illuminates the established trend away from mediation and, more generally, from political leadership by the Subbas, in favour of that provided by Notables who have achieved status as a result of army service:

In October, 1964, Kanak, the brother's son of Lajahang and Parsade,

1 Under the ranking system in the Gurkhas prior to 1947, a Gurkha lieutenant was an Indian commissioned officer, while a subedar was a Viceroy C.O. The latter ranks below the former.
2 They are among the Main Landholders (H and I) distinguished in Table 16.

loaned Rs 1 to Khem Bahadur, the son of Chongbung Subba Kabir Hang, so that Khem Bahadur could remain in a game of cards some boys were playing. The following January, Kanak asked for the return of the money. It is alleged that Khem Bahadur refused, and that there ensued an argument during which the Subba's son was beaten. When Kabir Hang heard what had taken place, he discussed the matter with another Chongbung Subba, the most highly respected Limbu headman in the Cluster, and both decided to hold a moot (in their *amal*, as they put it, using the term for the traditional Subba's court). Both Kanak and his father's brothers – but not Kanak's father, who is a poor man without influence – were summoned to the house of Kabir Hang, where the moot was to be held. After some time a messenger from Lajahang and Parsade arrived at Kabir Hang's house to say that any discussions were to take place at the former's house. Those who had gathered in Kabir Hang's courtyard then walked the half-mile to the new meeting-place.

Kabir Hang regarded the beating as a deliberate insult to the dignity of a Subba. He insisted that 'the Subba is a king, and to beat the son of a Subba is to beat a king's son' (and future king). The purpose of the moot for him was to seek redress for this affront. The incident was regarded in quite different terms by Lajahang. He pointed out that it is against the law to gamble and that both boys were wrong to do so. He then reminded Kanak that it is also against the law to beat another, and that a court would deal severely with such an offence. Kanak was then made to present a bottle of liquor to the Subba, and to signal his apology for the beating – but not for beating a Subba's son – by bowing to both Kabir Hang and Kanak.

Two points are worth noting. Firstly, Lajahang, by insisting on holding the moot in his own homestead, established his right to mediate against that of the Subbas. Although the two Subbas were elders and much respected, neither could compete in power or influence with the ex-army Notables. Moreover, their position was made untenable by the fact that they had not only mortgaged kipat fields to Lajahang and Parsade, but were also tenants of the lieutenant. Secondly, the different value frameworks within which each side interpreted Kanak's misdemeanour illustrates the divergent bases of the two kinds of leaders. Stated crudely, it is the distinction between, on the one hand, acribed leadership founded on traditional norms and, on the other hand, achieved leadership validated by the norms of the wider society.

Although it is often said of Limbus that their disputes are never aired before members of other groups, in fact mediation is sometimes sought from another category of Notables who are not Limbus. The status which most often leads to the recognition of a non-Limbu as a Notable is headmanship on raikar holdings, i.e. the title of Thari. Indeed, until recently it was unlikely that a non-Limbu could achieve the qualities associated with a Notable without the status and economic prerogatives enjoyed by a Thari. In rare instances, a local Brahman might rise to a position of prominence in the administration in Ilam Bazaar. When this happened, the wealth and prestige earned externally would be imported into the settlement and used to obtain a raikar holding and headman title, thus providing him with a political base in the settlement. Nowadays, in theory at least, a man can gain prominence through the new administrative structures, such as the Panchayat Committee. But in fact, as will become evident from the discussion below, this is highly unlikely. In the region of the Indreni Cluster, while not all Tharis are Notables, there are no non-Limbu Notables who are not also Tharis.

The nature of the relationship between a raikar headman and his dependents relates, to some extent, to the spatial distance between the Thari and his holding. Because of the early practice of sale and purchase of holdings as well as the introduction of a category of government-appointed headmen, a Thari's residence often does not coincide

TABLE 23
Holdings of Indreni Tharis

Thari[1]	Thari's residence	Location of holding (distance from residence)
Brahman A and B[2]	Dorumba	1 mile
Brahman C	Chitok	(a) 6 miles / (b) 2 miles
Brahman D	Bharapa	1 mile
Brahman E	Chitok	(a) 6 miles / (b) 1½ miles
Brahman F	Chitok	6 miles
Jaisi G	Dorumba	(a) Dorumba / (b) 3 miles

1 See Table 16 for their position among the Main Landholders.
2 At the time of field-work, the headmanship on this holding was being disputed by Brahmans A and B, two brothers, following the death of their father. See pp. 151–3.

with the location of his holding. Of the six Tharis resident in the Indreni Cluster, only one, a Jaisi of Dorumba, actually resides on his own holding. The other five Tharis – all Brahmans – have their holdings anywhere from one to six miles away from their homes. As can be seen from Table 23, three of the Tharis resident in the Indreni settlements have more than one holding.

The raikar lands within the Indreni settlements are divided among four Tharis, three of whom – the Jaisi being the only exception – live outside, but within a three-mile radius of the Cluster.

Due to the nature of raikar land, the Thari is separated from his dependents in more than a spatial sense. Other than the fact that holdings themselves could, at one time, be transferred by sale, raikar lands can be alienated so that, over time, the composition of the holdings' residents may change substantially. Thus, in contrast to the Subba, the Thari is unlikely to be a kinsman to more than a few, if any, of his dependents. The result is a relationship between Tharis and dependents quite distinct from that between Limbu headmen and their dependents.

For a number of reasons, it is to a Thari's advantage to keep in close touch with his holding. For one thing, by doing so he is able to exact the traditional five days of labour (or their cash equivalent), despite the fact that such exactions are now outlawed. For another, he can ensure that dependents turn up at Dasein with their tributary payments. Thirdly, since a fee (*teki*) following the sale of any land within his holding is paid to the Thari, it is in the latter's best interests to be in touch with all developments, so as to know if the price mentioned in the documents of sale is in fact the real sale price.

Still, it is not in a Thari's interests to emphasize his prerogatives to the exclusion of his responsibilities. A Thari should be ready to offer financial and other kinds of assistance to his dependents during times of distress. He should also be prepared to help his dependents in their occasional dealings with the administration. And he must be ready to offer his services in mediating their disputes. The Jaisi headman in Dorumba, for example, has on several occasions attempted to seek a solution to a bitter antagonism existing between two Kambo brothers and their wives who reside on the Jaisi's raikar holding in Dorumba. In the most recent incident the wife of the older brother was severely beaten during a drunken quarrel by the younger brother and his wife. Since the case was one of assault, it was cognizable by the court, but the Thari succeeded in persuading the injured party to settle the matter

13 A Limbu girl fetches water
14 A Limbu ritual to 'wash away bad feelings'

15 A Limbu *phedangma* performs a curing rite

without resort to litigation. He then held a moot, where it was decided that the aggressors would pay the offended woman Rs 1·60 to 'raise her head', i.e. prestige (*sir uthaune*).

A Thari who is known to be fair in his demands and generous in his assistance earns not only the accord of his dependents, but of his neighbours, even if the two categories of persons are spatially distinct. Thus the reputation earned by a Thari through his relationships with his dependents can give him Notable status in the area of his holding as well as in the settlement region where he resides. Two cases serve to demonstrate the foregoing remarks.

A poor Brahman from a settlement just west of Bharapa had asked a Limbu widow of Angbung if he might take some bamboo from a small wood belonging to her son. While he was cutting the bamboo he was approached by the woman's son, who threatened to beat him. At that point a Brahman Notable returning home from the market heard the two men quarrelling and suggested that they explain the matter to him. When it became clear what had transpired, the Notable exacted an apology from the Limbu for his hasty accusation and a promise from the Brahman that in future he would seek the Limbu's consent directly before taking any bamboo.

The Brahman mediator, who was a Thari residing in Chitok, had no specific kin or political relationship with either of the disputants. His holding was situated about six miles to the north of the Cluster, but his status as a Notable in the Indreni area derived from his reputation as a man of wealth and influence, and his mediation attempts were both welcome and effective.

In another instance, the mediator was a Brahman with similar Notable status, who was headman of a raikar holding within the Indreni settlements, though he was resident several miles away from the Cluster. The dispute involved a Chongbung of Chitok who had cut off the ear of a goat belonging to a Brahman from a neighbouring settlement because the animal had come unattended into the Limbu's potato field and destroyed part of the crop. The Thari, who was asked by the owner of the goat to settle the matter, upbraided the Limbu for not first tying up the animal and then claiming compensation for the crop damages. It was decided that the Limbu would pay the owner Rs 30 and keep the goat. The owner demanded a promissary note from the Limbu, but the Thari insisted that this was unnecessary and that he would guarantee the payment, since both men owned a plot of raikar land in his holding.

11

Thus Notable status within the Cluster can accrue, on the one hand, to Indreni Tharis who exercise at least part of their leadership roles in holdings removed from the Cluster and, on the other hand, to Tharis resident outside the area, but whose political base, as it were, is within the boundaries of the Indreni settlements.

The recently established Panchayat Committee has not created any new Notables, but has given a somewhat official sanction to the mediatory efforts of a few prominent men who have become Panchayat executives. Disputes, including those in which Limbus are involved, are nowadays, with increasing frequency, brought to the Committee chairman, who, sometimes alone and sometimes with the help of other Panchayat representatives, attempts to reach a settlement. The mediation is not, strictly speaking, formal in the sense that the Panchayat Committee is not authorized to act as a court,[1] although it may offer its good offices to effect compromises when both disputants voluntarily seek mediation. On the other hand, the chairman mediates with the full authority of his position, and there is all but the force of law in his decisions. I cite two cases to illustrate this kind of mediation.

In 1963, following the death of his wife, Budibal, a Nembeke of Dorumba, brought an Angu woman of Bharapa to live with him. The woman was separated from her own husband, whose whereabouts were not known, and so, since Budibal had paid no compensation, he did not consider her his wife, although she was referred to as such by everyone in the Cluster. The woman was subject to periodic moods of depression and sudden outbursts of violence. After one incident, during which she threw a *khukuri* knife, narrowly missing one of Budibal's young children, he decided that he could no longer allow her to stay in the house. Budibal and his two brothers met with several Angu men to seek a solution to the dilemma. The Angus insisted that this was a domestic quarrel and should be settled within the household. If a wife is troublesome, they pointed out, a man cannot send her away, but must take the good with the bad. The Nembekes, on the other hand, stated that a wife is brought to make a house happy, and if she is unable to do so another house must be built for her to live in, and an additional wife taken to care for the children. Budibal, however, would not accept the advice of either side. He was adamant about being rid of the woman, and based his determination on the danger to his children, thus shifting the nature of the dispute from a minor domestic quarrel to a public offence. Several representatives from each side were chosen

1 For a brief period from 1953–6 a Panchayat court did exist. See pp. 163–4.

to present the case to the Committee chairman. At this point Budibal enlisted the support of Lajahang, the ex-army officer, who was the father of Budibal's first wife and the grandfather of the children who were alleged to be in danger from the uncontrollable anger of the woman. The chairman, after hearing the problem, agreed that the woman constituted a danger to the children. He suggested that she be given Rs 50 to 'lift her prestige' and that she return to her natal home in Bharapa. This is in fact what was done.

The case provides an interesting contrast between what might be called the 'domestic' dimension of the dispute, in terms of which the supporters of both the husband and wife sought a solution, and the 'legalistic' dimension, which approach Budibal adopted, and in which both his father-in-law and the chairman concurred. This is not to suggest that the first is a traditional approach, while the second is a modern one, since the presence nearby of police and court has long ago brought the law into the Indreni peasant's perception of his surroundings. But it does indicate a more immediate and effective presence, in the form of the Panchayat Committee, of the force and authority of government. Indreni Limbus are increasingly encouraged to take advantage of this stress by the Committee mediators on the legalistic dimension of disputes.

A Chongbung of Bharapa, for example, had borrowed Rs 180 and agreed to pay interest at 20% per annum. When it came time to collect the interest the creditor, a Brahman from a neighbouring settlement, approached the Limbu, but the latter refused to pay, claiming the interest was too high, and suggested the matter be brought to the chairman. The latter scolded the Limbu for refusing to honour his obligations, but conceded that the law set a limit of 10% on interest payments. The initial document was torn up, and a new one made stipulating the legal rate, and the Limbu was instructed to pay the amount with a month.

In sum, then, there are a variety of mediators available to settle disputes in which Limbus are implicated. The decision as to which category of mediator to choose depends partly on who a man is quarrelling with, and partly on the disputants' assessment of their own status. The first is of importance because Limbus prefer, even if it is obvious from some of the examples cited that they do not always succeed, to have their quarrels mediated by other Limbus. The second determines the 'level' at which mediation will be sought. Thus,

'small' men turn to Subbas and elders of influence in their neighbourhoods; 'bigger' men seek mediation from one of several categories of
universally recognized Notables, including Panchayat Committee
executives. This explains the tendency for the decisions of informal
mediators to be respected. The acceptance of their superior status is at
the same time the strongest sanction of their mediation.

Informal dispute settlement within the Cluster does not exhaust
the range of choices open to those involved in disagreements. For the
redress of their grievances men can also turn to the administration in
Ilam Bazaar. In addition to the court, both the treasury department
(*mal*) and the office of the governor have traditionally provided
facilities for the settlement of disputes. This is due largely to the
blurring of jurisdictional boundaries between the various branches of
the administration. Decisions from all these sources have the force of
law. In consequence, inhabitants of the settlements of Ilam view the
administration as undifferentiated. Dealings with the governor or his
representatives, with the treasury officials or the court are seen as
dealings with the 'office' (*adda*). And it is not uncommon to seek
redress for grievances concurrently in more than one branch of the
administration.

Disputes taken to the governor or the treasury office involve less
time and cost than court litigation, yet few Indreni peasants possess the
resources – wealth and literacy – to exploit any of these possibilities.
As a result, a very small proportion of quarrels which concern any but
the most prominent of the Cluster's residents ever reach Ilam Bazaar
at all. I was not able to discover precisely what proportion of all disputes are brought to the Bazaar, nor how they are distributed among
the several branches of the administration. From a perusal of court
records since 1951, however, several facts emerge.[1] Firstly, a large
proportion of disputes reaching court are over land. Of forty-eight
cases involving litigants from the Indreni settlements, twenty-three
cases were about land. Another ten were complaints about assault.
Secondly, Limbus were litigants in only five of the court cases; three
of these dealt with assault on other Indreni Limbus, while two were
land disputes with Brahmans. Thirdly, in forty-two of the forty-eight
cases at least one member of a single Brahman lineage in the Cluster
was implicated. This latter fact relates to the existence of factional
cleavages in the Indreni settlements.

A discussion of the organization and activities of factions will help to

1 Most records of the court prior to 1951 were destroyed.

clarify the pattern of leadership in the Cluster and indicate the extent to which Limbus, to gain their own ends, are compelled to rely on the support of these Brahman-led units.

Factions

For most Notables, the display of leadership qualities is confined to contexts of mediation. Some, however, become political leaders by gathering about themselves a core of followers whose ranks are augmented on particular occasions by additional supporters. The immediate purpose for their recruitment is generally the waging of a dispute, but the underlying goal is the pursuit or maintenance of power and influence by the leaders. The aggregations formed in this way will be called 'factions'.[1]

Factional divisions bearing on the Indreni settlements are not confined to the Cluster, but extend throughout and, to an extent, beyond the village area. The activities of factions, however, will be considered only in so far as they concern alignments within the Indreni Cluster. The background to factional struggles will be discussed first.

Factions in the Indreni settlements are based on a schism within a single Brahman sibling group. The origins of the split can be traced to 1925, when Loka Narayan (see Fig. 5) purchased some raikar land in Chitok and Bharapa and moved with his wife and four of his five sons into the Cluster. The eldest son, Ram Chandra remained in the house where he and his brothers had been born, and which was situated in a settlement on the outskirts of Ilam Bazaar. The move corresponded with a division of property among the three eldest brothers, Ram Chandra, Narad Muni and Gobinda,[2] and their establishment of separate households. Gobinda came to Bharapa, while Narad Muni and his father, Loka Narayan, built their homes on neighbouring plots in Chitok. The two youngest sons, Bishnu Prasad and Tunka Nath, who were only seventeen and twelve years old, continued to live for a time with their parents.

1 By 'faction' I mean a leader-based quasi-group, recruited on diverse principles, and operating in the political field. This combines the definitions of faction given by Firth (1957) and Nicholas (1965) with Mayer's use of the term 'quasi-group' to indicate an egocentred, non-corporate collectivity of individuals (1966).
2 The letters in brackets beside the names in the genealogy correspond with those in the list of Main Landholders in Table 16.

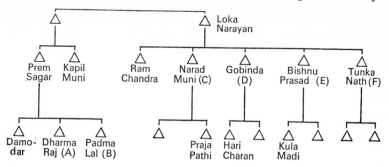

Figure 5

As is customary, not all the property was divided among the sons. A portion (*jiuni*) was kept by the parents to guarantee their own security in old age. The *jiuni* consisted mainly of forest and grazing lands as well as title to a holding on other cultivated lands, all of which were situated about six miles north of the Cluster. The lands and headmanship had all been acquired by Loka Narayan as a result of his attaining a high position in the district administration. At the time the division of property agreement was prepared, it was stipulated that, following the death of both parents, Narad Muni would succeed to the title of headman and receive the income from the holding. The remaining forests and grazing lands were to be divided among Narad Muni, Bishnu Prasad and Tunka Nath. But a further stipulation required that the son who cared for his parents in their old age would, following their death, receive a larger share of these lands than the others.

In 1931 Loka Narayan died. Shortly after, Bishnu Prasad established a separate household in Chitok. Loka Narayan's widow lived with her youngest son, Tunka Nath, until her death in 1953.

The death of Loka Narayan set the stage for a series of disputes among the sons, stemming initially from disagreements over the division of the *jiuni*, and then becoming generalized in a wide range of contexts. Within the sibling group, the brothers formed a series of temporary alliances which dissolved with the settlement of a particular dispute or succession of disputes, or upon the death of one of the brothers. Still, over a period of time, alliance patterns are discernible. The earliest quarrels, following the death of Loka Narayan, concerned mainly Ram Chandra and Narad Muni. Bishnu Prasad and Tunka Nath were still young men, while Gobinda spent most of his time in the Terai, where much of his inheritance was situated, and so was never involved in his brothers' disputes. At the time of the revenue settlement of 1936, Narad Muni succeeded in registering in his own name all the *jiuni* lands which he was supposed to share with his brothers following their mother's death. This led to prolonged court action, which eventually ended with a Supreme Court decision in favour of Ram Chandra, who had pleaded the case on behalf of his mother and his other brothers.

From 1940 to 1950 Narad Muni was aligned against each of his brothers in turn, although occasional disputes broke out between Ram Chandra and Bishnu Prasad. By this time, the contexts for strife were not only their own disputes, but quarrels concerning others as well. After the death of Ram Chandra in 1950, both Bishnu Prasad and Tunka Nath quarrelled separately with Narad Muni and, on occasion, allied themselves against him. In 1956, following the death of Narad Muni, the only two remaining brothers, Bishnu Prasad and Tunka Nath, became the principal protagonists. When I arrived in the Cluster these two men were the leaders of factions which ramified throughout the area of, and to an extent beyond, the village.

How were the factions composed? Each faction had established a 'core' of adherents who tended to support their faction leaders whether the immediate dispute concerned them directly or not. The core included, first of all, the members of a leader's household. This is not as obvious a statement as it may seem. The ethic which exhorts a father to distribute his property (and his love) equally among his sons is occasionally ignored in practice. Fathers often favour particular sons or the sons of a particular wife. Since property divisions are frequently determined before the sons establish separate households, such practices can result in a disenchanted son identifying with an opposing alliance against his father while still nominally a member of the latter's household. Thus the eldest son of Narad Muni became an adherent of his father's elder brother, Ram Chandra, because of grievances against the former over property division.

Generally, however, as long as an estate remains undivided, a father can count on the support of members of his household. Both Bishnu Prasad and Tunka Nath head joint-type households, with two sons each. One son in each household plays a key part both as adviser and as a highly important link with the administration in Ilam Bazaar, where the two are employed.

Aside from household members, factional cores also include men who, in the furtherance of their own ambitions, find it expedient to seek the support of faction leaders. Absorption into factional cores may also have a basis in a history of disputes. Those led by Bishnu Prasad and Tunka Nath included two brothers of a collateral line in the same lineage who had been at loggerheads for almost fifteen years. The initial antagonism developed at the time of their division of property. The elder, Dharma Raj (see Fig. 5), alleged that his younger brother, Padma Lal, had received a larger share of the estate than he did. The hostility between the brothers was exacerbated by the fact that their father, Prem Sagar, lived during his old age with his youngest son and was commonly known to favour the latter. Alignment with the primary faction leaders came about in 1952. At that time Padma Lal was discovered to have impregnated the wife of Damodar, an older brother who had emigrated to India. To cover up the scandal, one of the dependents of Prem Sagar, who was a Thari, was paid handsomely to take the woman away from the area. The arrangements were made by Tunka Nath in return for support given him by Prem Sagar on a previous occasion. Dharma Raj broke off commensal relations with his younger brother, as did a number of other men in the area. Padma Lal, to save caste, was forced to distribute much of his wealth in the form of bribes, and had to sell a number of his lands to meet the costs. Tunka Nath was one of those who agreed to interdine with him, and since that time the latter has supported and been supported by the faction leader. In consequence, Dharma Raj was brought, somewhat inadvertently, into the core of Bishnu Prasad's faction.

When Prem Sagar died in 1961 the two brothers, after observing a mourning period of one year, began campaigning for their father's title of Thari, along with Prem Sagar's younger brother, Kapil Muni. Each had in fact been sharing the income from a designated number of households within the holding, but the title itself could not be shared, i.e. the holding could not be formally divided. The treasury office, which makes the appointment, decided at one point to seek the 'advice' of the dependents on the holding. In preparation for the visit of the treasury representatives, each candidate enlisted the support of the faction leaders. Although Bishnu Prasad, by this time a Panchayat Committee executive, could not campaign openly in favour of Dharma Raj, it was commonly known where his preference lay, and another member of his faction core conducted the campaign. Tunka Nath himself spoke in favour of Padma Lal and, in an attempt to impress the treasury office of the strong opposition to Dharma Raj, who was the favourite by virtue of being the elder of the two contending sons of the former Thari, Tunka Nath encouraged another member of his faction core to bolster the claim of the third candidate, Kapil Muni. The meetings only ensured that each candidate would have the support of those households already paying taxes to him, since no dependent attended the meetings of his rivals. In the end the treasury office heard only a few mild speeches in favour of each candidate without bringing the matter to a vote. Although nothing had been decided when I left the field, the general consensus was that the contest was a façade, since the authorities generally follow custom in choosing the eldest son – in this case Dharma Raj – to succeed to a headman's title. The campaign continued behind the scenes by intermittent visits to the treasury office made by the competitors and their faction supporters.

Two other men resident in the Cluster belong, together with Dharma Raj and Padma Lal, to the core of the factions recruited around Bishnu Prasad and Tunka Nath. Here again alignment on a regular basis has resulted from the growth of intense hostility between a Jaisi and a Nembeke of Dorumba. The rivalry stems from a dispute over rights to land which the father of Jahare, a Subba, had granted as a holding to the father of the Jaisi, Bhagi Rath.[1] The latter allied himself with Bishnu Prasad, who had already been at odds with Jahare in a number of minor squabbles.

The first major test of the coalition came in 1961, when Jahare attempted to claim the title of Subba after the death of his brother's son, Dolpe (see Fig. 6), who had inherited the title while Jahare was in the army. Although both customary and legal rules stress succession

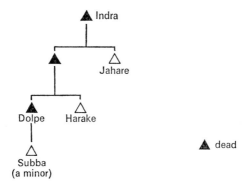

Figure 6

1 See above, pp. 129–30.

by primogeniture, Jahare challenged the right of the late Subba's son to succeed on the grounds that the latter was a minor. With the help of faction leader Tunka Nath, he was able to convince the treasury office that the Limbu dependents on the kipat holding should be allowed to decide the issue. They then went on to 'pack' the hearing held before the treasury representatives with twelve non-Limbu supporters recruited from all parts of the village, who added their considerable weight to the five Nembekes speaking on behalf of Jahare. The treasury subsequently ruled in Jahare's favour.

Bishnu Prasad and Bhagi Rath then persuaded Harake, the late Subba's brother, and also a dependent of Bhagi Rath, by virtue of owning a plot of raikar land on the latter's holding in Dorumba, to appeal against the decision. They pointed out that the hearing, on which the treasury office decision was based, could be shown to be illegal, since most of Jahare's supporters who appeared before the hearing were not in fact dependents on the kipat holding, but non-Limbus resident on other, raikar holdings. They then suggested that if Harake would emphasize that a minor's rights had been violated by the decision and would agree to act as the boy's regent until he came of age, the responsibilities of tax-collection on the holding could be properly discharged and the fears of the treasury office allayed. Harake agreed to appeal and documents were prepared by the faction leader and his core adherents. Capital to fight the case, which went as far as an appeal court in Kathmandu, was supplied by Bhagi Rath, who took some of Harake's kipat lands under mortgage. The original decision was eventually reversed, and the boy appointed Subba, with the stipulation that Harake would act on his behalf until he came of age.

In addition to their own households, Bishnu Prasad and Tunka Nath can count regularly on the support of four other households (between them) within the Cluster, and perhaps another six in settlements outside the Indreni area. Factional cores, then, are small. There are several reasons for this. Firstly, unless a man has political ambitions, the risks involved in commitment to a faction leader are too great. These risks are mainly financial.[1] A core adherent may have to

---

1 There are, of course, other considerations as well. Faction leaders and core adherents, although respected and even feared for their power, are thought by many to be trouble-makers, and a considerable amount of opprobrium attaches to their activities. Few peasants would care to exchange their relatively peaceful lives among amicable kin and neighbours for the rough-and-tumble arena of factional strife.

invest substantial sums of money in long-drawn-out struggles without any certainty of success. The costs of Jahare's battle for the title of Subba, for example, were in the region of Rs 1,200, with Jahare providing most of the money himself. Hence, few men are able or prepared to identify themselves with a faction unless they are regularly in need of support. There are circumstances when an ambitious man has no choice but to align himself with the core of a faction leader: as, for instance, when a traditional enemy gives his support to one leader, and forces his opponent to seek the security of the other.

A second reason for the limited size of cores is that faction leaders seek adherents who are more than mere sycophants. Core supporters must possess attributes which redound to the benefit of a faction. In addition to wealth, literacy is an essential criterion of core membership. Literacy in this context refers especially to a capacity to comprehend the Nepalese legal code, a formidable document of immense complexity, and a total mystery to all but a few.[1] Since most disputes involving substantial amounts of property or other wealth find their way to court, someone with a facility for supplying legal stratagems is a major asset to any faction. Men with ability to comprehend the written word and to prepare petitions and counter-petitions based on legal arguments are of prime importance to a faction leader.

The term 'core' suggests that a faction leader does rely on other occasional supporters as well. Both leader and core adherents generally possess the means to recruit supporters through relationships established in other contexts. Dependents on holdings are one such source, especially if they are near at hand. Although both faction leaders are Tharis, their holdings are at some distance from the Cluster. In 1965, however, Bishnu Prasad succeeded in obtaining the headmanship of a second holding, situated in a settlement a short distance from his home. Bhagi Rath resides on one of his holdings, while Dharma Raj and Padma Lal, who were disputing their late father's title, have both established headman-dependent-like ties with a number of households within the holding, which is situated nearby. The fact that headmanship ensures a fairly reliable fund of support was undoubtedly one of the motives for Jahare's attempt to gain the office of Nembeke Subba. And when Bishnu Prasad and Bhagi Rath opposed his claims to the title, Bhagi Rath was able to bolster his faction's case by recruiting

---

1 Until recently, court officials were political appointees without legal training, so that the court itself was less than capable of coping with the highly complicated law.

several of his own dependents to sign as witnesses on the petition presented to the appeal court.

Ties of kinship and affinity provide another source of potential recruits. Because Brahmans and Jaisis comprise the majority of the population in the region, members of these castes, especially wealthy families, are able to find spouses in nearby settlements, and so tend to have at least some of their relatives close at hand. Moreover, ties to certain kinds of relatives are strengthened in a ritual context, since, for example, sisters' husbands or sons, fathers' sisters' sons or daughters' sons can perform services as household priests (*purohit*). At one Shiva ritual sponsored by a core adherent of Tunka Nath, eleven relatives in the category of *purohit* to the host were invited to participate in the rite, and were appropriately fed and paid. Such men constitute an additional fund of occasional faction support.

Mortgages and tenancies create relationships which can be employed to mobilize backing. Both faction leaders and, with the exception of Jahare, all core adherents resident in the Cluster are among the Main Landholders; they are linked as landholders and landlords to twenty-four Limbu households on whom they can call for assistance now and again.[1] When Praja Pathi and Kula Madi (the sons of Narad Muni and Bishnu Prasad) accused one another of assault following an irrigation dispute, each presented a number of 'eye-witnesses' to the event testifying to his opponent's guilt. Several of these witnesses were Limbus dependent on the faction leaders for credit or tenancy rights, who were recruited to the factions for the duration of the case.

Finally, the status of Notable enjoyed by faction leaders places them in a position to do a variety of favours for others which accumulate as political debts to be collected at some future time.[2] Thus, a Limbu who had been accused of injuring a Brahman in a quarrel sought advice from Bishnu Prasad, who prepared his counter-petition to the Panchayat Court. Some time later a witness was required by Bishnu Prasad to attest to the latter's presence in a particular location and at a particular time to belie a charge that the faction leader had instigated an assault on a member of the opposing faction. The debt owed by the Limbu was collected, and the charge against the faction leader was

---

1 A few of the wealthiest political leaders also give some lands to non-Limbu tenants, and so have other potential supporters among them.

2 Faction leaders act both as 'patrons', when allocating favours to clients directly, and as 'brokers', when obtaining these favours as intermediaries (cf. Mayer, 1963).

dismissed. Notables also accumulate a store of favours because of their role in mediating disputes. A man who has sought and received justice at the hands of a Notable would be reluctant to refuse his support when called upon.

Faction leaders frequently seek to become involved in the disputes of others, and so make them their own. The struggle over the Nembeke headmanship is a case in point. Harake, in whose name the opposition to Jahare was mounted, was only to be regarded as a tool of Bishnu Prasad's faction, which seeks, at every opportunity, to thwart Jahare's ambitions. The motives for such tactics are often personal gain for the faction leaders and their core adherents, who charge for their various 'services', such as preparing petitions, and hope to share in the proceeds of any victory. Faction leaders themselves are quick to point this out, at least of their opposition. Thus, when a Limbu brought a petition against one faction leader the latter, in his counter-petition, noted that the Limbu was being 'carried' (*boknu*) by the opposing faction leader, whose 'tactics are to seek out two persons who are quarrelling and incite one side; and by this he hopes to gain something'. Support may be offered gratuitously only when failure to do so could result in economic or political loss to one faction or, alternatively, gain for its rival.

To what extent are disputes involving Indreni Limbus absorbed by factional rivalries? The bulk of cases in which Limbus are the disputants concern matters from which little profit is to be gained. This is to be expected because of the poverty of most Limbu households. But when a Limbu, especially one who is poor and illiterate, becomes implicated in a dispute where the stakes are high, allies with the necessary contacts, knowledge of law and court procedure are required to ensure any chance of success. To refuse the support of a faction leader in any important dispute would be to invite defeat and financial loss. Major quarrels are thus usually fed into the existing factional cleavage. The process is best illustrated by documenting a dispute over kipat land which has been smouldering for almost half a century and which has exercised two generations of faction leaders (see Fig. 7).

Following the death in 1922 of Tilbir, a Kambo of Chitok, Chinde, Tilbir's son by his first wife and Chinde's three sons opposed the right of Punja to inherit a portion of Tilbir's lands. Although Punja's mother had become Tilbir's second wife, it was widely believed that the woman had come to the Cluster in early pregnancy, and that Tilbir

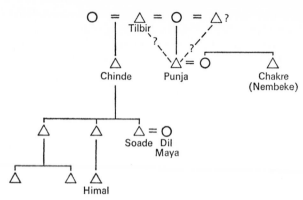

Figure 7

was not in fact Punja's genitor. Chinde and his sons were successful in their opposition and so, without adequate means to get a living, Punja went to Assam, where he worked on a tea plantation. He continued to return on occasion to the Cluster, since he had married the sister of Chakre, a Nembeke of Dorumba.

On one of his visits in 1945 he was approached by Ram Chandra, who was at the time leading a faction against his brother, Narad Muni, and urged to prefer charges against the latter for illegally encroaching on kipat land belonging to the Kambos.[1] Punja realized that if he could prove the case against the Brahman, then he might finally get the lands he had been denied as a young man. Moreover, no Kambo would contest his right, since by 1945 the sons of his half-brother Chinde had died or gone away, as had all their sons but one, Himal, who was in any case in India at the time. Of all those with rights to Tilbir's lands only Dil Maya, the wife of Chinde's youngest son, Soade, was resident in the Cluster. In any case, Ram Chandra pointed out, Dil Maya would not stand in Punja's way, since she had herself been victimized by Narad Muni on several occasions. Ram Chandra was certain that Punja could win his case, and offered to prepare the necessary documents.

In his petition to the court Punja argued:

'When I came back [from Assam] I found that my old house and the house of my brother's sons were no longer there. And there was a large house and

1 According to informants, Ram Chandra probably knew that Punja had returned from Assam with some money, which the former hoped to get for preparing the necessary documents.

there was Narad Muni. I said to him: "What is the matter that you have built a house on our kipat, and who gave it to you? You are a wicked person." Then I went to Dil Maya and asked her what had happened. She said that Narad Muni had driven away all the descendants of Chinde by his treachery. Narad Muni, she said, made her sign many documents. Dil Maya was afraid to refuse so great a man and anyway she is simple, so she signed. Now she does not know any more which lands are still kipat and which he has made raikar.'

Narad Muni's reply to the accusation was brief. He challenged the plaintiff to show that any of his transactions were illegal. He also brought up the fact of Punja's uncertain parentage and stressed that since Punja had not received an inheritance of kipat land he had no business inquiring about the lands. Narad Muni then directed the greater part of his attack towards Ram Chandra and Tunka Nath, since the latter was at the time aligned with his eldest brother. He accused them of inviting Punja back to the Cluster just to bring a case against him. In Narad Muni's words: 'They seek to destroy my property, and when they are through, they will send Punja back to Assam.'

Beside this explicit statement of the manner in which faction leaders instigate disputes, the alignment of support behind each faction leader illuminates the pattern of faction formation. Ram Chandra recruited his support for Punja on three bases. The first was hostility to Narad Muni. A father and son of the same Kambo lineage had recently quarrelled with Narad Muni and could be counted on to support a grievance against the latter. It should be noted, however, that the two were from an 'adopted' branch and so had no claim on Tilbir's lands. Consequently, Punja represented no threat to their own interests. A second basis was affinal ties. Three Nembeke men, among them the brother of Punja's wife, lent their support to the faction leader for the sake, as one put it, 'of our sister'. Thirdly, and to an extent this criterion subsumed the other two, was the feeling of hostility shared by all kipat-owning Limbus towards Brahman landholders. The kinds of accusations thrown at Narad Muni by Ram Chandra and Tunka Nath through the mouth of Punja echoed the common Limbu experience. On this basis four Chongbung elders, one of them a much-respected Subba, joined in support of Ram Chandra's faction. The fact that the latter was a Brahman as well was ignored in the circumstances of this particular quarrel.

Narad Muni, for his part, sought the kind of support which was meant to achieve two main purposes. The first was to attest to his status as a Notable, and *mutatis mutandis* his reputation as an honest man who accomplished his ends by legal means alone. This required several 'character' witnesses, whose own reputations were impeccable. To this end eleven prominent men were recruited from every corner of the village area. Three were affines, while another six, all Brahmans and Jaisis, were themselves landholders of kipat and undoubtedly saw in this case the threat of a precedent which could affect their own economic positions.

Of perhaps greater importance was the necessity for Narad Muni to present his opponents with a denial of Punja's right to kipat, and this could best be effected by recruiting the support of Himal, who was at the time working in India. The latter was sent for and brought to the Cluster, where he confirmed the denial of Punja's rights to kipat, and hence protected his own inheritance. On the basis of this latter evidence, and the lack of firm proof to back up Ram Chandra's allegations of dishonesty, the case was decided in favour of Narad Muni.

Another dispute erupted in 1964 following Himal's resettlement in the Cluster after a long residence in India. Although Himal, a Subba, owns a considerable amount of kipat land, 98% is under mortgage. To build a house and re-establish an estate in Chitok, he required capital, only some of which he could supply from savings accumulated during his residence abroad. He proceeded to raise the money by taking interest-free loans (*bard*) from those to whom his lands had already been pledged. The kipat lands of Tilbir which Narad Muni had taken under mortgage had been 'inherited' after the latter's death by his son, Praja Pathi (see Fig. 5). When Himal came to request *bard* from Praja Pathi, he was refused. At first Himal sought to transfer landholding rights from Praja Pathi to someone else willing to take the lands under mortgage. But the amount of the mortgage was out of all proportion to the value of the lands, and Himal could find no takers. In a rage, Himal decided to petition in court for the return of some of these lands on the argument that the landholders had falsified the figures on the documents so that they did not correspond with the amounts actually borrowed by the kipat-owners.[1] He requested the support of Tunka Nath, who welcomed the opportunity to involve his brother's son, Praja Pathi, in expensive litigation, since the latter had recently been making some embarrassing accusations about the

[1] Informants, including Praja Pathi, privately agreed that the figures probably had been altered by Narad Muni.

faction leader to government officials and, furthermore, had established good relations with the opposing faction of Bishnu Prasad.

The matter was brought to court, but before a decision could be reached several influential men in the district, most resident outside the village area, succeeded in convincing both disputants that by becoming involved in factional strife they were courting financial disaster. Subsequently, a compromise was reached which enabled Himal to repossess some of his lands.

This case indicates how attachment to faction leaders is temporary and lasts only as long as there is advantage to be gained. Himal first allied himself with Narad Muni against Ram Chandra and Tunka Nath, who were supporting his classificatory grandfather, Punja, and later joined forces with Tunka Nath against the son of Narad Muni. The basis for alignment in both instances was Himal's own interests. Similarly, a Kambo man who had supported Ram Chandra and Tunka Nath in the earlier dispute found himself urging mediation in this one because of ties both to Himal, as classificatory brother and next door neighbour, and to Praja Pathi, as tenant on the latter's land.

This case also illustrates the general tendency, evident from previous examples cited, for Limbus (including headmen such as Himal) to rely for support in their more important disputes on the Brahman faction leaders. Without the backing and know-how these men can provide, no impoverished and illiterate Indreni peasant can hope to gain satisfaction in a quarrel, however just his case may be.

The great majority of Limbus are able to avoid involvement in factions. Indeed, some are compelled to do so to avoid overlapping claims to their allegiance. Economic, political and kinship ties often place Limbu households under obligation to leaders of opposing factions. When a man finds himself in such circumstances he attempts to disengage completely from factional struggles. The dispute over the title of Subba provided one such occasion. Several of Jahare's affines were also dependents on Bhagi Rath's raikar holding in Dorumba, and efforts by both sides to enlist their support were assiduously and successfully avoided. Where this is impossible, however, a man tries to shift support from one faction to another as personal advantage or short-term obligation dictate.

But, in any event, the sanctions which a faction leader can bring to bear on those whose support he seeks are mitigated by several factors. One is the nature of the kipat system, which, as I pointed out in the

12

previous chapter, enables Limbus to manipulate land rights and so retain a measure of economic and political independence. But, as I suggested also, this freedom of manipulation is restricted where links between the Limbu and the landholder are more than single-purpose. And it is clear from the preceding paragraphs that a great many Limbus are beholden to the faction leaders and their core adherents not only for mortgage credit and tenancy contracts, but for their mediatory efforts, for occasional favours which only Notables are able to dispense, and for crucial assistance in waging disputes. *Vis-à-vis* such men, the 'freedom' conferred on Indreni Limbus by kipat-ownership counts for very little indeed.[1]

Of greater importance is the nature of homestead and settlement dispersion.[2] The inhabitants of Bharapa and Angbung, in particular, seldom have occasion to meet faction leaders and so are able to avoid becoming involved without too much difficulty. It is not surprising that the Limbus who are most frequently called on to support factions are resident in Chitok and Dorumba, where leaders and their core adherents reside.

But land tenure and household distribution are peripheral to a third factor: the nature of the political arena, i.e. the contexts within which factional struggles are waged. Faction leaders compete for economic prizes as well as power and influence. To make political gains supporters are, of course, necessary, but their effectiveness is not in numbers. As I have shown, faction leaders solicit core adherents who possess specific qualities which can be utilized in the furtherance of their interests. Other supporters are mobilized to lend credence to an argument, act as witness to an event, sign documents or attest to firmness of character. There is no context, however, in which the numerical strength of a faction is relevant. Although physical assault may lead to or result from factional strife, it is confined to two or three individuals, and does not lead to large-scale violence between factions. In brief, leaders do not attempt to employ coercive force as a means of achieving their ends, a practice which, if followed, could lead to the importance of sheer numbers as a measure of fraction strength.[3]

1 Kolenda, referring to *jajmani* ties, notes that the *jajman*'s power is greater if he and the *kamin* are linked in a variety of superordinate/subordinate relationships (1963, 23).
2 Residence patterns also bear on faction formation in Indian settlements in Fiji (Mayer, 1957, 324).
3 I cannot agree with Miller (1965, 26), who seems to suggest that the *number* of followers is always the chief test of faction strength.

Both Mayer (1957, 322) and Benedict (1957, 340) suggest that an emphasis on numbers might result from the establishment of an arena, defined by statute, within which elections for office can be held. The inclusion of the Indreni settlements within an administrative village and the creation of a statutory Panchayat Committee has provided a new context for factional activity. It has not yet (although it certainly might in the near future) brought about an increased awareness of the importance of numbers in the assessment of factional strength.

The Panchayat

The first attempts to introduce statutory Panchayats in Nepal date back to 1926. In that year, experiments in local government were carried out in the region of Kathmandu Valley and in 1930 were expanded to include four districts in both the hill areas and the Terai. It was not until 1948, however, that legislation was introduced allowing for the establishment of village Panchayats throughout the country. At that time a Panchayat Committee was formed of representatives from settlements in the Ilam-Darda sub-division of the district, which was constituted as a single 'village'. However, the revolution of 1951 aborted the Panchayats before they could begin functioning properly.

In 1953 the system was reintroduced, but this time Ilam-Darda was divided into three 'villages'. All inhabitants over twenty-one years of age became members of a Village Assembly (*sabha*), which met twice annually to approve the budget and discuss the development programmes before it. The members of the Assembly also chose nine men to represent them on a Panchayat Committee, and the latter, in turn, selected their own chairman and vice-chairman. The government appointed two prominent men of the area to act as president and vice-president, responsible for the proper conduct of the Panchayat Committee's business and, generally, to oversee its functioning. Additional supervision was provided by a District Panchayat and a specially created government department which audited the accounts of the Committee, approved its programme and had the power to suspend it or any of its members.

The main aims of the Panchayat, as set out in the Panchayat law, were to implement government programmes for welfare and development, collect essential census records and maintain law and order. The greatest emphasis was placed on the last-mentioned responsibility, and a Panchayat Court was established whose jurisdictional boundaries were defined by a special Act. The court was empowered to settle cases involving damages up to Rs 100 and for which fines of up to Rs 25 or imprisonment for up to three months could be meted out. In addition, it could offer mediation facilities for all cases, regardless of the amount of damages involved, provided they were not cognizable by government courts. The Panchayat Court consisted of five men chosen by the chairman of the Committee, two of whom had to live in or nearby the settlements of the litigants and so be familiar with them. Members of the Court had also to be rotated on a regular basis, with no member serving more than one month at a time. The chairman or vice-chairman of the Committee was required to attend all its sessions. During the four years of its existence the Court seldom used the powers given it by the law. Instead, it sought to effect a cooling of tempers and to promote compromises.[1] Acceptance of a Court decision in one dispute did not necessarily mean that the same litigants would not reappear before it under a different pretext. Where factional issues were involved, Court arbitration afforded only a temporary lull in the storm of litigation.

Under the present Panchayat system established in 1962, emphasis is laid on the encouragement of 'self-help' development schemes, and involvement in judicial matters is actively discouraged. Not only has a Panchayat Court not been established, but a Panchayat Committee which seeks to utilize the powers previously held by the Court must request special authority from the government.

The Panchayat Committee established in 1953 did not absorb the existing factional cleavages. The village contained an area and a population considerably larger than that within which any faction leader could exert his influence effectively. Also, the purpose and authority of the Panchayat system could not be readily understood at the time of its inception. It was, and to an extent still is, perceived as an instrument of government created to implement the instructions of district and central authorities. The appointment by the government

1 Indreni Limbus tended not to bring their disputes to the Panchayat Court. Of the 200-odd cases it entertained, Limbus were involved in only five; and in three of these the litigation was initiated by a member of another group. Their reluctance to bring quarrels to the Panchayat Court is explained partly by their preference for informal mediation (usually by other Limbus) and partly by their opposition to the Panchayat system in general. See pp. 168ff.

of a president to oversee the day-to-day workings of the first Panchayat Committee further served to prevent the use of the Committee as an arena for factional dispute. The man chosen to fill the position was a Brahman pandit highly respected for his learning and impartiality in mediating quarrels. He and the vice-president, another Brahman of similar status, were largely responsible for the formation of the nine-man Committee, although in theory the choice was that of the adult population. One faction leader, Tunka Nath, was chosen to be a member of the executive, but, being only one Notable among many on the Committee, most of whom were neutral to any faction, he had little opportunity to transform the Committee into an instrument for strengthening his faction.

Circumstances connected with the establishment in 1962 of the new Panchayat system changed the attitudes of faction leaders to the Committee.[1] For one thing, the area under its jurisdiction, i.e. Syawa village, was reduced to about one-third of its former size and so came within the purview of their influence. Secondly, the posts of government-appointed president and vice-president were abolished so that the choice of the Committee would be entirely an internal matter. The effective head is now the chairman, chosen from among the nine ward representatives who comprise the Committee. Thirdly, those who had controlled the previous Committee were either outside the new village, too old to assume the responsibilities of office, or refused to participate on the grounds that the responsibilities were not matched by commensurate gains. All these factors weighed on faction-leader Bishnu Prasad's decision to represent his ward, composed almost entirely of Limbu households in Bharapa and Chitok.[2] No attempt was made by Tunka Nath directly to oppose the candidacy of his brother. Informants I asked about this stressed the fact that Tunka Nath had been on the previous Committee and so 'had his chance'. Also, the idea that elections should be held to choose a representative was felt to be bad, as they would 'show our quarrels'.[3] Tunka Nath, however, tried to persuade one of the ex-army pensioners, Lajahang, to join the Committee, knowing that if he did Bishnu Prasad would stand down. Although there was some feeling in the ward that it should

---

1 Following the demise of the first system in 1956, another Panchayat Act was introduced, but no measures were taken in Ilam to set up Committees.
2 Households in Angbung and Dorumba are bunched together with those in neighbouring settlements to form two other wards.
3 No elections were held in any of the wards.

be represented by a Limbu, Lajahang refused and deferred in favour of Bishnu Prasad. Once it was known that the latter was to enter the Committee, it was a foregone conclusion that he would be its chairman. He was able to ensure that the majority of ward representatives were men of no consequence, and that they were either his own supporters or not attached to any faction. The notion that the Committee should reflect the caste composition in the village limited the choice somewhat. It was felt, for example, that at least one representative should be a Limbu. Since Bishnu Prasad was himself from a Limbu-dominated ward, Jahare was chosen to represent the ward which includes Dorumba. This was the only successful attempt by Tunka Nath to place one of his adherents on the Committee.

When the Committee came to elect its chairman, Jahare suggested that he might seek the office. But when he realized he would have no support he made no attempt to carry out his threat. Bishnu Prasad was then chosen by acclamation. Shortly thereafter Jahare became involved in a court case with the district administration – which, he alleged, was instigated by Bishnu Prasad – and ceased attending Committee meetings. He was replaced by another Nembeke of Dorumba – Budibal, Lajahang's son-in-law – who is not affiliated to any faction.

Thus Bishnu Prasad succeeded in packing the Panchayat Committee with men who would not oppose his will and who are, by and large, ready to rubber-stamp his actions. But the fact that one faction leader monopolizes the statutory authority which resides in the Committee does not preclude the existence of opposition on the level of policy-making. This is because decisions are arrived at by consensus of a body wider than the Panchayat Committee.

Meetings are seldom held, and important issues never broached, without the participation of at least some Notables who are not in fact members of the nine-man Committee. Except during the rainy season, meetings are held regularly, so that anyone interested in attending knows where and when to come. Although the Committee has the authority to initiate a wide range of actions, when an important decision is to be taken invitations are sent to influential men in the area requesting them to be present. Committee deliberations thereby take on the character of informal gatherings of Notables. This 'comprehensive committee', as Mayer (1960, 116ff.) calls a similar body in Ramkheri, is not given formal recognition and has no fixed membership or existence outside the framework of Committee decision-making.[1] It is also to be distinguished from a formally constituted sub-committee, with an executive and determinate membership which may be established to deal with special projects. Thus, for example, when it was decided to build a Panchayat house, a sub-committee consisting of twenty-four of the wealthiest village residents was set up to collect subscriptions.

The Panchayat Committee, then, is subsumed by a plenary body composed of men who are traditional leaders. Members of the former, other than Bishnu Prasad and one or two other articulate persons, voice no opinions in the presence of these men of influence. In such a setting, members of the faction opposed to Bishnu Prasad – who attend Committee meetings regularly – participate in decision-making. There is room for factional hostility to be expressed in opposing views of various Committee projects, but a middle way can be sought under the guise of working for 'national development' (*bikas*). Matters are never taken to a vote. Discussions which cannot be resolved at one meeting are carried over to the next until a suitable compromise is reached.[2] Often a decision taken at one meeting is countermanded at the next when news of the decision reaches the ears of Notables who were not present at the previous meeting. Minutes are kept, but they mention only those in attendance and what the Committee eventually decided.

Thus the established procedure of seeking consensus achieves the dual purpose of containing factional strife and enabling the Committee to carry out its tasks of local government. When the Committee attempts to ignore the wider consultative body on important matters it risks bringing factional opposition out into the open. This happened when Bishnu Prasad attempted to win the approval of the Village Assembly – which must ratify the Committee's annual budget – for a tax plan which had been prepared without the prior approval of the plenary body. The faction opposing the Committee chairman, Bishnu Prasad, gathered sufficient support to stage a walk-out, and so broke up the meeting before the required number of signatures could be gathered to legalize the proposal.

There are signs of a growing realization on the part of the faction

---

1 The 'comprehensive committee' in Ramkheri, however, was a more formal body, itself having officers.
2 Commenting on the nature of consensus in a committee, Bailey (1965, 8) states: '... everyone knows that if the decision is not the result of an agreed compromise, then it cannot be implemented'.

leaders that control of the Committee is an essential prerequisite for building a strong following. Kathmandu's emphasis on the development of a viable Panchayat system has meant that government officials at the district level are especially sensitive to anything they regard as an attempt to hamstring the work of the Committee. Opposition to proposals of the Committee, or to its manner of implementing government programmes, thus tends to be equated with opposition to the Panchayat system. A faction leader in control of the Committee can increasingly disregard the traditional methods of achieving consensus and pressure others to conform to his policies under the veiled threat of denunciation as 'opponents' (*birodhi*) of the Panchayat system. Several men, among them supporters of faction leader Tunka Nath who have been vocal in their disagreement with certain Committee proposals, have been called to Ilam Bazaar for a browbeating by various government officials.

Ultimately, of course, a determined Committee could exercise its statutory powers to take all necessary decisions without reference to a more comprehensive body. Thus, a new coercive weapon has been added to the arsenal of the faction leader entrenched in the Committee, and could lead to a shift in the delicate balance between the two factions. Given the continued development of this trend, it is possible to foresee the Committee becoming the principal arena for factional strife. In such circumstances, formal election procedures could replace the hitherto consensual methods of choosing representatives. It would follow then, logically, that new emphasis would be placed on the large-scale recruitment of factional following and, alternatively, on the need for residents of the village area, including Limbus, to take sides to a greater degree than they now need to do.

The Limbus, led by their Subbas, have all along opposed the Panchayat system. In 1952, when district authorities first invited the Subbas of Ilam to encourage support for the system among their followers, the response was a plea urging the government to withdraw its intentions to establish Panchayat Committees.[1] Indeed, Subbas are often given credit for the fact that the system was abolished in 1956. This opposition is related to the fact that as the Committee, at the government's instigation, becomes the main repository of authority in the settlements, it threatens to assume the few remaining prerogatives of the traditional Limbu headmen. At the same time, Limbu hostility

1 See p. 185.

to the Panchayat system must be viewed in the context of their relationships to the Brahmans, who dominate the Committee which encroaches, in a number of ways, on the daily lives of the Limbus.

During the time I spent in the Indreni settlements the issue which most exercised their antagonism to the Committee was a project to erect a Panchayat house. About 80% of the financing was to be raised from village residents. For the purpose of apportioning contributions, members of the Committee placed everyone in one of four categories on the basis of impressionistic (though fairly accurate) assessments of wealth. Although about 90% of Limbu households were placed in the two lowest categories (contributions of Rs 6 and Rs 20) the general feeling among the Limbus was that the level of contributions was too high. For months, whenever Limbus gathered in some numbers the topic of conversation turned immediately to the Panchayat Committee and the financial burden it had imposed. Resentment at having to pay what for most was a considerable sum was directed firstly at the Panchayat system as such. The Committee was seen to have replaced what for the Limbus was a far superior system based on the traditional ties between Subba and lineage dependent. At one gathering, an elder (who had been placed in the Rs 20 category) spoke at some length about how the Committee only makes demands for money, but never seems to accomplish anything. 'What kind of Committee is this which takes money from the government [which contributed 20% of the costs] and from the people, but shows nothing for it?' He went on to compare the Committee to the Subbas, 'who did everything for the people and who returned whatever they took'. The allusion was to the traditional balance of rights and obligations which characterized the Subba's relations with his dependents. By implication, he accused the Committee of emphasizing only its rights at the expense of its obligations.[1]

Although Limbus disapprove of the Panchayat system as a whole, they especially resent Brahman control of the Committee. In Syawa village five of the nine Committee members, including chairman Bishnu Prasad, are Brahmans; three of them – again including the chairman – members of a single lineage. The two wards in which Limbus are a majority are represented by Bishnu Prasad and his late brother Gobinda's son, Hari Charan. Limbu residents do not feel that

1 To be fair, not only the Limbus complained about having to contribute to the building; but members of other groups did not express their anger in quite the same terms.

their best interests are being served by these men. At one stage, protests were voiced about the lack of consultation over the categorization of the Indreni population for the assignment of contributions to the proposed Panchayat house. The Limbus were not satisfied with the explanation that the ward representatives had made the assignments. They complained bitterly that they had played no part in choosing their representatives in the first place, and had no confidence in them. Following a threat by the Committee executive that the police would be called in if contributions were not forthcoming, a number of Angbung residents met informally. One of the Subbas suggested bringing a complaint to the government against the Brahmans, 'who because they are rich and educated run the Committee and think they can do anything they want to do'. There was much talk of refusing to pay, and of fighting the matter in court, or, if necessary, resisting with force.

In the face of the government-backed authority of the Panchayat Committee, the Limbus knew from the start that resistance would lead nowhere. When I left the Cluster the building was nearing completion and the rate of payment of Limbu contributions was keeping pace with that of the rest of the village population. The occasion had provided an opportunity to express hostility to the Committee, regarded as a usurper of the power of the Subbas and an instrument of the Brahmans.

The intercalary position of Limbu Notables

To this point in the chapter I have shown how, since the end of the nineteenth century, due mainly to the improvement in their economic position, Brahmans have become politically ascendant in the region of the Indreni settlements. The Limbus accept their mediation in disputes, require their assistance in litigation, and are increasingly bound by the decisions of the Panchayat Committee, which they dominate. In a word, the Limbus are subordinate to the Brahmans in virtually every aspect of their political relations.

Recently, however, Gurkha service has created wealth and status differences within the Limbu community which have begun to alter the traditional ties between the two groups. The rise of a small class of affluent Limbus, recognized as Notables in the wider society, has introduced an 'intercalary' category into the Indreni settlements. On the one hand these Notables have interests in maintaining their ties with the Limbus and in promoting the unity of this group in opposition to the Brahmans. On the other hand, they have an equal, though contradictory, interest in stressing their association with the dominant section within the wider society. In the following paragraphs I consider each tendency in turn.

There is no question of Limbu Notables validating their status in terms of marriages with members of high Hindu castes. They tend, instead, to create marriage links, where possible, with Limbus of similar status in other settlement clusters, so developing a far-reaching network of affines who constitute an *élite* sector of the Limbu population.

A variety of considerations motivates Limbu Notables to maintain amicable relations within the Cluster. They require, certainly no less than others, the co-operation of kinsmen and neighbours in a number of contexts: lineage mates to conduct the proper rites following a death; supporters to help out in a number of crisis situations, such as those arising out of adultery; assistance in carrying out the manifold tasks involved in entertaining large numbers of guests at funerary and marriage feasts; witnesses to sign documents written at the time of land transactions, and so on.

Important economic benefits also attend Limbu Notables who cultivate their ties in the Indreni settlements. The wealthiest among them cultivate substantial land-holdings, requiring labour resources they are unable to provide from their own households alone. They are compelled, therefore, to meet their needs by exchanging labour with neighbouring households and, when this source is exhausted, by engaging agricultural wage labourers. I have pointed out how Limbu households which hire out labour accept less than 'market' rates from Indreni employers, since their links to the latter are more than single-interest in nature. By keeping active their ties to kinsmen and neighbours the Limbu Notables thus guarantee their supply of a relatively cheap source of labour.

The importance of identifying with the Limbu community derives also from their interests in maintaining the kipat system. The guarantee of perpetual ownership rights enables men to serve in the army for long periods of time in the knowledge that the lands they and their kinsmen own will still be intact and, if mortgaged, available for redemption on their return to active social life in the community. Thus, Limbu Notables who are all ex-army men share, in common with all Limbus, a fundamental interest in kipat tenure and in combating any attempts to compromise their rights. Lajahang, the Cluster's most prominent Limbu Notable, was on the organizing committee for a mass meeting held in 1958 to draw up a petition urging the government to make no changes in the kipat system.[1]

Indeed, wealthy Limbus benefit most from the system. They obtain access to land at a reasonable cost and on a relatively secure basis. I have noted how a serviceman or pensioner utilizes his relationships within the Limbu community to obtain landholding rights to kipat. Since the land is in all likelihood already mortgaged, he expects the kipat-owner to co-operate in transferring the rights away from the present landholder, probably a member of another group. Once installed as landholder himself, he seeks to hold the mortgage at the lowest possible level by keeping the demands of the kipat-owner for incremental loans (*bard*) to a minimum. Table 24 compares the percentage of the total amount of land held under mortgage by three categories of landholder with the percentage of mortgage credit provided by these persons.

TABLE 24
Comparison of mortgage distribution (in units and cash value)

	Percentage of mortgaged land held	Percentage of mortgage credit provided
	%	%
Limbus resident in Cluster	21·3	15·5
Brahmans resident in Cluster	11·3	12·1
Brahmans resident outside Cluster	35·6	41·3

It will be noted that Limbus resident in the Cluster have provided only 15·5% of all mortgage credit on Indreni kipat while holding 21·3% of the land mortgaged. The proportion is equally favourable for the two Notables Lajahang and Parsade, who are the largest Limbu landholders. Between them, they hold 10·1% of the land and have provided only 6·5% of all mortgage loans. The multiplicity of convergent ties with Limbu neighbours would also provide an explanation for the fact that Brahmans resident in the Cluster – among whom are the faction leaders and their core adherents – have provided a lower amount of mortgage credit in relation to the lands they hold under

1 See the next chapter for a discussion of the moves to preserve kipat land.

mortgage than those resident outside the Indreni settlements. The latter must 'pay' a higher price for their land because their links with the kipat-owners are by and large only single-interest.

Limbu Notables are also concerned to obviate the threat of the land they have taken under mortgage being transferred to yet other land-holders. I know of only one case where a kipat-owner took land away from a Limbu Notable, and in this instance the former needed the land to trade off to an Indreni Brahman with whom he was involved in a complicated transaction. These Notables, by meeting the expectations of kinsmen and neighbours, can enjoy a reasonable measure of security on their landholdings.

What are these expectations? There are, of course, obligations attached to the roles of kinsman and neighbour. They are supposed to assist one another in disputes, come to the aid of one another in times of need, behave in a ritually acceptable manner if they are agnates, etc. But those regarded as Notables, because of their wealth and pro-minence, must expect the demands of others to exceed the normal expectations. Limbu Notables are continuously under pressure to provide loans and tenancies, or to create jobs either as agricultural labourers[1] or domestic servants for Indreni relatives who have no other means of livelihood. Their overall importance in the economic life of the Cluster is evident in the number of Indreni households which are in one way or another dependent upon them. The two wealthiest Notables, Lajahang and Parsade, for example, aside from being linked as landholders to twenty-two (30%) kipat-owning households in the Cluster, are landlords to ten Limbu tenant households and have loaned money to another seven households, three of them already linked by mortgage or tenancy ties. Hardly a household in the Indreni settlements has not at one time or another worked for wages on the fields these men cultivate, and at least two households provide regular domestic services for them. Their economic relationships extend to all four Indreni settlements and reach beyond the boundaries of lineage or clan segment.

Other kinds of demands are made on Notables by virtue of their prominence in the community. I have already described the im-portance of these men as mediators in disputes. Their help is also sought in a variety of other matters. Men from every part of the Cluster request their support in a quarrel, urge them to reverse a

---

1 Notables frequently hire kinsmen and neighbours who are too old to be employable elsewhere.

decision of the Panchayat Committee, or merely seek their advice on the wording of a document or the advisability of giving a daughter to a suitor. On most mornings a handful of men are to be found in the adjacent courtyards of Lajahang and Parsade arguing, pleading, gossiping or merely enjoying the company of others whom they might otherwise seldom meet. In a very real sense, these Notables have become the focus of social life in the Limbu community.

This suggests that the existence of a nucleus of very wealthy men among the Limbus serves a latent purpose, viz. the exertion of a centripetal influence on social life in the Cluster. This tends to counteract the centrifugal forces of the terrain, settlement distribution and the highly individuated character of the household. Because of their wealth and status, Limbu Notables bring together at such important occasions as weddings and funerals residents from every part of the Indreni settlements. At the wedding of Lajahang's grandson, for example (which Lajahang financed, since the boy was a part of his household), every Indreni household was represented. In the absence of other Cluster-wide rituals, these events serve as an important means of stressing the links among all Limbu residents in the settlements, and bolstering their awareness of themselves as a distinct community.

Wealth and high military rank earned in Gurkha service also confer on Limbu Notables a high status within the wider society beyond the confines of the Cluster. I have noted how Brahmans must adjust their attitudes and behaviour towards a traditionally undifferentiated Limbu population to take account of this newly emergent category. Commensal barriers between Brahmans and wealthy Limbus by no means disappear, but they are restricted to ritually relevant exchanges only and are not extended to include neutral foods, as happens when other Limbus are involved. Notables are also addressed by high grade honorifics (*tapai*), and greeted as equals by Brahmans who normally behave towards other Limbus as superiors to inferiors.[1]

Notable status within the wider society gives these Limbus certain interests which they share in common with wealthy Brahmans, and the protection of which imposes co-operation between affluent sections of both groups. The intercalative nature of their position was dramatized in the spring of 1964, when rice prices in the area rose in response to seasonal shortages. The District Panchayat offered to

[1] See Chapter 4.

import rice from the Terai and sell it to the Committee for resale in the village at controlled prices. In common with other poor sections of the population, Indreni Limbus supported the idea. But at the meeting of the Committee where the matter was discussed, the 'comprehensive committee' composed of Notables opposed the scheme. The argument centred on the difficulty of transporting the rice to the village and the problem of distribution. Informants, however, were quick to point out that the Notables, most of whom sold rice in the area, were concerned about the threat to their commerce. The Limbu Notables, who in fact sell very little rice, at first appeared to support the plan, since they realized that the Limbus would be among those benefiting from controlled prices. Under pressure from other Notables, however, they agreed to a proposal for 'further investigation', which effectively shelved the idea.

The nature of Limbu antagonism to the Brahmans conflicts with the desire of Limbu Notables to maintain good relations with Brahmans, especially those in the Cluster. The manner in which one minor dispute was settled indicates how highly amicable relations are prized. When cattle tended by Parsade's son destroyed some wheat growing in (faction leader) Tunka Nath's fields, the latter tied up the cattle and asked both Parsade and Lajahang to assist in estimating the crop damage. Tunka Nath reminded them that this was the third time such a thing had occurred and that if someone other than Parsade's son had been responsible he would have 'tied him to a post and beat him'. The entire procedure of negotiation over the amount of damage was quite unlike any similar occasion I had witnessed. It was characterized by extreme politeness and constant reassurances on both sides that there was no quarrel between them, only a need to arrive at a fair figure for compensation, so that Parsade's son would realize that he had to be punished for endangering the good relations which had always existed between these men. Tunka Nath addressed both Limbus in high-grade honorific terms and referred to them as his elder brothers (*dajyu*). Agreement was reached (over tea) without the need for mediators. Several passers-by were asked only for their opinion of the amount of damage, since wheat is a new crop in the region. The only note of discord was sounded by one of these observers, who inquired if a promissary bond was not required. He was turned on by both the Limbus and the Brahman, who reminded him that the word of a Notable is sufficient bond.

Limbu Notables are of two minds about their relations with the

Panchayat Committee. On the one hand, prominent men are expected to associate themselves with the aims of the Committee, and they are continually pressured by other Notables (and now by the government) to participate in its deliberations. There are advantages to be gained from such association, since the Committee provides the opportunity for a periodic display of notability. On a variety of holidays the village's most influential residents are given the platform for several minutes, during which they comment appropriately on the significance of the particular occasion for the gathering. The order of speech-making reflects the assessment of status, and the right to speak is usually awarded those who attend Committee meetings with some regularity. There is another advantage to be gained by attending meetings: the opportunity to influence decisions taken by the Committee. When one Notable complained about the amount he was being asked to contribute towards the erection of the Panchayat house, he was reminded that he was invited to attend but had not shown up at the meeting at which the assessments were decided. Thus a Notable who refuses to associate with the Committee invites criticism from his peers and perhaps from officials of the administration, forfeits the opportunity to display his prominence and risks being left out of decisions which might affect him.

On the other hand, if Limbu Notables were to be too closely identified with the Committee, they would be regarded as working hand-in-hand with the Brahmans against the interests of the Limbus. Since the Committee is seen by Limbus as a direct challenge to the traditional rights and privileges of the Subbas, the Notables could well jeopardize their ties within the Limbu community by becoming too involved in Committee affairs. Since the Panchayat's inception in 1953, they have carefully avoided serving as Committee members. When the present system was established in 1962, Tunka Nath sought to encourage Lajahang to represent the Chitok-Bharapa ward instead of Bishnu Prasad, who had announced his intention of becoming the candidate. Lajahang refused on several grounds. Firstly, he was determined to avoid becoming involved in factional strife, and it was obvious that an overriding motive for Tunka Nath's suggestion was to keep his brother out of the Committee. Secondly, Lajahang knew that involvement in a contest for domination of the Committee would change the amicable relations he enjoyed with Brahman Notables in the area, and especially with those in the Cluster – relations which he was anxious to preserve. Finally, despite the support of the Limbu residents in the ward, Lajahang realized that he would be highly vulnerable to accusations of being in league with the Brahmans if he did accept the position. As he explained: 'They [the Limbus] begged me to be a representative, but if I had accepted, then whatever the Committee would decide would anger them, and they would murmur among themselves that I was working with the Brahmans against them.'

The same reasoning was behind the Limbu Notables' decision not to serve on a special sub-committee established to collect subscriptions for the building project. Both Lajahang and Parsade were elected to the sub-committee's executive at a Committee meeting which they did not attend. At the following meeting they resigned their posts, pleading impending absence away from the Cluster on other business. The level of assessments was deeply resented by the Limbus, a fact of which the Notables were aware. The sensitivity of the latter to any suggestion that they were in any way responsible for categorizing the Limbus for purposes of assessment is illustrated by the following incident: During a meeting with several members of the Committee a number of Limbus demanded to know the person responsible for deciding how they were to be differentiated for purposes of assessment. In an attempt to assuage their resentment, the Committee members stated that Lajahang had been present at the meeting in question (which he was) and had taken responsibility for assigning the Limbus to the various categories (which he had not). The Limbus thereupon met with Lajahang, who assured them that not he but the Brahman representative of the ward had suggested the categorization.

What can be described as the balance of conflicting expectations on the small class of wealthy ex-servicemen thus defines the limits of their political activities based on the Committee. They participate in its activities in so far as such participation is consistent with their status as Notables, but they are careful to avoid being too closely associated with its decisions, for fear of jeopardizing their relationships among the Limbus.

Recently, however, new associations have been created under the aegis of government, which provide for political expression by Limbu Notables. What is more, by participation in the new associations, they avoid the conflicting demands inherent in their intercalary positions. This is because these bodies, by their very nature and definition, exclude anyone other than ex-servicemen, which in effect means most Brahmans and certainly all Brahman Notables.

13

The primary school in the Indreni Cluster was built in 1958 with funds provided by the District Soldiers' Board, an organization of ex-Gurkha servicemen with branches throughout those areas of Nepal which contain heavy ex-army populations. The Board was established in 1952 to administer a fund given by the India government to the government of Nepal for the benefit of Nepalese who had served in World War II.[1] The money has been used to build dispensaries and schools throughout the country. The District Soldiers' Board provided an initial grant of Rs 750 to build the Indreni school, and continues to pay the salaries of its three teachers.

The organization of the Soldiers' Board in Ilam provides for a three-man district executive to administer financial allocations and to handle matters of liaison with education authorities. The executive appoints a representative in each of the district's four sub-divisions, who is responsible for working with the local school committees. Lajahang is the vice-president of the District Soldiers' Board in Ilam and Parsade is the Board's representative for the Ilam-Darda subdivision of the district.

The former has also been president and the latter treasurer of the Indreni school committee since its creation in 1958. Because the curriculum of the school is laid down by the education authorities, the committee has a largely administrative and watchdog function. Meetings discuss payment of school fees, employment of teachers and maintenance of the school building. In contradistinction to their attitude to the Panchayat Committee, Indreni Limbus regard the school committee as representing their own interests. Because it is effectively controlled by Limbu Notables, other Limbus attend its meetings and accept minor responsibilities if asked to do so by the executive. Of the twenty members, excluding the president and treasurer, nine are Limbus from the Cluster, though only four of these have children attending school. The remainder are mainly Newars and members of 'drinking' caste groups.

The Ex-Servicemen's Association provides Limbu Notables with yet another framework for political activity. The Association is one of seven 'class organizations'[2] created along with the Panchayat system in

1 The fund is called the 'Central Co-ordination Board Post-war Reconstruction Fund'. Cf. Hitchcock, 1963, 80.
2 The other six 'classes' are peasants, labour, women, students, youth and children. By 1964 only the Ex-Servicemen's Association had established an organization in the settlements of Ilam.

1962, and is designed to serve the interests of veterans of the Indian, British and Nepal armies. The organization of the Association parallels the four-tier Panchayat structure with executive bodies at the village,[1] district, zonal and national levels, and sends two representatives to the National Panchayat.

Lajahang and Parsade are chairman and treasurer of the village executive, and Jahare, the only other Limbu regarded as a Notable in the Cluster, is its secretary. Parsade is also treasurer of the district executive, while Lajahang is a member of the zonal executive. The Association concerns itself with improving pension-paying facilities and money-transfer arrangements for servicemen, so that its activities are conducted outside the arena of settlement politics. Recently the district executive obtained a grant of land in the Terai adequate for the resettlement of 200 families of ex-servicemen in the first stage. Conceivably, membership of the village executive, hitherto a post conferring prestige but little other advantage, could become important for dispensing patronage. But this is still in the future.

[1] To establish a 'village' executive there must be 100 ex-servicemen who are paid-up members of the Association. For this reason Association 'villages' may extend beyond the boundaries of Panchayat villages. There are forty-nine units of the latter kind in Ilam, and only thirty-eight units of the former.

Chapter 7

Land, culture and politics

Certain political attitudes and activities within the Indreni Cluster can only be understood against the wider background of the Limbu struggle to preserve their lands under the traditional system of tenure. In this chapter I discuss first the movement which has provided a framework for common action against the government's threats to reduce or abolish kipat lands. I then consider how cultural exclusiveness serves as a weapon in the political struggle.

Because kipat has for some time been unique to the Limbus, they virtually do not distinguish between their land-tenure system and their way of life. Kipat is fused with and articulates the culture. Indeed, many Limbus (and some members of other groups) believe that 'kipat' is a term in the Limbu tongue and, having been granted only to Limbus, is symbolic of their exclusiveness as a community and their 'apartness' from the rest of Nepal society.[1] In the words of one Limbu spokesman: 'Our social, cultural and religious beliefs, way of life, and administration under the kipat system are completely different from those prevalent in the rest of the country' (quoted in Regmi, 1965, 131).

In so far as the system of land tenure is included under the rubric of culture, any assault on kipat is seen as a threat to the very existence of the Limbus as a separate community within the society. Thus cultural identity becomes political identity in the context of the struggle to preserve the kipat system.

---

1 Some writers (Pradhananga, 1953; Chemjong, 1961) insist that kipat applies only to land cleared and brought under cultivation by Limbus. Regmi, however, argues that the term probably originated in the western part of the country and reached Limbuan some years after the imposition of Shah rule (1965).

The Limbu movement[1]

Since at least the late nineteenth century there have been sporadic attempts to organize opposition among the Limbus to stem the tide of kipat conversions to raikar tenure. There is no evidence[2] that any permanent political association to represent Limbu interests was ever set up or that any single leader arose to give clear direction to the movement. Rather, *ad hoc* committees of Subbas on a district-wide and occasionally even Limbuan-wide level were established from time to time, usually to protest against adverse legislation or the threat of such legislation.

Thus between 1913 and 1917 the Limbus of Ilam were compelled to present a united front against the authorities when the district became the locus of a concerted effort on the part of Kathmandu severely to restrict – indeed, virtually to abolish – lands held under the kipat system.[3] The restrictions of 1901 on the permanent alienation of kipat had intensified an already growing practice by Limbus of giving their lands to non-Limbu creditors under usufructuary mortgages. Even those diminishing wastelands brought under cultivation by Limbus had to be mortgaged almost as soon as they were reclaimed. In 1913 the government sought to freeze the amount of kipat land in Ilam by ruling that any new lands brought under cultivation by the Limbus between the revenue settlements of 1890 and 1912

1 I might have referred to the activities here described as those of a 'pressure group', since their main aim has been to bring about political change. But the term 'movement' is preferred because it better conveys the fact that these protests and pressures and the manner of their organization lacked the corporate character of formal group action.

2 In the absence of proper documentation, my information is far from adequate, and I have no doubt that the events mentioned in these paragraphs represent only a small proportion of Limbu protests over the years. This is not intended, therefore, as an historical account of the movement, but only as an indication of one kind of political activity employed to protect Limbu interests.

3 By this time members of non-Limbu groups formed the majority of the population in Ilam, so that the amount of land under kipat tenure was out of proportion to the number of Limbus inhabiting the district. Moreover, from the viewpoint of the government, Ilam was the most vulnerable part of Limbuan, due to its smaller ratio of Limbus. Kathmandu would often test its kipat proposals there to gauge the reaction before deciding whether or not to apply them in other kipat areas.

would be converted into raikar tenure. The rule was then amended to allow that 10% of these reclaimed lands could remain under kipat tenure and the amount in excess of that figure would become raikar. In 1917 legislation was proposed to convert into raikar tenure all mortgaged kipat lands which were not redeemed within six months, and to register as raikar any lands pledged in future.[1] If the pattern in the Indreni settlements was anything like typical of the situation in the district as a whole, it is unlikely that less than half of all kipat lands were mortgaged at the time. The introduction of such a ruling would in effect have abolished the kipat system in Ilam. At the same time it would have transferred ownership rights to the predominantly Brahman creditors who held the usufruct of these lands.

To counter these proposals, meetings were held in Limbu settlements throughout the district, and over 300 men, most of them Subbas, were delegated to appear before the government officials hearing the case. I was not able to discover how the Limbu campaign was conducted nor precisely what arguments were conveyed to the officials. Indreni informants with whom I discussed the matter suggested that the officials must have realized that if they had tried to enforce such regulations there would have been widespread unrest in the district. In any event the authorities were impressed by the intensity of the opposition to both the 1913 and the 1917 proposals and withdrew them, apparently after receiving vague promises – which they knew could not be kept – that kipat lands would in future not be mortgaged.

Disparities between the country's legal code and special regulations enacted to deal with the land problems of Limbuan led to the formation of another *ad hoc* committee of Subbas in 1946. Several headmen from Ilam, including one from the Cluster, were invited to join the committee, consisting of about forty-five members, to make recommendations for the avoidance of contradictory rules pertaining to kipat land. The Subbas pointed out that in cases where the law of the state conflicted with customary laws relevant only to kipat, the courts tended to ignore the latter. They urged that a Subba familiar with the 'customary rules' be attached to the court as a consultant, since the officers of the court were not always aware that such contradictions did in fact exist. They also suggested that a special law be written for Limbus. Neither of these suggestions was adopted, but the authorities did issue an

1 Government of Nepal, order regarding kipat land in Ilam and Das Majhia, 1917.

order (*sanad*) reaffirming many of the regulations issued in the past and promising to resolve some of the discrepancies in the law. Whether any concrete action was in fact contemplated is doubtful, since similar promises had been made in the past. Shortly after the issuance of the order the government released its plans for a Panchayat system which the Subbas regarded as inimical to their interests. Before the plan could be effected, however, the Rana government was swept out of office.

The suggestion to create a special law for the Limbus is noteworthy because it demonstrates that the pressures directed against the government were not – indeed, could not be – confined to questions of land tenure alone. Limbu leaders attempted to preserve and at times to resurrect other features of what they regarded as their traditional way of life, especially those which related to their own positions within the political system. For a number of years there were exchanges of views with the government over the question of administrative backing for the judicial authority of the council of Subbas (*amal*). The last exchange took place as late as 1951, long after the traditional *amal* had ceased to play a significant part in the rural system of social control. In their petitions and representations the Limbu headmen spoke as if the *amal* was not only very much alive, but a vital Limbu institution, and urged the government to recognize its powers officially. Later, when the authorities mooted the introduction of a Panchayat system, the Subbas attacked the idea on the grounds that Limbus 'had their own administrative and adjudicative structure', so that the new system would be 'an encroachment upon their rights' (Thulung, 1961). Any attempts by the authorities to modify existing or introduce new economic or political institutions were represented as a menace to the traditional customs and values of the Limbus and, along with threats to kipat tenure, had to be resisted.[1]

This tendency for the Limbu movement, while focused primarily on the defence of kipat land, to expand its activities to include other related issues was highlighted in a dramatic way during the revolution of 1950–1. At that time the movement threatened to transform itself into a separatist political organization.

In the interval of several months between the collapse of Rana authority and the firm establishment of the new government the Limbus sought to organize themselves for political action on a broad

1 The term used to refer to the rules governing kipat land – *riti-thiti* – is the same as that ordinarily employed for 'custom'.

front. A mass meeting (*chumlung*) was held, to which representatives from all areas of Limbuan were invited. The more moderate voices urged the meeting to limit its purpose to the formulation of proposals for presentation to the incoming government. They sought firm guarantees for the maintenance of the kipat system and a greater voice for Limbus in the affairs of Limbuan. This was to be assured by the appointment of Limbus to senior posts in the administrative bodies of the area.

More extreme elements, however, taking cognizance of the temporary power vacuum in the region, demanded the establishment of an independent state.[1] Several Indreni Subbas who were present at the meeting stated that these elements spoke of storming the administrative offices in the Limbuan districts and declaring independence forthwith. Some of those in attendance are even alleged to have designed a Limbu flag. In one area of Limbuan where relations between Limbus and Brahmans had been particularly strained there were some outbreaks of violence, and it appears that a number of Brahmans were killed and much property destroyed. It is very doubtful, however, that these acts of violence were directly connected with what went on at the meeting.

There is no evidence to suggest that even the mild proposals put forward by those responsible for organizing the gathering ever got beyond the talking stage. 'They drank and boasted of what they were going to do,' was how one Limbu who had been present summed up the meeting. But the significance of all this 'talk' lay not in what it led to or did not lead to, but in the sentiments expressed – for the continuity of kipat tenure, for a greater political role for Limbus in the existing Nepal state, and even for sovereignty.

In Ilam, following the transfer of power, which was swift and uneventful, a number of Subbas sought to test the attitude of the new régime towards Limbu claims by drawing up a list of demands. It is worthwhile listing them here, since they are, by and large, typical of those presented to the authorities over the years. They illustrate the focal issues in all these rather diffuse and on the whole only partially successful attempts at political pressure. There were eight proposals prepared by 195 delegates – including three Indreni Subbas – from

1 One author claims, in what appears to be a reference to the Limbus, that in January, 1951, some 'independent-minded tribesmen' actually declared a 'Free Kirat State'. None of my informants could confirm this and I have seen no documents to support the statement (cf. Driver, 1963, 85).

thirty-five settlement clusters throughout Ilam. Two Chongbung Subbas in the Cluster were on the special committee of three chosen to present these demands to the district governor. The proposals were as follows:

1 Most of our kipat lands have been pledged to landholders. One-third of these lands should be returned to their Limbu owners (without repayment of the mortgage sum).

2 At present, a kipat-owner must repay the mortgage in full before he can repossess his land. Landowners should be allowed to repay mortgages piecemeal and repossess their lands piecemeal.

3 Any raikar land purchased by a Limbu should be converted to kipat tenure and the tax on the land included within the household tax already paid by the kipat-owner.

4 At present, when a new household is registered at the time of a revenue settlement, it must pay a fixed tax assessment. But the number of households increases while the amount of tax remains the same. Henceforth, the amount of tax paid by newly registered households separating from one main household should not exceed in total that paid previously by the main household.

5 At present, Tharis submit taxes collected from their dependents directly to the treasury office. Henceforth, they should be made to submit these taxes to the Subbas, who would then pass them on to the office.

6 The Subba's court (*amal*) should be given the right to hear disputes (and to collect fines).

7 If these proposals are introduced, we will accept responsibility for the maintenance of law and order in our areas.

8 Limbus are 'backward'. Something should be done to bring them up to the level of the other castes.

Seven of the eight proposals are concerned either directly with kipat land or the special position of the Subbas as a consequence of their traditional relationship to that land. The first three suggest ways of altering the balance of control of land, while the fourth proposal seeks to alleviate the tax burden on the land. Nos. 5–7 aim to re-establish the authority of the Subbas which grew out of their initial roles as custodians of kipat, as grantors of holdings to immigrant settlers, and as the principal channels of administration at the settlement level. Proposals 6 and 7 are also veiled attempts to forestall the establishment of Panchayat Committees in the area, which were regarded as likely to undermine the few remaining prerogatives of the Subbas. The last proposal is meant to refer to the specific educational needs of the Limbus and, more generally, reminds the government that Limbus are a distinctive group requiring special consideration.

In Ilam this was the last organized attempt to bring pressure on the government to alter its kipat policy, although efforts to mobilize opinion on a Limbuan-wide basis continued. When a series of demands similar to those proposed by the Ilam Subbas were presented to King Tribhuvan in 1951, a statement was issued reminding the Limbus that east Nepal was inhabited by many different ethnic groups and that only the wishes of all the people could be taken into account in determining policy. This represented not so much a change in the government's attitude to kipat and the Limbus as the adoption of a more blunt method of treating Limbu demands for special consideration.

At the approach of elections in 1959 kipat seemed likely to become an issue when the Congress Party came out in favour of abolition, while another party, the Gorkha Parishad, supported its retention. Perhaps it is an indication of the numerical strength of non-Limbu residents in Limbuan or a reflection of the tactful exclusion of its kipat plank from the Congress campaign in the east that the latter won all eight seats it contested in the region.[1] In any case, the threat of abolition was not implemented even after Congress formed a government. In December, 1960, after only fifteen months of rule, parliament was dismissed and the monarchy resumed direct control of the affairs of state. The 'traditional rights and privileges' of the Limbus were once more guaranteed by a royal decree, although again this meant no basic alteration of the government's kipat policy.

Because the Subbas have led the movement to protect rights in kipat land they are regarded by the Limbus as symbolizing the unity and the continuity of the group. This fact helps to explain their continued prestige and influence in the settlements, despite the considerable diminution of their powers. The lineages with which the Subbas were traditionally associated are no longer important groups in respect of land. Many of their administrative functions are being transferred to other government-backed agencies. In the overall wealth structure of the community the Subbas are no less impoverished than the majority of their followers. They can give little support or assistance to their

---

1 None of the Limbus in the Indreni Cluster with whom I spoke was aware of Congress attitudes to kipat, and apparently did not hear of them from the opposition candidates.

lineage mates in disputes and their offers of mediation are mostly ignored in favour of that provided by more powerful figures in the settlements. Yet Limbus make a point of honouring their Subbas, and demonstrate this by continuing to pay them tribute. They do so because the Subbas are seen as their front line in the struggle to preserve ancestral land under a traditional system of tenure.[1]

The reasons why the Subbas were in the forefront of the movement are not hard to seek. Firstly, the government which had absorbed them into its administrative apparatus recognized them as the official spokesmen for the Limbus and frequently directed the Subbas to present for its consideration the Limbu viewpoint about proposed changes in kipat legislation. Secondly, as the main beneficiaries of the kipat system, the Subbas were the principal victims of any alterations in the system. They therefore had most to gain by organizing the resistance to change.

Leadership of the movement has transformed the Subbas from headmen of small kin groups to more broadly-based leaders.[2] They have assumed the role which in a tribe with a traditional 'centralized' polity would likely have fallen on the paramount ruler. Their followers, accordingly, have recognized that, however ineffectual the Subbas are as leaders within the settlements, their role as the chief articulators of Limbu demands has to be acknowledged and applauded. As the Limbus see it, the Subbas are defending not only a form of land tenure, but a whole way of life.

There is some indication that, as of late, the Subbas no longer completely monopolize the movement's leadership. This first became apparent in 1958, when there was a major effort to establish a unified kipat policy in view of the elections which were impending. It is of interest to note that one of the organizers of the mass meeting was an ex-Gurkha officer from the Cluster (Lajahang) whose stake in kipat land – discussed in the previous chapter – reflects that of many rising Limbu leaders whose prominence is based, not on hereditary headmanship, but on wealth and status acquired in army service. Of perhaps even greater significance is the fact that of the seven committee

---

1 In a similar vein, Gluckman (1958, 44) points out how opposition to white rule in South Africa has heightened allegiance to Zulu chiefs. In particular, the 'sentiment about the king grows, *helped* by his *lack* of power, for he has no power to abuse' (my italics).

2 Worsley (1957*a*) notes how leaders of millenarian movements no longer belong to a local unit or group, but to a greater unity.

members two were Brahmans and another a Chetri. This was not merely an attempt to give voice to all sections of the population in east Nepal as the government had recommended, but an expression of the importance which many rich non-Limbu mortgagees of kipat land attach to maintaining the present tenure system. For as major creditors they, like affluent ex-servicemen, have access for lengthy periods of time to lands on which the taxes are minimal and at a cost considerably less than that required to purchase raikar land.

To my knowledge, this was the first time that a significant proportion of those responsible for organizing a political meeting were not Subbas. The outcome, nevertheless, was similar to that of previous meetings: proposals were put forward and promises were received that they would be considered.

It is tempting to suggest that these trends which point to a change of leadership in the movement represent a projection of political realities at settlement level on to the wider regional plane. But this is impossible to verify, as no other mass meetings of the kind described have been held since 1958. The more usual kinds of pressure continue: individuals or groups of Limbus – either self-appointed or invited by the government itself – continue to present the Limbu case for preserving the kipat system. And these are usually Subbas.

For more than a half-century, then, Limbus have attempted to protect their interests in land. The movement, by and large, has been unco-ordinated and ill-organized. Limbu demands have often been unrealistic, occasionally irrelevant and, more recently at any rate, far from effective. But by circulating petitions, holding mass meetings and sending delegations to present their views to government, the Limbus have, on the one hand, succeeded in allaying the ultimate menace of kipat abolition and, on the other, cultivated a widespread awareness of their special position *vis-à-vis* the rest of the population. In this latter respect the Limbu movement has served, as might a separatist church in Africa or a cargo cult in Melanesia, to express internal solidarity and differentiation from other groups (Mair, 1959).

What is in essence a confrontation over land comes to be seen as a battle for the survival of a way of life. Conceptualized in this way, cultural distinctiveness serves as an important weapon in the struggle for land. It becomes essential for the Limbus to reiterate the peculiarity of their own customs and values. When cultural practices and beliefs are promoted and their uniqueness stressed, they not only maintain group boundaries, but become what Cohen refers to as a 'political ideology'.[1] Culture, in other words, comes to have a political role.

The political role of culture

The process of Sanskritization has been much discussed in the anthropological literature on south Asia. Essentially, it is a means whereby a subordinate group in a society recognizes the superiority of another by emulating its cultural practices.[2] It might be expected that members of tribal groups in east Nepal would model their behaviour on the dominant Brahmans in their midst. All do so to a much greater extent than the Limbus. Members of other tribal groups worship deities of the Hindu pantheon, cremate their dead, and rely almost exclusively on Brahman priests to conduct their important rites. I think this is at least partly explained by the fact that no other tribal group possesses some vested economic interest like kipat which would make it worthwhile, perhaps essential, to resist emulative tendencies and emphasize instead their uniqueness. Only among Newar shopkeepers, who dominate retail trade in the towns of east Nepal,[3] is there a strong feeling of exclusiveness as among the Limbus. Unlike Newar farmers, often living in nearby settlements, these shop-keepers actively celebrate all Newar festivals, keep up traditional ritual practices and strive in every way to retain their identity as a separate community. There is a clear parallel here with the Hausa migrants described by Cohen (1969) who are able, by exploiting cultural affinities, to dominate certain kinds of trade in the western region of Nigeria. And there is a similar process at work among the Limbus. Periodic worship reminds them of their common religious beliefs; weddings, funerals and a host of other rites emphasize the special quality of their customs. The common factor on many of these occasions is the Limbu ritual specialist, who is not only the repository of

1 Cohen (1969). After reading this interesting discussion of the political uses of cultural exclusiveness I was able to clarify many of my random thoughts about this process among the Limbus. I am most grateful to Dr. Cohen for allowing me to read his manuscript prior to its publication.
2 Srinivas (1967) defines Sanskritization as 'the process by which a "low" caste or tribe or other group takes over the customs, ritual, beliefs, ideology and style of life of a high and, in particular, a "twice-born" caste'.
3 In several towns in the east, including Ilam Bazaar, there is also a sizeable proportion of Indian (Marwari) traders.

religious knowledge and techniques, but whose officiation attests to the determination of the Limbus to retain their cultural independence.

It is important to stress that the Limbu refusal to Sanskritize is not due to any notions of their own cultural superiority. I have already related a Limbu myth accounting for the possession by Brahmans of the written tradition of Hinduism which the Limbus regard as superior to their own oral tradition.[1] This myth bears a striking resemblance to those explaining the European monopoly of 'cargo' where religious cults have appeared. Among the Mambu, the 'primal myth' (Burridge, 1960) relates how one of two protagonist brothers, representing black men, commits a sin and is doomed to a life of servitude. He is not endowed with understanding; he can copy, but not invent, and he is unable to write. By contrast, the other brother has all the attributes of a European. Similarly, Lawrence (1964) shows how a creation myth in the Madang district of New Guinea was merged with the biblical myth of the fate of Ham. Because of the latter's sin, the cargo was taken away from him and he was sent to New Guinea to become the ancestor of the native people, who therefore inherited only an inferior material culture. In some versions of the myth they were offered a choice of cargo or traditional material culture and chose the latter. This theme of being at least partly responsible for their own dilemma is similar to the explanation offered in the Limbu myth, where wrong choice is regarded as an important reason for the possession of what is accepted as an inferior culture.[2] The notion of guilt leads Limbus frequently to disparage their own customs and beliefs ('jungalee', 'simple'), so much so that the observer is struck by the tendency to self-contempt. This certainly emerges clearly in a Limbu creation myth. It relates how God (Bhagwan) made man of gold, but he refused to speak. He then made man of silver, and he too refused to respond. In a third attempt, man was fashioned out of ashes and the droppings of a jungle fowl. And only then did man speak. 'God was disgusted and hated it and spat upon it. This is why men die. Had man spoken when made of gold or silver he would have lived forever.'

I am neither competent nor concerned here to comment upon the psychological implications of these myths. The point being made is that stress on cultural exclusiveness, to which myths make an im-

1 See p. 69.
2 Brahman deceit is the chief explanation offered in myth form for Limbu inferiority in the politico-economic sphere. See pp. 64–5.

portant contribution, need imply no notion of superiority to the cultures of other groups and, indeed, can rest on, perhaps even be encouraged by, a people's conviction of their own cultural inferiority.[1]

A sense of identity is fostered in a number of ways. Within any settlement cluster kinship and contiguity create an intricate pattern of intense relationships among Limbus. At the same time endogamy combined with clan exogamy envelop them in a widespread series of overlapping kin networks which extend throughout the district, and beyond the district into other regions of Limbuan. These links are strengthened and expanded through a continuous process of inter-action demanded by the norms of kinship.

The custom of visiting during Dasein provides the occasion for a renewal of ties between daughters and sisters who have married out and their natal kinsmen, as well as between the husbands of these women and their affines.

During the three years following a marriage, a son-in-law is expected to pay his annual respects to his father-in-law. Since a variety of payments in meat and liquor must be transferred on each visit, the couple is accompanied by anything from three to six young men from the husband's settlement cluster, who carry the payments. Such visits, obviously, not only discharge the obligations of kinship, but enable fledgling affinal ties to be bolstered. The presence of so large a number of guests also requires the provision of hospitality which absorbs the attentions of a circle of affines wider than members of the bride's household alone.

Marriage and mourning rites are other important occasions for the strengthening of ties. The former rites, in particular, bring together large numbers of kinsmen not normally resident in the groom's settlement area. The marriage of a son calls for invitations to be sent to the groom's mother's brother and other close matrilateral kinsmen, to the groom's sisters and their husbands, and to the sisters of the groom's father and their spouses. In addition, the bride is accompanied to the wedding by a number of women from her settlement area, some of whom may already be related to residents in the settlements of the hosts.

These occasions serve not only to strengthen ties between relatives,

---

1 There is, of course, inherent in a longing for their traditional ways and customs a belief that this tradition was or would be better for the Limbus than what they have at present.

but provide appropriate contexts for rehearsing customs, relating myths and legends and in other ways demonstrating shared cultural background. Even when Limbus from different areas meet for the purpose of settling disputes there is reference to a common framework of moral precepts. I have suggested that in such instances, since there are no accepted mediators, the idiom of tradition provides an 'umbrella' under which discussions between the disputants can proceed and to which their claims and counter-claims can be referred. Negotiations to determine compensation following adultery, for example, generally include numerous allusions to the legendary Ten Limbu (*Das Limbu*) brothers, from whom all members of the tribe are believed to have descended.[1] In the midst of what might be a heated discussion the reminder of a common tradition keeps the dispute within bounds until other, more concrete considerations bring matters to a successful conclusion.[2]

Kinship provides only one channel through which Limbus reinforce their links within and beyond the area of settlement. A common language forms an instant bridge among Limbus, just as it provides a barrier which can be erected at any time between themselves and members of other groups. Most Limbus in Ilam are bilingual. This is in contrast to members of other tribal groups in the district, like the Gurungs and Magars, who no longer speak their traditional tongue. And again, it is interesting to point out that whereas Newar peasants speak only Nepali, Newar shopkeepers residing only a few miles away in Ilam Bazaar can speak Newari fluently.

Knowledge that they share a common language and background serves to overcome the initial reserve with which Limbu strangers are regarded. In their long-distance trading ventures Limbus from the settlements of Ilam meet others from different parts of Limbuan. During the mandarin season, in particular, the main road leading to the market town of Sanisare in the Terai carries a heavy traffic of porters bringing the fruit from areas to the north. Since the trip takes several days, men camp at night in or nearby a number of roadside shops where they can buy beer or liquor and find a place to sleep. Here Limbu porters establish contact with one another and exchange information about prices in the market. In Sanisare, which is a heterogenous town, they seek out the company of other Limbus, with whom they camp and make up parties to return together to the hills. Porters

1 This myth has been recorded by Vansittart, 1915, 101.
2 See pp. 134ff.

from the Indreni settlements frequently invite travelling companions from settlements to the north of the Cluster to spend a night with them on their return from the plains, and a dancing party is organized in their honour. Friendships created in this way are sustained beyond the portering season and a pattern of mutual visiting may endure for years, or eventually lead to the formation of affinal links.[1]

When Limbus travel long distances for any purpose, be it trade or visiting, they invariably seek out Limbu households or wayside inns run by other Limbus at which to spend the night. When I trekked for several weeks in parts of Limbuan my Limbu travelling companion would speed up or delay the daily journey in order to arrive at dusk in an area of Limbu settlement. Only by so doing could he feel certain that we would spend a pleasant night in congenial company. And the initial reserve with which we were met was invariably dispelled when the persons on whom we had imposed ourselves heard the familiar and evidently welcome sound of Limbu.[2]

The avoidance of contact with non-Limbu strangers is virtually a credo informing most situations which bring Limbus together with members of other ethnic groups. For example, the twice-weekly market in Ilam Bazaar provides an occasion for people from settlements in the surrounding area to meet one another. But Limbu petty traders occupy one section of the market square. When shopping chores are complete, Limbu visitors to the market frequent only certain shops selling liquor and in this way demonstrate their preference for the company of other Limbus.

This kind of spatial separation is evident, too, at a number of annual fairs held in various parts of the district. At two such events I witnessed attendance was not confined to Limbus, but brought together a large mixed population for as many as four days at a time. In each instance Limbus – mostly young men and women – segregated themselves in one section of the grounds and had no contact with members of other groups. Through the medium of familiar songs and dances, Limbus from a large number of settlement clusters mingled easily with one another. Mixed dancing and much drinking contributed to keep many members of other ethnic groups away from the Limbu

---

1 The persons involved in these friendships do not become ritual brothers (*mit*), since this would eliminate the prospect of marriage links being forged between members of their immediate families.

2 Needless to say, on those few occasions when we were the guests of non-Limbus we were treated every bit as courteously.

14

area. But some who showed interest and even sought to join in the dances, although not turned away, were certainly not made welcome. Embarrassment at not knowing the dance steps or the language of the songs soon encouraged them to return to another area of the fair grounds.

Thus a common language and a pattern of self-imposed segregation assist in creating social relationships among Limbu strangers dispersed over a wide area, just as kinship imposes obligations which intensify links among relatives living scattered throughout Limbuan. In these and other ways exclusiveness is recognized and fostered. In a sense, the Limbu community in east Nepal is more important than any local settlement cluster which includes members of other ethnic groups. Opposition to the 'outside' is conceptualized not merely in local terms, but in the context of wider community membership. When an Indreni man refers to 'we Limbus' he indentifies with all Limbus, not only with those in the Cluster.

Conclusion

In this chapter I have not tried to relate the political history of the Limbus, nor even to analyse their political relations with the government. Rather, it has been my intention to select certain historical events which help us to understand social relationships in the Indreni Cluster.[1] Fully to comprehend the attitudes of Indreni Limbus to the Brahmans and to their own Subbas, and to appreciate the kinds of conflicts which confront Limbu Notables in behavioural choices, it was necessary to consider the district- and Limbuan-wide movement to preserve land under kipat tenure. In relating some of the activities which comprise the movement, I was led to examine the relationship between land and culture and between culture and politics.

The Limbus strive to remain a distinct community by resisting Sanskritization and, alternatively, by emphasizing their cultural apartness. They do so not because of any inherent propensity to tribal solidarity, but because it enables them better to maintain their defence of kipat land. This is not to suggest that wherever or whenever a people cultivates a sense of cultural exclusiveness it does so to serve a

1 Cohen (1969) would refer to such an examination as 'micro-history', which, in his words, 'deals with grand historical events as they are manifested in the local, small-scale, face-to-face community'.

political end. But where such an end is given, so to speak, a stress on shared customs and values increases the self-awareness of the community involved in the political struggle. At the same time the reiteration of exclusiveness tends to obliterate any distinction between cultural and political identity. What is seen to be at stake is not only a politico-economic interest – in the Limbu case, kipat land – but the very survival of the community as a cultural entity.

Chapter 8

Conclusion

This book has considered the interrelations between Limbus and Brahmans in east Nepal, and has attempted, by focusing the discussion on a single cluster of settlements inhabited mainly by Limbus, to assess the impact on an indigenous tribal community of a dominant Hindu group settled in the area.

Broadly speaking, Limbu-Brahman relations are characterized by two opposed tendencies: cleavage and interdependence. The former has grown out of and expresses a confrontation over land; it is evident in attitudes of hostility and in an absence of many kinds of social interaction, and it is reinforced by deep cultural divisions between the two groups. Interdependence derives from the separate but complementary roles they play in the agricultural economy as a result of the distinct type of access to land which each enjoys. Interdependence is evident, too, in the political configuration which reflects economic realities. The interrelations between Limbus and Brahmans are therefore to be understood primarily in terms of their differential rights and interests in land.

These rights and interests, and so the relationships between the two groups, have altered in the course of the past two centuries. This study, then, has been concerned to examine some processes of social change. It has tried, firstly, to indicate the ways in which certain economic and political institutions were interconnected in a systematic way at different points in time and, secondly, to suggest which factors contributed to bring about changes in these institutions, and in the systems within which they were interconnected.

No single dramatic event allows us to pinpoint a specific moment before which a certain social pattern obtained and after which it was replaced by a different pattern. But the facts suggest that during the last quarter of the nineteenth century a variety of changes in economic and political institutions were set in motion, leading to a fundamental transformation in the relationships between Limbus and Brahmans which had existed during the century following the absorption of Limbuan into the Nepal state.

This period was characterized, first of all, by a subsistence economy, in the sense that agricultural requirements were met largely within the settlement cluster. Some of the produce was undoubtedly traded in the region to acquire the few goods which could not be made or grown locally, and to find the cash needed to pay taxes, but by and large the economy was self-sustaining. Mair (1957, 46) has argued that 'in such an economy there could be no commodity more valuable than land, no circumstance in which it would be profitable to dispose of land'. I would stress also that an abundance of land was as much a reason for this fact as the existence of a subsistence economy *per se*. Land in Ilam had no exchange value because it was a free good. This meant that production was limited primarily by technological know-how and the supply of labour. Availability of land explains the readiness of the Limbus to make generous grants of holdings to the Hindu immigrants who entered the district following the pacification of Limbuan. Land was given in return for economic assistance and political support, so that, in Gluckman's terms, the 'series of estates in land' (1943, 45) was mirrored in the political gradations of Subbas, Tharis and dependents. This structure was bolstered by the various prerogatives enjoyed by persons in superordinate positions *vis-à-vis* their subordinates and symbolized in the system of tributary payments. Limbu headmen, then, stood at the summit of a political hierarchy based on differential rights to land.

In so far as the government employed the Subbas as tax-collectors and made them the main instruments of administrative control in the settlements, this hierarchy was sanctioned by the authority of the State.

The political roles of the Subbas had another dimension as well. As lineage headmen they were the dominant leaders within the Limbu community. Here, too, control of essential land resources provided the basis of their power. Households obtained secure rights to an estate by virtue of membership in a patrilineage which implied, among other things, allegiance to a Subba. It was shown how, in conditions of land-plenty, the lineage appeared not overly concerned with defining membership criteria too narrowly. As a result, outsiders were occasionally absorbed into the lineage or 'accommodated' in other ways.

The desire to enhance a political following would seem to have been an important motive for this practice.

The politico-economic system found today in the Settlement Cluster follows from several linked developments related to pressures on land and government kipat policy, the effects of which crystallized around the end of last century.[1] Serious land shortages resulted from a steady growth of population due to natural increase and the continued influx of mainly Hindu immigrants into east Nepal. These new settlers gradually came to outnumber the indigenous Limbus and, partly to meet their demands for land (and in keeping with Kathmandu's long-range policy towards Limbu land), the government converted all grants made by Subbas to the immigrant settlers into raikar tenure, thereby removing them from Limbu control. In the course of the analysis, the effects of these developments on the social system were noted.

First of all, a dearth of land meant that the recurrent and contingent obligations of Limbu households could only be met by pledging kipat lands to Hindu creditors, who assumed the usufruct pending repayment of the loans. There emerged the familiar syndrome of agricultural indebtedness: as more and more lands were pledged to raise non-productive capital, the Limbus gradually lost the means to repay these debts and resume their lands.

Secondly, the Brahmans, as the most numerous and literate of the Hindu groups, and controlling the majority of raikar headmanships (Thari), were best placed to benefit from government kipat policy. In a number of ways, they managed to acquire many lands which had previously belonged to Limbus under kipat tenure. They thereby became the economically ascendant sector of the population and, as such, the chief source of credit and tenancy for the Limbus.

Thus the economic foundation on which the political hierarchy of the earlier period had been built eroded as the amount of kipat was reduced and as the Limbus then lost access to the productive potential of their remaining kipat lands. Moreover, the conversion of Limbu land grants into raikar tenure secured the rights of the non-Limbus to these lands and freed them of any economic or political dependence on the Subbas. Thereafter, the Tharis were beholden to the government and not to the Limbu headmen for their titles and authority.

1 In studying social change, as Ginsberg (1958) points out, we must ignore many conditions because social phenomena are so complex, and cite only the most important causal factors.

When the system of tax-collection in Ilam was rearranged so that Tharis paid taxes directly to the treasury office instead of to the Subbas, the last remnants of the hierarchy in the district were dissolved.

The impoverishment of the Limbus, Subbas and followers alike, and the enrichment of the Brahmans – in particular, the Tharis among them – altered the balance of power and influence within the settlements. Limbus increasingly accepted mediation of their disputes by Brahmans, and began to turn to Brahman faction leaders for assistance in serious quarrels. The latter, too, dominated the new Panchayat Committees, which more and more came to influence events in the settlements.

Land-shortages affected the definition and structure of Limbu kin groups as well. The criteria for lineage membership became more stringently defined in order to limit the numbers with rights to kipat. Patrilineal descent became the sole charter for obtaining such rights, and Limbu 'outsiders', who had previously been accommodated in the settlements and given land, no longer found themselves welcomed in the same way. In some circumstances Limbus did come to live with affinal or matrilateral kin, but they could not expect to receive any grants of land from their hosts. As a result settlements like those in the Indreni Cluster are now inhabited by a number of Limbus who own no kipat land there.

Household composition, too, has been affected by land-pressures. There is no evidence to suggest that the Limbu household ever approximated to the traditional Hindu joint family. However, a common interest in land kept a group of brothers together until the death of their father. But as household estates have become smaller and less viable, the tendency has been for young men to press for partition and a division of property shortly after marriage. The trend has become even more pronounced with the growth of new commercial opportunities outside the agricultural economy. As young men begin to recognize their importance as earners of wealth in the cash economy, they are more reluctant than ever to share these earnings with a large family group.[1] The efforts of their elders to keep the household estate intact for as long a period as possible are rendered ineffective, and only the wealthiest households can hope, by holding out the prospect of an expanding estate, to delay the process of division. Thus as the rate of land-fragmentation has increased, household size has become smaller

---

[1] This kind of trend has been noted in areas where labour-migration is an important part of economic life. See Firth (1954).

and these groups progressively less able to support themselves from the land.

During the late nineteenth century, therefore, several key developments brought about a profound transformation in the relationships between Limbus and Brahmans, as well as within the structure of Limbu kin groups. But the contemporary social pattern in east Nepal is by no means static. The changes which are going on today, moreover, can be seen to relate to three principal catalysts which have been introduced since the turn of the century. These are the government ban on the alienation of kipat land, the opportunities presented by Gurkha service, and those offered by economic developments in the area after 1951.

The government decree of 1901 prohibiting the permanent alienation of kipat land gave Limbu mortgagors of kipat an increased manœuvrability in seeking credit. Since pressures on raikar land have been growing steadily, Brahmans and other non-Limbus have been forced to compete for access to the usufruct of kipat lands. This has placed Limbus in a position from which to exploit their ownership rights by demanding interest-free loans (*bard*) against the security of lands already pledged. In addition, they retain the right of first refusal of tenancies in the event that the creditors can or will not cultivate the lands themselves. These rights, moreover, are sanctioned by the threat of transferring the usufruct to new landholders. The effects of impoverishment are thereby mitigated, so that the pattern of total economic dependence which characterizes the relations between, for example, landlords and non-Limbu landless has not developed.

I have suggested, however, that a kipat-owner is not completely unhampered in his freedom to manipulate his land rights so as to gain the maximum credit advantages for himself. His freedom to withdraw landholding rights from an existing creditor and transfer them to a new one is limited by the nature of the ties binding the former and his Limbu debtor. Where these are single-interest, based only on a credit contract, the Limbu can withdraw from the relationship with impunity. Where they are convergent or multiplex, so that the credit link is only one of many between the two persons, the ability of the Limbu to break the credit link alone is obviously restricted. I have shown that a small category of mainly Brahman landholders of kipat are also landlords and neighbours to their Limbu debtor/tenants, and are called on by the latter for a variety of political favours as well. These few Brahman creditors are seldom if ever turned off the land they take under mortgage. Where such convergent linkages exist, the boundaries of Limbu choice are much curtailed.

The legislation of 1901, securing Limbu ownership rights to kipat, takes on a new significance with the growth of opportunities since the First World War for Limbus to earn cash incomes from military service. Because land-rights remain intact during their lengthy absences, servicemen are encouraged to accumulate substantial savings and pensions, which are used to regain the usufruct to their own lands or to take the lands of other Limbus under mortgage. This means that the proportion of kipat lands to which the Limbus now have unrestricted access has begun to increase at the expense of the Brahmans and other non-Limbus who previously held their usufruct. Thus as cash from military service finds its way back to the settlements the agricultural sector of the Limbu economy improves accordingly.

The growth of government services since 1951 has stimulated economic activity further, and Limbus are increasingly able to earn some money in the local commercial economy. These incomes, while not sufficient to repay loans and take back mortgaged lands, nevertheless contribute to slowing down the rate of kipat-pledging. And reliance on non-agricultural sources of wealth, of course, reduces Limbu dependence on the Brahmans who still dominate access to their lands.

The political effects of these new developments have been far-reaching. Gurkha service has given rise to a small class of affluent Limbus, who through wealth and status earned in the army have appropriated much of the power and influence once reserved for Limbu headmen in the settlements. At the same time they have become leaders in the wider society – the all-Nepal arena, so to speak – expressed in their control of new political associations created by government. These developments have begun to alter the character of the relationships between the Limbus and Brahmans. The latter have had to adjust their attitudes and behaviour, which were previously directed towards an undifferentiated Limbu community. The Limbu Notables, for their part, are in the difficult position of having to reconcile the conflict between, on the one hand, the benefits which accrue to them from maintaining their identity with Limbu kin and community and, on the other hand, the interests they have in common with wealthy and powerful Brahmans.

Inasmuch as a struggle for land ensued from the penetration of tribal areas by Hindu immigrants in many parts of south Asia, this paradigm of changing group relations undoubtedly has a relevance beyond a particular cluster of settlements in east Nepal. Looked at from a different point of view, the phenomena discussed in this book touch more broadly on the universal problem of the response of one community to domination by another.

Most studies of domination have concerned themselves, understandably enough, with the European impact on small-scale societies. And a significant number of these have treated with the many kinds of religious movements which, as Worsley points out, 'serve as an expression of reaction against what is felt as oppression by another class or nationality' (1957). This statement of the conditions which give rise to religious movements might well be applied to the situation described in these pages.

Why, we might ask, did a religious movement not emerge among the Limbus? What appear to be two essential preconditions for such a movement are both absent in east Nepal. The first is a markedly uneven relation between expectations and the means of their satisfaction (cf. Firth, 1955). This, in turn, is related to the degree of economic differential between the indigenous and the foreign communities. Religious movements such as cargo cults emphasize not only the inability of the deprived group to obtain the sophisticated manufactured goods which accompany European domination, but their total failure even to comprehend the white economy (Worsley, 1957a). This suggests, then, a crucial difference in the kind of deprivation which has followed from contact between European and tribal, on the one hand, and between Hindu and tribal, on the other. In contrast to the profound economic impact of European conquest, Hindu invaders introduced relatively little innovation into the areas they came to dominate. Immigrants into Limbuan may have brought more sophisticated techniques of cultivation than those in use by the Limbus, but there were no mysteries about these techniques and the Limbus apparently adopted them without difficulty. Almost from the moment of incorporation into the State, both communities have enjoyed access to the same material standard of living. If the Hindus have managed to obtain more of the available resources, the difference has been confined to magnitude and not kind. In a word, the distinction in economic levels between the tribal and the dominant Hindu sections of the society was never such as to create an unbridgeable chasm between Limbu aspirations and their means of satisfaction.

A second precondition for a religious movement is the absence of any avenue for political expression. Where such action is possible there is little need for 'fantasy compensation' (Mair, 1959). In east Nepal, as I have shown, political activity has certainly been possible, not merely in the sense that the Subbas have been incorporated into the formal political system, but that Limbus have been able openly to exert pressure for special privileges on a communal basis. The Limbu reaction to domination has been to wage a persistent struggle to defend ancestral lands under the kipat system of tenure, regarded as an integral part of their way of life. Limbu customs and values have been reiterated and fostered so that cultural exclusiveness could be mobilized in this all-out struggle.

Epilogue

In 1964 a comprehensive series of land reform measures were announced by the government, with the intention of introducing the programme in all areas of the Kingdom. Although nowhere in the original legislation was specific reference made to the future of the kipat system, it was apparent that the successful implementation of such a scheme would probably mean conversion of all kipat lands to raikar tenure. At the end of October 1968 the central government introduced an amendment to the Lands Act of 1964 which allowed (a) for the alienation, i.e. sale of kipat land and (b) that these lands would be assessed at rates of tax equivalent to those prevalent on raikar. The authorities in Kathmandu thus seem at long last determined to abolish once and for all the kipat system. In the light of this study it is safe to assume that these developments will, in time, bring about further changes in the existing pattern of relationships between the Limbus and the Hindus who live amongst them in east Nepal.

Appendix A

The measurement of land

The problem of measuring land arose early in my field-work and produced something of a dilemma. The last revenue settlement in Ilam took place in 1936, so that the records were out of date and of little value. Moreover, only irrigated lands were in fact surveyed, but dry fields were not.

Hill peasants themselves have no exact knowledge of the size of the fields they cultivate. They speak only of the amount of seed they sow in the case of paddy lands, and of the number of *hul* they own when referring to dry plots. A *hul* means a pair of bullocks, and in this context implies the number of mornings it takes to plough a dry field. This gives no indication of its size, since the figure varies with the condition of the soil, the time of year, the strength of the bullocks and the skill of the ploughman.

Under these circumstances the only alternative was to use the figures for production. A 'unit' therefore is not, strictly speaking, a measurement of land, but of its productivity. The figures given in the text are for the year I spent in the field. There is nothing to suggest that 1964–5 was a year of abnormal yield – either above or below par.

There are two weaknesses in this approach which become immediately apparent. The first is this: how was I to know whether the production estimates given me by my informants were accurate? Limbus, like peasants everywhere, are never happy to speak about their yields. But the fact that the great majority of their fields were mortgaged made them less reluctant to give me the information I asked for, and at the same time made it possible for me to check their statements. Since in most cases two and often three persons had rights to the same plot of land, I was able to verify the production figures by relying on more than one source. Then again, certain areas were known to yield a determinate quantity of grains per seed planted. So that, for example, most cultivators knew that fields along a specific ridge produced twenty times the amount of seed sown, while others in another area produced twenty-five or thirty times the amount. This provided an additional means of verification. Finally, I was present on a number of occasions when grains were counted at harvest-time, and was able to check personally the statements I had taken.

Perhaps a more serious drawback of attempting to employ production figures as an objective measurement of land relates to the fact that yields can vary from year to year. In this regard I can only point out that any significant variations in production would occur 'across the board', and so would not substantially alter the land pattern I present.

Because agricultural techniques are standardized, the skills of individual cultivators would have little bearing on yields. The figures given in this book are therefore presented as a reasonably accurate estimate of the production of Indreni kipat fields.

To enable me to compare production with consumption requirements, I have defined the 'unit' as the amount of food an adult (aged fourteen and over) eats in one day (two meals). With the husks removed, two measures of paddy will give one measure of rice. A measure of maize on the cob will give three-quarters of a measure of edible grain. Millet, on the other hand, is reckoned to give full 'measure for measure'. The figures used, then, are for net edible grains.

Crops are normally measured in *muri, pathi* and *mana*. One *mana* is equivalent to about 1 lb. There are eight *mana* in a *pathi* and twenty *pathi* in a *muri*. One *muri* corresponds to 2·4 bushels. An adult eats one *mana* of grain (whether rice, maize or millet) at a single meal.

Appendix B

Agricultural income

To arrive at the total agricultural income from lands owned or cultivated by Indreni Limbus, I have added together production figures from (a) unmortgaged kipat lands cultivated by the owners; (b) raikar lands owned and cultivated by Limbus; (c) mortgaged kipat lands cultivated by Limbu landholders; (d) mortgaged kipat lands cultivated by Limbu tenants; (e) raikar lands cultivated by Limbu tenants. To these figures must then be added (f) the rent received by Limbu landlords from non-Limbu tenants. Finally, from the total of all these I have subtracted (g) the rent paid by Limbu tenants to landlords other than Limbu resident in the Cluster. I have omitted the costs of cultivation.

	Units
(a)	41,100
(b)	7,500
(c)	14,000
(d)	28,700
(e)	2,400
(f)	1,700
	95,400
(g)	−8,400
	87,000

References

BAILEY, F. G. (1957), *Caste and the Economic Frontier*, Manchester: University Press.

— (1961), ' "Tribe" and "Caste" in India', *Contributions to Indian Sociology*, 5, 7–19.

— (1965), 'Decisions by Consensus in Councils and Committees', in M. Banton (ed.), *Political Systems and the Distribution of Power* (A.S.A. Monograph 2), London: Tavistock Publications.

Tribal Economy', *Bulletin of the Cultural Research Institute*, II, 2, 19–22.

BANERJEE, S. K. (1963), 'Land Alienation: Causes and Effects Thereof on

BENEDICT, B. (1957), 'Factionalism in Mauritian Villages', *British Journal of Sociology*, 8, 328–42.

— (1962), 'Stratification in Plural Societies', *American Anthropologist*, 64, 1,235–45.

BHANDARI, K. P. (1959), 'Kipat', in *Samyuakta Prayas*, Kathmandu, September 13th and 20th (Nepali text).

BOSE, N. K. (1953), 'The Hindu Method of Tribal Absorption', in *Cultural Anthropology and Other Essays*, Calcutta: Indian Associated Publishing Co.

— (1964), 'Integration of Tribes in Andhra Pradesh', *Man in India*, 44, 2, 97–104.

BOTT, E. (1955), 'Urban Families: Conjugal Roles and Social Networks', *Human Relations*, 8, 345–84.

BURRIDGE, K. (1960), *Mambu*, London: Methuen.

CHEMJONG, I. S. (1952), *Kirati Itihas (History of the Kiratis)*, Gangtok (Nepali text).

— (1961), *Limbu-Nepali-Angrezi Shabda Kosh (Limbu-Nepali-English Dictionary)*, Kathmandu: Nepal Academy.

CLARK, T. W. (1963), *Introduction to Nepali*, Cambridge: W. Heffer & Sons, Ltd.

COHEN, A. (1965), *Arab Border Villages in Israel*, Manchester: University Press.

COHEN, A. (1969), *Custom and Politics in Urban Africa*, London: Routledge & Kegan Paul.

COLSON, E. (1953), *The Makah Indians*, Manchester: University Press.

— (1953a), 'Social Control and Vengeance in Plateau Tonga Society', *Africa*, 199–212.

DAVIS, K. (1951), *The Population of India and Pakistan*, Princeton: University Press.

DONALDSON, F. (1900), *Lepchaland*, London: Sampson Low, Marston.

DRIVER, J. E. S. (1963), 'Party and Government in Nepal', in S. Rose (ed.), *Politics in Southern Asia*, London: Macmillan.

ELWIN, V. (1943), *The Aboriginals*, Oxford Pamphlets on Indian Affairs, No. 14, Bombay: O.U.P.

FIRTH, R. (1954), 'Money, Work and Social Change in Indo-Pacific Economic Systems', *International Social Science Bulletin*, 6, 400–10.

— (1955), 'The Theory of "Cargo" Cults: A Note on Tikopia', *Man*, 142, 130–2.

— (1957), Introduction to 'Factions in Indian and Overseas Indian Societies', *British Journal of Sociology*, 8, 291–5.

FORTES, M. (1938), 'Culture Contact as a Dynamic Process', in *Methods of Study of Culture Contact in Africa*, London: International African Institute, O.U.P.

FREEDMAN, M. (1958), *Lineage Organization in South-eastern China*, London School of Economics Monographs on Social Anthropology, No. 18, London: Athlone Press.

FRIED, M. H. (1957), 'The Classification of Corporate Unilineal Descent Groups', *Journal of the Royal Anthropological Institute*, 87, 1–29.

FÜRER-HAIMENDORF, C. VON (1956), 'Elements of Newar Social Structure', *Journal of the Royal Anthropological Institute*, 82, 15–38.

— (1960), 'Caste in the Multi-ethnic Society of Nepal', *Contributions to Indian Sociology*, IV, 12–32.

— (1967), 'The Position of the Tribal Populations in Modern India', in P. Mason (ed.), *India and Ceylon: Unity and Diversity*, London: O.U.P.

GHURYE, G. S. (1959), *The Scheduled Tribes*, 2nd revised edition, Bombay: Popular Book Depot.

GINSBERG, M. (1958), 'Social Change', *British Journal of Sociology*, 9, 205–29.

GIUSEPPE, FATHER (1790), 'An Account of the Kingdom of Nepal', *Asiatick Researches*, 2, 307–22.

GLUCKMAN, M. (1943), *Lozi Land and Royal Property*, Rhodes-Livingstone Papers, No. 10, London: O.U.P.

— (1956), *Custom and Conflict in Africa*, Oxford: Basil Blackwell.

— (1958), *Analysis of a Social Situation in Modern Zululand*, Rhodes-Livingstone Papers, No. 28, Manchester: University Press.

GLUCKMAN, M. (1965), *The Ideas in Barotse Jurisprudence*, New Haven, London: Yale University Press.

GOODY, J. (1961), 'The Classification of Double Descent Systems', *Current Anthropology*, 2, 1, 3–26.

GOULD, H. (1964), 'A Jajmani System of North India: Its Structure, Magnitude and Meaning', *Ethnology*, 3, 12–41.

GURUNG, C. B. (1949), *Report on the Study of Agricultural Conditions of the Eastern Nepal Hills, East No. 1 to Ilam* (Mimeographed).

HAMILTON, F. (1819), *An Account of the Kingdom of Nepal, and of the Territories Annexed to this Dominion by the House of Gorkha*, Edinburgh: Constable.

HARPER, E. B. (1959), 'Two Systems of Economic Exchange in India', *American Anthropologist*, 61, 760–78.

HITCHCOCK, J. T. (1963), 'Some Effects of Recent Change in Rural Nepal', *Human Organization*, 22, 75–82.

HODGSON, B. H. (1880), 'Route from Kathmandu, the Capital of Nepal, to Darjeeling in Sikkim', Section XI in *Miscellaneous Essays Relating to Indian Subjects*, Vol. II, London: Trübner.

JACKSON, R. D. (1940), *India's Army*, London: Sampson Low, Marston.

KARVE, I. (1965), *Kinship Organization in India*, 2nd revised edition, Bombay: Asia Publishing House.

KIRKPATRICK, COLONEL (1811), *An Account of the Kingdom of Nepaul*, London: William Miller.

KOLENDA, P. M. (1963), 'Toward a Model of the Hindu Jajmani System', *Human Organization*, 22, 11–31.

KUMAR, D. (1965), *Land and Caste in South India*, Cambridge: University Press.

KUPER, H. (1947), *An African Aristocracy: Rank among the Swazi of Swaziland*, London: International African Institute.

LAMA, S. B. (1959), *Ilam Darpard (Mirror on Ilam)*, Darjeeling (Nepali text).

LANDON, P. (1928), *Nepal*, 2 vols., London: Constable.

LAWRENCE, P. (1964), *Road Belong Cargo*, Manchester: University Press.

LEACH, E. R. (1954), *Political Systems of Highland Burma*, London: Bell & Sons.

— (1962), 'Introduction: What Should We Mean by Caste?', in E. R. Leach (ed.), *Aspects of Caste in South India, Ceylon and North-west Pakistan*, Cambridge Papers in Social Anthropology, No. 2, Cambridge: University Press.

LLOYD, P. (1962), *Yoruba Land Law*, London: O.U.P.

MAIR, L. P. (1957), *Studies in Applied Anthropology*, London School of Economics Monographs on Social Anthropology, No. 16, London: Athlone Press.

— (1959), 'Independent Religious Movements in Three Continents', *Comparative Studies in Society and History*, I, 2, 113–36.

MALHOTRA, R. C. (1958), 'Public Administration in Nepal', *Indian Journal of Public Administration*, 4, 451–64.

MAYER, A. C. (1952), *Land and Society in Malabar*, London: O.U.P.

— (1957), 'Factions in Fiji Indian Rural Settlements', *British Journal of Sociology*, 8, 317–28.

— (1960), *Caste and Kinship in Central India*, London: Routledge & Kegan Paul.

— (1963), 'Some Political Implications of Community Development in India', *European Journal of Sociology*, 4, 86–106.

— (1966), 'The Significance of Quasi-Groups in the Study of Complex Societies', in M. Banton (ed.), *The Social Anthropology of Complex Societies* (A.S.A. Monograph 4), London: Tavistock Publications.

MILLER, D. F. (1965), 'Factions in Indian Village Politics', *Pacific Affairs*, 17–31.

NAKANE, C. (1966), 'A Plural Society in Sikkim', in C. von Fürer-Haimendorf (ed.), *Caste and Kin in Nepal, India and Ceylon*, Bombay: Asia Publishing House.

NEBESKY-WOJKOWITZ, R. VON (1956), *Where the Gods are Mountains*, London: Weidenfeld & Nicolson.

NICHOLAS, R. W. (1965), 'Factions: a Comparative Analysis', in M. Banton (ed.), *Political Systems and the Distribution of Power* (A.S.A. Monograph 2), London: Tavistock Publications.

O'MALLEY, L. S. S. (1907), *Bengal District Gazetteers*, Darjeeling, Calcutta: The Bengal Secretariat Book Depot.

ORANS, M. (1965), *The Santal*, Detroit: Wayne State University.

PATTERSON, G. N. (1962), 'Recent Chinese Policies in Tibet and Towards the Himalayan Border States', *The China Quarterly*, 12, 191–206.

PIGNEDE, B. (1966), *Les Gurungs: une population himalayenne du Népal*, Paris, La Haye: Mouton & Co.

PRADHANANGA, G. B. (1952), *Limbuan-ko Kipat Samasya (The Kipat Problem of Limbuan)*, Kathmandu (Nepali text).

REGMI, D. R. (1961), *Modern Nepal*, Calcutta: K. L. Mukhopadhyay.

REGMI, M. C. (1963), *Land Tenure and Taxation in Nepal*, Vol. I, *The State as Landlord: Raikar Tenure*, Berkeley: Institute of International Studies, University of California.

— (1964), *Land Tenure and Taxation in Nepal*, Vol. II, *The Land Grant System: Birta Tenure*, Berkeley: Institute of International Studies, University of California.

— (1965), *Land Tenure and Taxation in Nepal*, Vol. III, *The Jagir, Rakam and Kipat Tenure Systems*, Berkeley: Institute of International Studies, University of California.

ROCK, J. F. (1953), 'Excerpts from a History of Sikkim', *Anthropos*, 48, 925–48.

ROSE, L. E. (1963), 'The Himalayan Border States: "Buffers" in Transition', *Asian Survey*, 3, 116–21.

ROY, S. C. (1931), 'The Effects on the Aborigines of Chota Nagpur of their Contact with Western Civilisation', *Journal of the Bihar and Orissa Research Society*, 17, IV, 358–94.

SRINIVAS, M. N. (1967), 'The Cohesive Role of Sanskritization', in P. Mason (ed.), *India and Ceylon: Unity and Diversity*, London: O.U.P.

SRIVASTAVA, R. P. (1966), 'Tribe-caste Mobility in India and the Case of the Kumaon Bhotias', in C. von Fürer-Haimendorf (ed.), *Caste and Kin in Nepal, India and Ceylon*, Bombay: Asia Publishing House.

STIRLING, P. (1965), *Turkish Village*, London: Weidenfeld & Nicolson.

THULUNG, N. M. (1961), '*Panchayati Parampara ra Kirat*' ('Panchayat Tradition of the Kirats'), *Gorkhapatra*, July 29th (Nepali text).

VANSITTART, E. (1915), *Gurkhas*, Calcutta: Superintendent of Government Printing.

WHITE, C. M. N. (1958), 'Terminological Confusion in African Land Tenure', *Journal of African Administration*, 10, 124–30.

WORSLEY, P. (1957), *The Trumpet Shall Sound*, London: MacGibbon & Kee.

— (1957*a*), 'Millenarian Movements in Melanesia', *Rhodes-Livingstone Journal*, 21, 18–31.

Glossary*

aḍḍā	lit. office; the administration p. 148
amāl	Subba's court or council p. 129
aputāli	childless person p. 40
baḍ	lit. increment; an additional loan taken against security of land already pledged p. 96
baḍā hākim	governor of a district p. 15
bāhun	Brahman or Jaisi p. 70
bālak	infant p. 136
bāli	annual payment in grain made to a member of a service caste p. 79
bārī	dry, unirrigated land p. 13
bayad [L]	dependent, lineage mate of a Subba p. 126
beʃyā	whore p. 89
bhalādmi	notable, important person p. 83
bhāt	cooked rice, maize or millet p. 73
bhog bandhaki	possessory mortgage p. 91
bikās	development p. 167
birodhī	opponent p. 168
boknu	to carry, to support in a dispute p. 157
buḍeuli	spokesman, also a functionary appointed by a Subba p. 29
buḍo	an elder p. 136
candā	contribution p. 88
chumlung [L]	mass meeting p. 184
cori bihā	theft marriage p. 84
culo	hearth, kitchen p. 35

* The number beside the English translation refers to the page in the text on which the term first appears.
[L]=Limbu word.

215

dāijo	dowry p. 90
dājyū	elder brother p. 175
dāl	lentils p. 73
dāmāsāhi	a proportion of tax paid by landholder to the owner of kipat land p. 63
dhān nāc	Limbu paddy dance p. 68
dhārā	water-source p. 20
dhoti	loincloth p. 67
dukha	hardship p. 114
gāū	settlement, village, cluster of houses p. 7
ghar	home, household p. 32
goṭhālo	cowherd p. 111
guhār	lit. help; assistance given without expectation of immediate return p. 108
hal	amount of land ploughed by a pair of bullocks in one morning p. 205
jā̃ḍ	millet beer p. 67
jāl	treachery p. 61
jāri	marriage by abduction of another man's wife p. 84
jārikal	compensation paid to a cuckolded husband p. 89
jāt	caste p. 70
jeṭhā	eldest sibling or son p. 25
jiuni	property kept by parents for support in their old age p. 36
jūṭho	ritually impure p. 66
kam [*L*]	soil p. 25
kartā	functionary appointed by Subba p. 29
kārbāri	functionary appointed by Subba p. 29
khas-bāhun	refers to the high Hindu category in the caste hierarchy p. 70
khet	irrigated land p. 11
khukuri	curved knife p. 146
kipaṭ	form of land tenure associated with Limbus p. 3
kiriyā putra	principal mourner p. 81
kul deutā	ancestor god p. 66
lālmohar	decree bearing the royal seal p. 29
lāṭo	simple, stupid p. 65

māgh	Nepalese month—falling during January–February p. 68
māgi bihā	arranged marriage p. 84
māl	treasury office p. 15
mana	unit of measure equal to about 1lb. p. 206
marcā	yeast loaf used in making liquor p. 111
māsikāṭṭā	kind of possessory mortgage whereby principal is reduced annually by a fixed amount p. 91
matvāli	member of a 'drinking' caste, ranked below twice-born castes p. 70
māuli	mother's natal family p. 52
mit	ritual friend p. 193
mūl ghar	main house from which sons divide p. 34
murī	unit of measure – 2·4 bushels; also 1,369 sq. ft. p. 57
nāū kamāunu	to make a name, earn a reputation p. 114
navamī	ninth day of the festival of Dasein p. 133
nūn tel chunu	touching salt and oil – a ritual lifting pollution after a death p. 81
pãc khat	certain offences which can be dealt with only by government courts p. 129
pakkā	real, genuine p. 47
pānī na calne jāt	untouchable caste p. 71
pareli	mutual labour exchange p. 108
pāthi	unit of measure equal to 8 manas p. 206
pāṭhfālā	religious school p. 61
perengo [L]	small wicker purse containing meat – given as part of marriage payments p. 87
phedangma [L]	Limbu ritual specialist p. 110
polāhā	informer p. 62
purohit	Brahman priest p. 156
rāi	functionary appointed by a Subba p. 29
raksi	liquor p. 67
ratyɔwli	performance by women of a groom's settlement on the night of his wedding – practised by high castes only p. 69
rɔykar	form of land tenure akin to freehold p. 3
rɔyti	dependent of a headman p. 126
rin	interest-bearing loan p. 93
rit	marriage payments, other than bridewealth, made by groom p. 86

riti-thiti	custom, tradition p. 183
sabhā	assembly of village adults p. 163
sanad	government order p. 183
sapat	short-term loan without interest p. 93
sarap bagāunu	ritual performed to expel bad feelings within a lineage p. 66
sel roṭi	kind of doughnut made on special ritual occasions p. 74
sīdur	red powder worn by woman to signify marital status p. 89
sikya [L]	nettle p. 25
silok	lit. verse; usually a verse competition engaged in by relatives of bride and groom at a high-caste wedding p. 69
sir uṭhāune	raise one's head, i.e. prestige p. 145
soranni	land grants given by Subbas to immigrant settlers in Limbuan p. 56
subbā	Limbu headman p. 28
sunauli [L]	bridewealth p. 85
tāgādhāri	denotes twice-born caste p. 70
tapāĩ	high-grade honorific form of 'you' p. 174
tarkārī	vegetable or meat curry p. 73
thar	generally refers to clan, but occasionally to any descent group p. 24
thari	headman on raikar land p. 126
ṭheki	lit. perquisite; fee or commission paid to a Thari by a dependent selling raikar land which is part of the former's holding p. 144
thum	sub-division of a district p. 13
ṭikā	ritual mark on forehead p. 126
tongba [L]	bamboo container with millet beer p. 68
upādhyāya bāhun	Brahman p. 70

Index